Washington D.C.
for Families

Also by Larry Lain

Paris for Families
London for Families
New York City for Families
London for Lovers

Washington D.C. for Families

by Larry Lain

illustrations by Barb Lain

Interlink Books
An imprint of Interlink Publishing Group, Inc.
New York • Northampton

First published 2003 by

Interlink Books
An imprint of Interlink Publishing Group, Inc.
46 Crosby Street • Northampton, Massachusetts 01060
www.interlinkbooks.com

Copyright © by Larry Lain 2003
Illustrations copyright © by Barb Lain 2003

Library of Congress Cataloging-in-Publication Data

Lain, Larry, 1947–
  Washington D.C. for families / by Larry Lain ; illustrated by Barb Lain.
    p. cm.
  ISBN 1-56656-471-9
  1. Washington (D.C.)—Guidebooks. 2. Family recreation—Washington
(D.C.)—Guidebooks. I. Title.
  F192.3.L35 2003
  917.5304'42—dc21

                    2002156668

Printed and bound in Canada

To request our complete 40-page full-color catalog,
please call us toll free at **1-800-238-LINK**, visit our
website at **www.interlinkbooks.com**, or write to
Interlink Publishing
46 Crosby Street, Northampton, MA 01060
e-mail: sales@interlinkbooks.com

Contents

For the latest updates to *Washington, D.C. for Families*,
check out our page on the web at:

www.interlinkbooks.com/dcforfamilies.html

Acknowledgements

Everybody is part of a family. They have kids, or they want to have kids, or they were kids themselves. And just about everybody has either memories of or plans for family trips. The plans are always idyllic—the perfect family holiday. Sometimes the memories are just as good, and sometimes there are stories of trips gone humorously or unhappily awry. But everybody wants to share their stories or their hopes with somebody who writes books about family travel.

I'm deeply grateful for that. It is the stories, the memories, the plans, the help, the advice, and the encouragement that I get from other people that have made the books in the Family Travel Series successful, and that provide me with the incentive, the enthusiasm, and the help I need to write them. The support of friends and the kindness of strangers are evident on every page that follows.

In particular I'd like to thank my wife and friend of a lifetime, Barb, who has not only provided her usual assistance and encouragement, but has also taken over as series illustrator. Our three sons and the fabulous wives they've made a wonderful part of our family have all provided ideas for the book. So thanks to Mike and Beth, Rik and Elizabeth, and Doug and Sunnie for ideas, advice, and the memories of many, many happy travels.

I've never specifically thanked the people at Interlink Books in this section, and it's high time I did so. I work most closely with publisher Michel Moushabeck, editor Pam Thompson, and designer Juliana Spear, and their enthusiasm for these projects and their careful shepherding of each word, photo, and drawing through the publication process produces good books, and frequently brings out more in me than I realized was in there to start with. They and the rest of the staff are delightful folks to work with.

Many other people have provided help, often unlooked for, but always appreciated. In particular I want to acknowledge Alan Beiber and his family for their stories and advice; Adrian Bess, Department of Commerce security guard; Folger docent Mona Dingle; Carolyn Hadley at the Octagon; the delightful and informative Florence Marvil at Woodrow Wilson House; Linda McElroy from Colonial Williamsburg; the great jazz pianist Kahlid Moss; the very new and very helpful Washingtonian Susan Stavenhagen; and congressional staffer Douglas Weaver.

I also have to tell this story of kindness. I met David Marks and his young son as I sat on a bench outside the Children's Museum while I was resting from many weary hours and miles of walking. We chatted and I explained the project I was working on, my reason for being in a place like that unaccompanied by a little kid. When he asked me where my next stop was, I said I was about to trudge down to the Folger Shakespeare Library, a mile or so away. His response couldn't have surprised me more. He said, "Let me give you a ride. We're just on our way there now. My wife is Director of Public Relations at the Folger." That's just the sort of happy coincidence that often happens to travelers. I accepted the ride and the respite from walking, and he introduced me to his wife Garland Scott (the very person I would have asked to see), who treated me like visiting royalty. So a very special thanks to David and Garland, and countless people like them, who are quick to make strangers feel like lifelong friends, and who make the chance for all of us to travel to new places and to meet new people so very worthwhile.

Introduction

As world cities go, it's hard to believe that Washington, D.C., has made all that profound an impression. After all, has anyone ever written songs about it, like they have about Paris?

No. If there's even one song about Washington, I've never heard it.

Is it an ancient city, filled with castles and the faded footsteps of the kings and queens of a thousand years ago like London?

Sorry. No. There's a building that's called a castle, but it hardly compares to a real one, and there's not a solitary king to be seen. And London is about ten times older.

Is it a huge, sprawling city like New York, streets buzzing 24 hours a day, packed with millions of people, including young, hip celebrities from every imaginable field?

Again, no. Washington is about one-fifteenth the size of New York, it's quiet at night, and the biggest celebrities are middle-aged lawyers and politicians.

So why are you reading this book?

Is it because Washington, D.C., has the highest concentration of powerful people on the planet?

Or because every country in the world is affected by some decision that's made in Washington every day of the year?

Or because Washington is associated with as many or more important historical artifacts, events, people, and buildings as any other city on earth, no matter how old or large it is?

Or because the city has an incredibly high concentration of some of the world's finest museums, as well as spectacular architecture recognized by people from all around the world?

Could be.

Whether you're an American or a visitor from another country, you'll discover things in Washington that you've heard about all your life, have seen on television every week, and are affected by every day. Washington, D.C., is one of the most popular tourist destinations in the world, and in the pages that follow, you'll see exactly why.

The idea of a family trip to Washington, D.C., is a special one to me, because it was one of the first major trips the Lains took, and we learned a lot about traveling with each other and making the most of a new experience. The Lains know what's in store for your family—a wonderful, unforgettable time filled with spectacular sights and amazing memories.

Talk to our kids now and, years after that first D.C. trip together, they'll roll their eyes if you utter the words "Keep to the right." That's a story for Chapter 5. After you read Chapter 2 you'll know why our kids chuckle whenever they see a lawn sprinkler. And in Chapter 7 I'll tell you how we mixed algebra and Washington, to the disgust of our youngest son.

As the years go by, it's those little memories that mean as much—maybe more—as craning your neck to look up to the top of the Washington Monument or gawking at the Capitol Building. The chance to do neat things together... as a family... is the very best part of travel. If all you want to do is to see famous buildings, you can rent a video tape. But if your idea is to give your family a trip that will stay with them forever, that will produce one more memory to share when you're together, even after they've grown up, moved away, and have families of their own, traveling together to special places is one of the very best ways.

Like other books in my Family Travel Series, this one is meant to be your complete guide to the destination. This book will lead you to the most interesting, entertaining, and memorable family sites and activities in the Washington area, but it will do much more. The books in this series are complete guides to family travel: How to get there most efficiently, whether you're coming from 50 miles away or from halfway around the world. How to find affordable places to stay, including some options you may never have thought of. How to manage your money and your meals. How to beat the crowds at popular attractions. (In fact, if I'd finished this book sooner, a neighbor's family might have had a better trip. They had trouble getting into several places they wanted to see because other people had advance tickets and they didn't.)

Most important, we'll talk about how to get the most out of your travels by living like a local. This book will show you how to make your family more than tourists, how to become temporary Washingtonians instead, with the savvy and insider information of the native.

Not only that, but the travel tips in *Washington D.C. for Families* will show you how to banish the friction that too often is a part of travel, so you return home better friends than you were when you started. Family vacations where everyone actually returns home feeling rested and in good spirits are a rare and wondrous thing. But I hope they're a little less rare than they were before I started writing travel books!

One unique aspect of the books in this series is the information in Part III, a checklist of all the attractions discussed in the book, suitable for review, discussion, even family voting; suggested daily itineraries that show you exactly how to structure and pace a trip like this; and easy-to-use forms for managing your money, comparing accommodations, and finding affordable airfare if you fly.

Your kids might spend 12 years, 15 years, 20 years or more going to school, but most of what they learn about the world they'll live in for the rest of their lives will come from their experiences, not their schoolbooks. Travel develops an appreciation for the cultures and diversity of the world. Travel promotes a grasp of history and an understanding of the traveler's place in the world. Travel teaches openness, flexibility, and curiosity. All these were qualities we wanted our own kids to grow up with, and I suspect you want the same thing for yours. Travel is the grandest classroom imaginable.

At the same time, travel has to be affordable. We're not rich— we're teachers! So if we wanted our kids to see something of the world outside their home town, we had to find ways to cut financial corners without diminishing the experience. What we learned are the techniques that go into these books.

Let's spend the next couple of hundred pages together now, seeing how to put together a family trip that will linger in everyone's memory for a lifetime, a trip that will still be a topic of dinner-table conversation when you gather decades from now, a trip that will give your kids a first-hand feel for one of the world's greatest capital cities.

Let's all go to Washington!

I
The Trip You've Always Wanted

Whether you've dreamed for years about taking your family to Washington or the idea came to you last Tuesday after lunch, this is the book that can make it possible, even if you've never taken a family vacation this complex before. It doesn't matter whether you're coming from a nearby state or a distant country, *Washington D.C. for Families* gives you everything you need except plane tickets (and will show you how to get those for the best price). If you've got questions, this book has the answers.

In this first section, I'll deal mostly with the logistics and attitudes of travel: how to get there, where to stay, what to eat, how to dress, how to be comfortable in a new place... everything you can think of. I want your family to arrive in Washington eager and filled with ideas, confident that, even if you've never been here before, you can feel right at home in this city and have the time of your lives.

Now sit back, turn the page and let me help you get ready for one of the best vacations you'll ever have—in Washington!

1. Washington, Here We Come!

As you begin the process of planning a big family holiday, it's easy to feel what engineers at NASA must have felt when they decided to go to the moon: How can we possibly afford that? How will we get there? Where will we stay? What will we do there? Is this really a good idea after all?

But maybe that's not such a good analogy. Whether you're coming from halfway across Delaware or halfway around the world, taking an entire family on vacation is a lot more complicated than merely going to the moon.

This book is here to de-complicate the trip. If this is your first big family outing, we'll walk together step by step through the entire planning process so you're as well informed and as confident as any safari guide when you lead your own tribe through the exotic landscapes of the nation's capital. And even if you've already mastered the elements of family travel, *Washington D.C. for Families* will offer you a wealth of information and insider tips specifically for this terrific destination. I'll start—right here in the very first chapter—with the most important advice in the book: Planning is the key.

Washington, Here We Come!

I have nothing at all against being spontaneous. It's fun, challenging, and perfectly possible as part of a well planned vacation. But there are limits to that sort of thing, particularly when an entire family is involved. Barb and I are able to be more flexible now that the kids are on their own and finances are a little less tight than they were twenty years ago. But there are real restrictions on how impulsive you can be when the welfare of your whole family is at stake. So we learned how to plan well in order to be able to do what we wanted to do.

Besides, unplanned travel can be terribly expensive. We learned early how to stretch a penny so far that we could have set up a copper-wire manufacturing plant in our basement. We didn't let ourselves be deterred by the cost of travel; we just found ways to beat the system, doing what was important to us, and coming home with money still in our pockets.

I'll share a secret with you: Planning is fun! As soon as we decided to take a major trip, we started planning, even if it was months away. I absolutely loved that part of a trip because we learned all about the destination at our leisure, read up on the things we wanted to see (or avoid)—really had a chance to talk about the trip, to anticipate it, to get excited over it. It was almost like taking the trip twice: once before we left and again while we were there. And the planning made us feel like locals, knowing our way around, knowing how to use public transportation, knowing how the city worked. As a result, we spent less time getting oriented when we arrived and more time doing what we came for—having fun! We had discovered how to Live Like a Local. Even without kids in tow, that's still my favorite way to travel.

If taking your family to Washington—but doing it on your terms and within your budget is what's on your mind—you've picked up the right book.

When Should We Go?

Depends on what you mean by the question. So let's look at it from both ways.

First: How old should my kids be to get something out of it? I think it depends at least a little on where you're coming from. If you're an American, and your kids have been exposed to American politics and presidents, history and culture on a daily basis, they'll get something out of the trip by the time they're in school, although they won't remember much of it when they're older (which will give you a good excuse to go back again). By the time they're 9 or 10 years old they'll be ready for almost anything Washington can throw at them. But if you're coming from outside the United States, especially from a non-English-speaking country, the kids might get more out of the trip if they were a couple of years older than that, unless they've studied a lot about the U.S. and watched a lot of American TV (which I wouldn't wish on anybody).

On the other hand, kids older than age 4 or 5 from any culture will enjoy many of the non-governmental attractions—the zoo, the aquarium, the Air and Space Museum, the dinosaur bones at the Natural History Museum, the parks, the bustle of the big city. If my oldest child were 5 or 6 I don't think I'd plan a family trip to Washington yet; I'd wait a few years. But if my youngest were that age, and my oldest were at a good age for the trip, I wouldn't hesitate a moment to begin planning. I'd buy this book right away.

If, by the question "When should we go?" you mean, "What time of year is best for visiting Washington?" we can talk about that for a minute, too.

Many of Washington's most popular attractions are open 364 days a year, closing only on Christmas Day, so you'll probably see whatever you want whenever you decide to go. While Washington has throngs of visitors at all times of the year, it's most crowded in the summertime. That makes sense, since the kids are out of school and people have more of an opportunity to travel. But summers are stressful in Washington. The weather can be miserably hot and humid (much of Washington was once a swamp) in July and August, with temperatures sometimes topping 100 degrees (38°C). Crowds are at their worst then, with long lines everywhere.

But if that's the only time you can travel, it doesn't matter. Do it! Your attitude is much more important (and easier to control) than the weather or the crowds. Besides, there are more hours of daylight so you can get an earlier start (with kids? yeah, right!) and attractions are open later. You'll find more family-friendly events going on in the summer, and you'll probably run into somebody you know from back home. That's happened to us several times in Washington.

Things are least crowded in winter, and even the post popular attractions seldom have lengthy waits. It gets dark earlier in the winter and some attractions close an hour or two earlier than they do in summer, but by late afternoon, everybody is probably tired and ready for a rest anyway. Washington seldom gets heavy snow (although it's certainly possible) or frigid temperatures,

What a great time you'll have!

and the holiday decorations, including the National Christmas Tree, are things you can't see in summer.

Spring is lovely in Washington, and the weather is usually wonderful. This is the time many junior and senior high schools take class trips to the city, which means you always run the risk of being inadvertently trampled by a band of marauding 13-year-olds. Crowds are worst in the spring around the Tidal Basin, because the Japanese cherry trees are in bloom in late March and April, producing bumper-to-bumper traffic and enough people to intimidate a Tokyo subway passenger.

Fall—September through November—might be the nicest time to visit. Kids are back in school, people are back at work, the weather is pleasant and the days are still long. But the operative words are "Kids are back in school." That probably means yours. And a family vacation isn't nearly as much fun without the kids.

Go when you're able. If summer is all you have available, go in June, if possible. You'll beat the worst of the crowds and the weather will be more pleasant. Otherwise work around school holidays as well as you can. Every time of the years has its charms; you can't make a bad choice. What's important is that if this is something you want your family to do together, get busy. What got the Lains out of the house and onto the road and into the air was the realization one day that the "growing-up" time we had with our kids was half over, and that if we didn't do the things we wanted with them during that second half, we'd never get another chance. Don't miss that chance.

How Long Should We Stay?

You want to stay long enough to see the things that are important to your family—but to leave before your money runs out. I don't know how much money you've got, so I have no idea how long it's possible for you to stay, but I might be able to give you an idea or two for a minimum.

Travel can be tiring. Anticipation builds during the planning stage, but the act of travel wears everyone down. A trip that's too short is especially unsatisfying, because you feel you've gone to a lot time and trouble—not to mention expense!—for not much of a payoff. So… when is a trip too short?

Many travel veterans would suggest that this simple formula works well: Stay at least one night for every two hours of travel time.

Our own experiences make this seem like a pretty reasonable approach. We live about a 10-hour drive from Washington. Driving out over a three-day weekend would seem like a waste of time, because the time we'd spend confined in the car wouldn't be offset by the time we had to enjoy the destination. On the other hand, we can fly there in less than two hours. A weekend stay seems perfectly reasonable. Three hours on a train from New York? Stay at least a couple of nights. A six-hour flight from Seattle? A minimum three days before you move on. Are you starting with a one-hour flight to Frankfurt, a two-hour layover, and an eight-hour transatlantic flight? You'll feel disappointed if you spend much less than a week.

Every family has its own comfort level, of course. Experienced travelers or visitors who are making a return trip to a destination know how to squeeze the juice out of a city more quickly than a young family taking its first big trip, the way our first excursion to Washington was. What's important is that every member of your family feels content and energized after the trip. Use the 2 hours = 1 night formula as a starting point when you begin your planning, and adjust up or down from there as you need to.

Can We Really Afford It?

I don't honestly know, but I'll bet you can, because I'm going to show you some ways to make your stay in Washington as economical as possible, without sacrificing a bit of the fun. If you've picked up this book in the first place, taking your family is something you already would like to do, apparently, so I don't have to try to talk you into it—I just have to show you how easy it can be to make that family dream come true.

The key is planning. Fear of how much a trip is going to cost keeps more people at home than anything else. Note that I said the fear of the cost. Too often the dream ends right there, even before anybody actually investigates those costs. So right here, in the first chapter of the book, we'll rough out a budget together. Then, in the chapters that follow, I'll go into detail so you can see how it all works, and the many ways in which you can cut costs without cutting into your comfort or into the fun your family has. While Washington can be a terribly expensive city because of the many restaurants and hotels geared to people doing business with the federal government (and harrumph! —spending my tax dollars on those $100 lunches), there are bargains galore for families like yours.

A major trip like this one has two types of costs for you to analyze: Costs you have only a little control over, and costs you have a great deal of control over. We'll start with the toughest one.

The U.S. Capitol is one of the world's most familiar buildings

Costs You Can't Control

You will find really only one item in this category: Getting to Washington.

Even at that, some of you will have more control than others.

If you're coming from abroad or, probably, from west of the Mississippi River, your choices are very limited. You're probably going to fly. And if you have to fly, you have to pay whatever the airlines charge. Don't wring your hands (or your travel agent's neck) yet, though. Chapter 4 will lay out some terrific strategies for cutting your airfare.

Visitors from the eastern United States have more choices. Washington is a manageable drive from as far away as St. Louis (although I don't entirely relish the thought now of a 16-hour drive with a car full of kids, however much I love them. We've done that sort of thing, though, when we were younger and perhaps more patient). East Coast residents can even take the train. So many of you are not without choices. We'll look at those in more detail later, but for many Americans and nearly all international visitors, you'll have to fly.

Costs You Can Control

Here is where frugal people like us (OK—cheapskates like us) excel. Getting to Washington might account for half your travel budget if you're flying from Asia, and almost nothing if you're driving from Richmond, and you can't do much about it either way. But once you get there, choice abounds. Where do you want to stay? How elegantly do you want to dine? How will you get around? You can go as financially hog-wild as you like, but you can also stretch a dollar so far that it will reach from the Capitol to the Washington Monument.

Let's look at the areas I get the most questions about: what it will cost for someplace to stay, what it will cost for food, what it will cost for local transportation, what it will cost for admission to attractions, and what it will cost for shopping. We've always found it useful to figure our budget on a Per Person/Per Day basis, so that's what I'll do as we go along. This is a help especially when you're visiting a new place, and lets you compare costs readily.

Accommodations: After travel (for those of you who aren't driving from nearby), this will be your biggest single expense. Washington has some fabulous hotels, and if you own a couple of oil fields or are traveling on somebody's tax money you can probably afford to stay in them. I guess it would be really convenient to stay at a place like the Hay-Adams, which is just across a park from the White House, especially if you're having breakfast with the President in the morning. But I can find accommodations nearby for one-tenth of what a place like that could cost me, and I'd get just as good a night's sleep. (Probably better because I wouldn't have to worry about being thrown into debtors' prison when I couldn't pay the bill.) Washington has a wonderful variety of hotels, and inexpensive places just outside of the city are just minutes away by Metro.

But you don't have to stay in a hotel. One of the very best Lain money-saving strategies over the years has been to rent an apartment—something that would seldom occur to a first-time visitor. It sounds odd if you've never done it, but the financial advantages for a family are enormous. Chapter 3 will tell you how to go about it. While American cities don't have short-let apartments in the same profusion as major European cities, they do exist.

What do you give up by not staying in a hotel? Not a lot, really. There's no Room Service staff to deliver snacks at 3 a.m.— but how often would you use a service like that? Besides, you have your own kitchen. You can't get a wake-up call from the Front Desk—but if you're traveling with kids, what are the chances of oversleeping anyway? Apartments have more space than the largest hotel rooms (and when you're traveling, even the closest, most loving families can use a little extra space!) and can cost much, much less. One of the biggest advantages to this sort of place is that you can fix your own meals, just like you do at home: You Live Like a Local.

There's a sort of halfway option between an apartment and a

hotel, often called a Suite Hotel. Accommodations usually have a bedroom plus sitting room with a couch that opens into a double bed. They'll include a kitchenette, but sometimes only have a microwave to cook with. But they're still roomier than any standard hotel room and are excellent value.

A third money-saving possibility is a less-expensive hotel or motel outside the city. Because Washington is compact and its Metro is able to take you almost anywhere, you can save money by staying in suburbs like Arlington, Virginia, or Silver Spring, Maryland. If you're near the Metro you can still be in Central Washington within twenty minutes of leaving your front door. Sometimes you can save enough money like this to get two rooms with a connecting door for less than you'd have to pay for a single small room downtown.

Bottom line: You shouldn't have any trouble finding roomy, comfortable accommodations for under $35 or $40 Per Person/ Per Day. And you should be able to do much better. If we could make our kids young again and the five Lains were going to Washington next summer, my target would be $20 PP/PD.

The Lincoln Memorial is familiar to every visitor

Food: One reason apartments or suites with kitchenettes are a money saver is because you don't have to eat every meal in a restaurant. The amount of money you'll pay for one family meal in a mid-level restaurant will probably be enough to buy supplies for breakfast and dinner for a week, if you do your own cooking.

The strategy is to have breakfast in the apartment or hotel, have lunch in the city as a welcome sit-down break from sightseeing (most restaurants are much cheaper at lunchtime than at dinnertime), and head back to your apartment or hotel in the late afternoon. Everybody can take their shoes off and sprawl on the furniture for awhile, and one person (Be fair: Take turns!) can fix a simple supper that would cost ten times as much if you ordered exactly the same thing in a restaurant.

Remember, too, that you'd have bought food even if you had stayed home, so it's even less expensive than you think. Even if you don't have cooking facilities where you're staying, you can visit a local convenience story for boxes of cereal and cartons of milk for breakfast, and take along the fixings for sandwiches. Have your main meal at midday when restaurant prices are lower and just fix "lunch" in your room in the evening. Keep perishables in a cooler in your room; nearly all hotels and motels have free ice available.

Bottom Line: There's no reason to spend more than $10 to $25 PP/PD on food. Much depends on the ages of your kids, of course. Preschoolers are easy to fill up. Hungry teenagers can nibble their way through twice that between lunch and dinner if you're not paying attention. (All three of our sons were teenagers at the same time for a total of 33 months. We'll never forget it....) But that much ought to pay for everything from in-room meals to simple restaurant meals.

Sightseeing: I've got terrific news for you. Washington is one of the cheapest places in the world to see marvelous attractions. While there certainly are plenty of places that charge admission, some of the very best things in the city are absolutely free. All the Smithsonian museums, all the government buildings and monuments, many of the private and semi-private exhibitions are completely without charge. You can easily spend a week here seeing top-flight attractions without spending a dime. Budget about $5 PP/PD. You're not likely to need that much, but that will leave you some extra cash to use for an occasional afternoon ice-cream break.

Local Transportation: If you plan to drive to everything and park as close as possible, better double your travel budget. Parking, when you can find it, is stratospherically expensive. Here are the two words that tell you almost everything you need to know about getting around: "Feet" and "Metro."

Washington is incredibly walkable. It's a very compact city and as often as I've been there, I'm still amazed at how close together everything is. There is certainly nowhere else in the world where so many world-class attractions are so densely packed. But when you do want to go a bit farther afield, or to travel quickly from one side of town to the other, Washington's Metro is one of the country's very best subway systems: fast, clean, and inexpensive. Chapter 5 tells you everything you need to know about that and one ride will make you an expert.

For a few attractions, you might find your car useful, if you brought one, or take a taxi. But you'll almost certainly walk or take the Metro to 90 percent of the places you visit.

So how much to budget? $5 PP/PD is probably plenty unless you're visiting a lot of places in the more remote parts of the area.

Shopping: I always have trouble answering this one, because on my personal list of favorite things to do on vacation, shopping ranks somewhere between standing for an hour in a cold rain and losing my passport. But I've lived in a family that has recreational shoppers among its members, so have had to learn in self-defense. And I have to be honest here: Not many people go to Washington for the shopping.

Oh, Washington has a full measure of wonderful things to buy or to fantasize about; there's a lot of money in Washington, and that gives inevitable rise to numerous ways to separate all that money from its owners. You can shop as spectacularly in Georgetown or along Connecticut Avenue as you can in midtown Manhattan or London's Knightsbridge. But it's really not why people come to Washington. Most family shopping is likely to be of the tee-shirt / baseball cap / postcard / miniature Washington Monument variety, and $5 to $10 PP/PD will more than cover that.

But you know your family better than I do. Some members of your group won't feel like they've really been on vacation without at least one big shopping excursion, and that's fine with me. Your budget can be as high as your credit card company will allow.

Adding It Up: So now we've got a rough budget for the part of the trip you actually spend in Washington, as opposed to what it costs to get there. Let's recap:

Accommodations	$20 to $40 Per Person/Per Day
Food	$10 to $25
Sightseeing	$5
Getting Around	$5
Souvenir Shopping	$5 to $10
Estimated Cost	**$45 to $85 PP/PD**

Remember, that's for everything. And I think it would be possible to do even better without giving up anything you really wanted to do or sleeping in a cardboard box behind the railway tracks at Union Station. You can certainly spend more than that if you're not careful. But careful research and planning make a holiday like this not just possible, but easy and fun. We've taken the first step by outlining the budget. Now let's go into details about how your family can get the most out of Washington.

Recommendations

✔ Any time is good for visiting Washington, but avoid July and August, if you can, when crowds and heat are at their worst.

✔ Save whirlwind trips for after the kids are grown. Stay long enough to unwind and become part of the city, one day for every hour or two of one-way travel time.

✔ Keep close track of your costs by budgeting on a Per Person/Per Day basis.

2. The ABCs of DC, USA

You'd better get used to a lot of initials, abbreviations, and acronyms in Washington. You'll see signs leading you to the FDA, NTSB, DoD, FBI, USDA, USPS, HHS, FTC, OMB, SSA, VOA, HUD, GSA, and about a million other offices that will make you feel like you're wading through a vat of alphabet soup. Washington has a language all its own, because it's one of the few places left in America where just about everybody, directly or indirectly, works for the same company.

Decades ago, the United States was dotted with what were called "company towns." These were communities where a single major industry like mining or steel-making owned and controlled everything, and where nearly everyone worked in that industry. Sometimes even the grocery stores and theaters were owned by the company. Welcome to Washington, a modern "company town." There is only one business here that matters: the government of the United States. Everything else is very little more than support services.

Washington is an interesting place. If you're an American citizen or legal resident, allow yourself to be amazed by the fact that you personally are paying the salary of almost every man or woman you see wearing a uniform or a business suit. Okay— that's a little exaggerated, but probably not as much as you'd like to think. But the point is, visitors don't come here for the nightlife, the culture, or the cuisine (although all are available in abundance), but to absorb the rich history, the dazzling museums, and the seat of American politics. That's undoubtedly why you've decided to come as well. All that is possible because Washington truly is a company town—and the "company" is the United States government.

To be completely fair, though, there is a second major industry in Washington. Tourism! But without government, there would be no tourism. That's why the tourists come. The two are inseparable. So we're back to where we started: This is a one-industry town. Washington is a city of 572,000 people. Even the Washington Chamber of Commerce seems unsure how many government employees work here. (The usual line is "About half of them.") But 260,000 people work in the tourism industry, because an astonishing 20 million tourists visit the city each year—not more than about five of whom would bother to come if this were not the seat of the American government. And roughly 2 million of those tourists are from outside the United States.

Does D.C. Mean Directionally Challenged?

There are four abbreviations visitors must remember: NW, SW, NE, and SE. If you don't, you'll end up confused at best—and miles from where you want to be at worst.

Washington is divided into quadrants: Northwest, Southwest, Northeast, and Southeast, with the U.S. Capitol Building at its center. North and South Capitol streets form the east–west dividing line and East Capitol Street and the National Mall form the north–south dividing line. Check out the map on page 19 to see what I mean. All Washington addresses are followed by NW, SW, NE, or SE to tell you what quadrant of the city the building is in.

This is important because many streets in Washington have the same name, but are located in different parts of the city. For example, two congressional office buildings, the Russell Senate Office Building and the Cannon House Office Building, are both at the intersection of 1st Street and C Street. It sounds like they must be right across the street from each other, doesn't it?

Wrong! They're more than one-third of a mile (0.6km) apart.

The Russell is at 1st and C NE, and the Cannon is at 1st and C SE. While they are on the same 1st Street, there are two different streets called C Street. (For that matter, there are also two different streets called 1st Street, which means that if you tell somebody you'll meet them at the corner of 1st and C streets, there are four different places in the city they might turn up, each many blocks from the other. If this is giving you a headache, take two aspirin and look at the map. It will help.)

Why ever did they do it that way? And why don't they change it!

Regardless of the answer to that, we're stuck with it. Just remember the four most important abbreviations in D.C.

A State of Confusion

Lots of Americans are uncertain about what the District of Columbia is, exactly, so imagine the bewilderment of visitors from other countries. Here's a thumbnail history lesson.

When the United States ratified its Constitution in 1787, its capital city was New York. But the states were about equally divided between North and South, and Southerners wouldn't tolerate placing the capital in the North. So a compromise was reached: the states of Maryland and Virginia would each contribute a little bit of land for a small federal territory that would stand between the two halves of the country. That territory (which included a lot of swampland that neither state really cared much about anyway) was named the District of Columbia. The new capital would be built there, in this small rectangle that now includes just 61 square miles.

President George Washington, a surveyor in his youth, personally chose the area where the new federal buildings

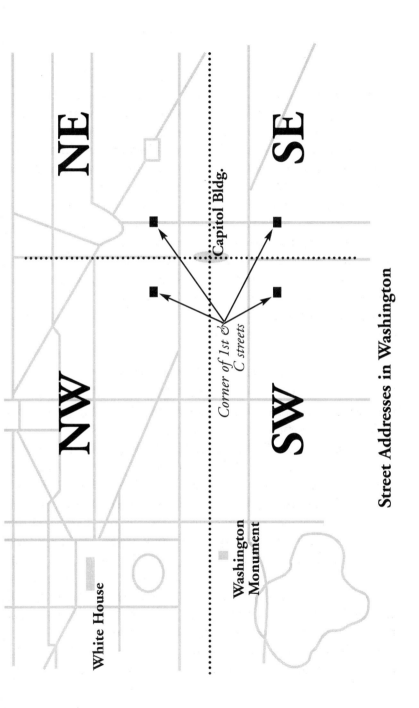

Street Addresses in Washington

would be located and, in 1793, personally laid the cornerstone for the new Capitol Building. Washington, however, did not approve of naming the new city after himself, and referred to it only as "Columbia."

John Adams, the second president of the United States, was the first president to live in the new capital, moving into the half-finished President's House (now known as the White House) in 1800.

But the District of Columbia was never considered a state. It has no voting members in the U.S. Congress (although it has a non-voting member in the House of Representatives) and its residents weren't even allowed to vote in presidential elections until 1964. Ironically, the residents of the nation's capital have

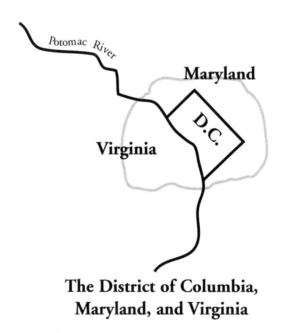

**The District of Columbia,
Maryland, and Virginia**

less say in their own government than any other citizen of that nation. Even today, many Washington, D.C., license plates are emblazoned with the words "Taxation Without Representation," now a complaint about their ambiguous political status and not an echo of the Colonial dissent of 250 years ago.

Today, while the District has fixed geographic limits, its influence oozes over into the states it adjoins. If you're visiting the top Washington attractions, you're almost certain to venture into Virginia or Maryland for some of them. A visit to Arlington National Cemetery or Mount Vernon will take you just across the Potomac River into Arlington, Virginia, and Alexandria, a wonderful place for shopping and walking, is also in Virginia. A ride on the C&O Canal or a trip to the National Wildlife Center will send you into Maryland. And you might find, within walking distance of the Metro, more affordable accommodations in either state that you'll find in downtown Washington.

A Suitable Place for Tourists

Some people don't like traveling to places where they can easily be spotted as tourists. That's not an issue in Washington. Everybody will know you're a tourist. It doesn't matter, though, because most of the people you see will be, too. And you'll be a lot more comfortable than the Washingtonians anyway. While the frequent advice in this book is to Live Like a Local, that doesn't mean you have to dress like them.

You see, I made a sarcastic crack a few pages ago (I didn't say untrue—just sarcastic) that almost everybody you see in a business suit is working either for or with the government. I should have described the full uniform as business suit, briefcase, and cell phone. The tourists are the ones who, in 98° summertime heat (that's 37°C), are wearing shorts, sandals, and tee-shirts. The locals are the ones in gray suits, long-sleeved shirts, and neckties, or blue blazers, nylons, and sensible shoes. And perspiration.

The locals are also carrying briefcases (probably containing bologna sandwiches and proposals to increase postal rates) instead of maps, and they all have cell phones glued to their ears. I'm certain I've seen two bureaucrats walking down the street side-by-side, talking to each other on their cell phones. A character on one popular British television comedy describes the incessant cell-phone use of another character by saying, "It's like an extra organ, that thing!" Nowhere is that more true than in Washington. But you can always spot the really important people—they have assistants to answer the phone for them.

> *Tip:* *If you want to blend in with the locals, or sound really in the know, never call this city "Washington." Just say "D.C." and you'll sound just like a senator.*

It does seem strange at first to walk along Pennsylvania Avenue, right in front of the White House, and see a crowd of young men (some with suit jackets tossed aside and ties tucked into shirts) playing roller hockey in the middle of the street. Undignified, somehow. But the street is closed to traffic, so at least it's getting used for something. Besides—why not encourage people to play games and enjoy themselves in front of their country's most famous house? The "Pursuit of Happiness" was one of the key ideas in the Declaration of Independence, after all. Besides, we've seen soccer games in front of the Paris city hall and cricket matches next to Buckingham Palace in London. Why not play in Washington, too?

Like most big cities, Washington always has lots of construction and lots of noise. If you follow my advice and do lots of walking (or ignore it and try to drive around the city), you're bound to come across lots of street work, renovation, and repair that will cause you to have to dodge and detour a bit. I found so much construction in one downtown area on a recent trip that I started keeping score. On a six-block walk in the

Judiciary Square area, I had to switch sides of the street, walk along a temporary path, or dodge a building site eleven times.

But the good side of that is that the city is in good repair and things work when they're supposed to.

Signs around here aren't always up-to-date, though. I was intrigued by one pointing the way to the U.S. Mint Museum. As a one-time coin collector I was excited, and headed off to the new Treasury Department office building on 9th Street NW. The security guard on at the door admitted that the signs were a little premature. "They haven't even started it yet," he told me. "It's supposed to be open in about two years." Perhaps.

But as a tourist you'll be welcomed everywhere you go that's actually open, and Washingtonians are notoriously friendly and helpful to visitors. I've never encountered a rude or uncooperative native in Washington. Quite the reverse, in fact: They're usually all too willing to talk my ear off and I sometimes have trouble escaping from friendly people. Even the animals are obliging.

Baltimore's Inner Harbor is the city's most popular gathering spot

Beyond D.C.

I'm encouraging you, even pleading with you, to take your family to Washington, because I know what a great time everyone will have. But I'm not suggesting for a moment that you confine yourself to it. Some of the best attractions you'll see are outside the District of Columbia, in the adjacent states of Maryland and Virginia.

You'll see those places described in detail in Part II of the book, but I think it's worth putting in a plug for them now. If you drove to Washington, or plan to rent a car, all of them are easy to get to. If you're relying on public transportation, most of them are still available to you. I'll tell you just how to get there. Let's look at the highlights now.

Maryland

Baltimore is easy to reach by rail from Washington; MARC trains run from Union Station and several Metro stations with a frequent and inexpensive service that takes less than an hour. That makes Baltimore an ideal daytrip, but there's so much to do there, you might want to put it at the beginning or end of your trip and stay two or three days.

The National Aquarium is the centerpiece of Baltimore's revitalized Inner Harbor. But Port Discovery, the Maryland Science Center, the U.S.S. Constellation, and the Star Spangled Banner House are nearby. Not far away are Fort McHenry, stadiums for professional baseball and football, and a wealth of other fascinating places.

As you head toward Washington from Baltimore, you can do what the Lains have done, stopping at some of the many other Maryland attractions like the National Wildlife Visitors Center, the Cryptologic Museum, the National Capital Trolley Museum, or the C&O National Historic Park. All are easy to reach by car if you're driving, but public transportation is dicey.

Virginia

Go south from Washington and you're in Virginia. Several attractions, like the Pentagon, Arlington National Cemetery, and Old Town in Alexandria, are available on the Metro. You can drive or get a Tourmobile bus to Mount Vernon, but if you want to go to the Claude Moore Colonial Farm or Leesburg Animal Park, or shop your way through the countless malls and outlet centers from Tyson's Corner to Leesburg, you'll need a car—or a large truck to hold all your purchases. Little more than an hour's drive away is Manassas National Battlefield Park, the moving site of two of the bloodiest battles of the American Civil War.

The ABCs of DC, USA

About three hours away by car is the country's most comprehensive historical recreation, Colonial Williamsburg, frozen in time in 1774. This one-time capital of Virginia Colony is still home to dozens of original buildings and hundreds of others rebuilt on the original foundations. Nearby are Jamestown, site of the first permanent English settlement in America, and Yorktown, where the British army surrendered to Washington and American independence was won.

Everywhere you go, inside the District of Columbia or outside it, you'll find fascinating places to visit for an hour or a week. A trip to Washington that's just a trip to the city of Washington will miss some of the best, most family-friendly attractions in the area.

I'll pardon you if you refuse to believe this story, but it's true, and happened while I was working on this book: I spent a full ten minutes one Thursday morning watching a squirrel patiently sitting on a park bench, posing for a group of tourists from Japan, who one by one, crept to within a foot or two of him to take a closeup photo. When they all had their pictures, he chattered cordially, then scurried off to investigate a nearby litter basket.

That's not to say that the locals are above having a little fun at your expense. On the Lain family's very first trip to Washington, we came out of the National Museum of American History just before 5 o'clock in the afternoon. We were tired and footsore, and it was a warm June day. Like a couple of dozen other tourists, we sat along a low concrete wall on Constitution

Washington is home to people from everywhere

Avenue, nibbling ice cream treats from one of the seven or eight mobile concessions stands parked along the street selling food and souvenirs. But we did notice something odd: All the vendors were watching the tourists with the same secret smile.

I felt to see if I had ice cream on my nose and was looking around to see if someone was making rude gestures behind me when I heard the bell in the Post Office Tower strike 5 o'clock. Suddenly the automatic lawn sprinklers behind us clicked on, and all the way down Constitution Avenue you could see wet tourists leaping to their feet like somebody had electrified the wall. And all the way down Constitution Avenue you could see a line of grinning vendors, taking part in what was obviously a daily ritual. There was nothing we could do but smile back. We'd been had.

It will take you no time at all to get used to the acronyms of Washington, and to its government/tourist dichotomy. You'll learn your way around, learn what the important abbreviations stand for (and ignore the rest), and revel in your status as a visitor. You'll be approached by strangers and asked to take their photos in front of famous monuments, and you'll ask strangers to take your picture, too. And you'll learn Washington, A to Z, in no time.

Recommendations

✔ Always double-check addresses to make sure you're heading for the right part of town.

✔ Play a game one day: Have everyone write down every abbreviation and acronym they encounter and make a list. Or tally the number of cell phones you see.

✔ Remind your kids to be just as cheerful and helpful to people who ask them for directions or to take a picture as you want others to be when you ask for help.

3. Make Yourself at Home

When we're at home we don't live in a big fancy house with enormous rooms, designer furniture, plush carpeting, and significant art adorning the walls. Our house is comfortably broken in, informal, and filled with the unmatched bits and pieces of our lives, an accumulation of things from here and there, not a planned décor where everything fits together to make a fashion statement. In fact, if I ever got a fashion statement, it would just tell me my account was overdrawn.

We have nothing whatsoever against beautifully decorated homes, and really admire people who have the aesthetic sense and good taste to pull it off. But to me, at least, a house has always been primarily a handy device to keep the rain off. So when I travel, I'm pretty easy to please. I don't need to stay at the Hay-Adams (a shockingly expensive hotel favored by visiting dignitaries) to be happy; I'll settle for clean and comfortable. The only time I stay somewhere posh is if somebody else is paying the bill—something that doesn't happen very often!

On the other hand, some people see travel as a perfect opportunity to live the way they wish they could in real life—to be pampered a bit, to experience for a week or two the things they couldn't possibly afford the rest of the year. That's fine, too.

Sleep Cheap

How can you be sure you're getting the best possible price for accommodations? You probably can't. If there are 100 rooms in the building you're staying in, the occupants are probably paying 99 different rates. But here are some tips for getting the best deal.

Do some research. Decide from the questions in this chapter and the forms in Chapter 20 what's important to you, and what you are not willing to pay for. Get information from your travel agent, if you're using one, although they usually have very little information about apartments. Go to the websites listed at the end of this book. Make a list of three to five places that look promising.

Check "rack rate" prices—standard price, in layperson's terms—and obvious discounts like those often available to auto club members, retirees, military personnel, and government employees. Many chains have their own incentive programs, often free, that provide discounts or upgraded accommodations. The most consistent piece of advice hotel managers provide (privately!) is this: Never pay rack rate.

Be flexible in your dates, if you can. Some places charge less on weekends, when the lack of business travelers leave more rooms empty. Sometimes moving your stay to a different week will get you a better price.

During the regular business day, telephone the places you're considering (not their toll-free reservations numbers) and ask to speak to the manager. This is the person who can provide the most flexibility in prices. Explain that you're excited about bringing your family to Washington and are trying to make this very

When you take your family to Washington, you have plenty of choices. You can spend more per night on your room than the annual salary of the CEO of a multinational corporation, or you can live frugally and save your money for shopping, dining, transportation, or your kids' college funds. Washington is a city where it's easy to live lavishly (remember, it's filled with politicians living on taxpayer dollars) but quite possible to live economically: There are more than a half million real people who live here, too, who are just like the rest of us. If they can afford it, so can we.

In this chapter, we'll talk about strategies for finding a place to live as a temporary Washingtonian. When we travel, we try as much as we can to Live Like a Local, an approach that extends to how we get around the city, what we eat, and where we stay.

Notice that I said strategies for finding a place. I don't like to recommend specific places, as a rule, because they change. The first place we stayed in Washington was terrific … and it's not there any more. One hotel I listed on my website for another book devolved into a place that didn't have a clean and safe feel to it—and just in the short time between my

special family holiday affordable. Get the manager on your side with your courtesy and enthusiasm. Ask for the best possible price, then ask if there are ways to reduce it further, perhaps by changing dates, bringing a sleeping bag for one of the kids instead of using a rollaway bed, foregoing the daily maid service, or something else.

Telephoning the manager is good strategy even if you're calling internationally. In fact, if you are phoning from abroad, be sure to say so. It will probably get you a faster response and a better price. If language is a problem, use a fax instead, but be sure to address it to the manager—by name, if possible.

Do some research, talk directly to the manager, and ask good questions by using the form in Chapter 20: Those are your tickets to the very lowest rates, no matter what sort of place you're staying in.

visit and the publication of the book. So rather than list a dozen places that might not be in your price range or located where you want to be, I'll talk about how you can find a place that meets your own needs—convenience, price, neighborhood character, and amenities.

Types of Properties

It was our first family trip to Washington that got us thinking about how creative we could be with finding accommodations, and how much money we could save by going beyond the obvious. What we learned on that trip—some of it accidentally—has saved us hundreds of dollars… and given us more comfortable trips… ever since. Here's the story:

Affording the trip to Washington was going to be a strain on our budget, taking every bit of the money we'd saved for it. But we'd promised the kids and we were excited about it ourselves, so we began looking for ways to cut corners.

One big expense, we knew, would be meals. Restaurant meals are expensive because you're not only paying for food, you're paying the salaries of the people who cook it, who bring it to your table, who clear the dirty dishes away, and who vacuum the floors after the customers go home. You're paying for building rental, heat, light, furniture, and upkeep. And you're paying for hundreds of things more than I haven't the space to list, plus a profit to the owner. At home you're paying for the food—period.

So we decided to save on food. With three hungry sons, one already a teenager, we knew that didn't mean fewer meals—but it did mean fewer restaurant meals. Everyone agreed that to make the trip possible, no one would complain about a lack of varied or elaborate meals, so we stocked up on inexpensive things from the grocery store like peanut butter and store-label breakfast cereal that didn't need refrigeration, and we bought a large boneless ham we could keep iced in our big picnic cooler. We'd have simple

Maybe you'll be able to see the Washington Monument from your window

breakfasts, lunchtime picnics of peanut butter sandwiches and fruit, and easy dinners we could fix in our hotel room, eating only occasionally at restaurants. That way, we figured, we would cut our food costs by more than 75 percent.

It worked beyond our wildest hopes, but only partly because of our frugality. When we got to the hotel, they had given us their "family room" for just about the same price as a standard room. This was a space about twice the size of a regular room and it had a kitchenette! Now we could do our own cooking, something that had never occurred to us! The extra room made life a lot more comfortable for everybody, and the cooking facilities saved us almost as much in meals as the room itself cost.

That was a turning point for us in learning how to travel. We discovered that we could save money and have more fun if we tried to Live Like a Local. Apartment life, simple cooking, and becoming part of a neighborhood are not just economical choices, they're ones that will make you feel closer to the city you're visiting.

Let's look at what types of accommodations are available in Washington, including one you might not have thought of, and the plusses and minuses of each.

Motels

If you're coming to Washington from overseas, this is a term that might be unfamiliar. Short for "motor hotel," these accommodations dot American roadways from coast to coast. They began in the vast rural areas between large cities, providing motorists with reliable places to stop for the night on a long drive. Now they are found in cities of every size and at the conjunction of all major highways.

While size and amenities vary widely, motels generally offer free parking, small rooms, two double beds, bland décor, rooms that open directly onto the parking lot, and clean if often spartan accommodations. Prices tend to be low.

You'll find motels located in downtown Washington, and the prices will be lower than those of full-service hotels. But the rooms are likely to be uncomfortably small for a family to spend a week or more in, unless the kids are very small. You can often, however, get two rooms joined by a connecting door for much less than twice the cost of a single room. This is great if you have older kids—and you have the real bonus of having two bathrooms!

Some motels include a continental breakfast in the room cost. While this is usually just donuts, bagels, coffee, and juice, you might sometimes find cereal, fruit, toaster pastries, and other items. Better yet, some places offer small refrigerators and microwave ovens in the rooms, useful for storing and preparing simple meals. Some motels even offer rooms with kitchenettes that include a small stove, pots and pans, and tableware. This can be a wonderfully inexpensive option for a family. After all, if you're going to Live Like a Local, you should remember that few locals eat in restaurants all the time.

Don't just look in downtown Washington. We've stayed in quieter neighborhoods in the city, within walking distance of the Metro, and in nearby suburbs like Alexandria, Virginia, and Silver Spring, Maryland, where we've been able to walk to the Metro or drive to a Metro station and park nearby for about one-tenth of the cost of parking downtown. In fact, this is a strategy we've used in numerous cities. Room prices are usually lower in the suburbs, and if you've got Metro passes anyway, there's no additional commuting cost.

Hotels

These full-service lodgings are often the automatic choice of foreign travelers who aren't aware of other options and many Americans who think these are the best places for being close to the attractions in Washington, D.C. But hotels are often mostly inhabited by government and business people who can afford to stay at fancy hotels because someone else (often we taxpayers) is paying the bill.

In truth, the best thing about hotels is that, as a rule, they charge so much that you're sure to get a bit of pampering. Hotels are likely to have good restaurants, swimming pools, room service, carpeted hallways, valet parking, and a fawning staff—although none of these is guaranteed. All this comes at a price.

There are places like New York City that are so hotel-oriented that it can be difficult to ferret out other housing options. But a traditional hotel is usually my last choice in Washington. The city is compact enough that you can get from place to place quickly on public transportation (or by car, if you have one), and hotels have a lot of amenities a family just doesn't use. Anyway, hotel quality varies a lot, and it's possible to end up in a place with rooms that are no larger or nicer than those in the motel down the street... but at twice as much money as the motel charges.

Speak to the manager personally

Apartments

Our experience on that first Washington trip was a revelation. What we'd actually ended up with was just one big room, but we could cook there and we had room to spread out: Although it wasn't called that, basically what we had was an efficiency (or studio) apartment! That became part of our travel strategy, when possible, from then on.

Renting an apartment for just a week or two seems like a pretty far-out thing to do if you've never done it. But the advantages are easy to spot once you arrive. There's much more room than you'll ever get in a hotel room, giving family members a chance for a little privacy now and then—something you never get sharing a single room. You can save great wads of money by cooking some of your own meals in the mornings and evenings instead of eating at restaurants all the time. You're more likely to stay in a normal neighborhood, surrounded by local people than in a more congested business area, surrounded by other tourists. You shop where the locals shop, relax in the parks with local residents, and get to know your neighbors a little, just like at home. You're Living Like a Local!

Not only do apartments have more space than even the largest hotel rooms, they often have amenities hotels usually don't.

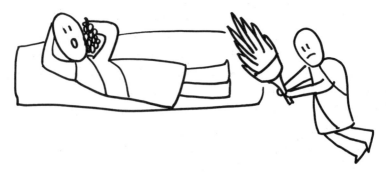

Take some time to relax in your room

Make Yourself at Home

These can include VCRs or DVD players, CD players, laundry facilities, and full kitchen facilities, of course. You can find studio apartments, usually with separate sitting and dining areas, that will sleep up to four people comfortably. Apartments with a living room sleeper sofa and one or two bedrooms are especially nice for longer stays.

How much will this cost? It varies, of course, according to the size and location of the apartment. But Washington has short-stay apartments for less than $1,000 a week, or about $35 per person/per night for a family of four. If that seems like a lot, consider that an ordinary hotel room at $150 per night (a realistic hotel price, though you can do better) would cost $1,050 for a week, and you'd have just one room, and no realistic way of avoiding restaurants for most of your meals. What you'll spend on just one family dinner in a restaurant will probably buy you a week's worth of groceries. And less expensive apartments are available.

Short-stay apartments are not as common in the United States as they are in Europe, but they are available. Because Washington has so many visitors from around the world in town to do business with some government agency or other, apartments are often marketed to business travelers. But there's no reason why defense contractors and labor union lawyers should be the only ones to enjoy the benefits of having a genuine home away from home. There's no reason for you not to Live Like a Local.

Landlords sometimes advertise a one-month minimum for these apartments, but many will accept bookings for shorter periods if you ask nicely. We always found that telling the landlord about how much our kids were looking forward to the trip and how being able to save money on accommodations was the only way we could make it possible usually got a helpful response.

Renting an apartment isn't the norm, but a little looking can help a family put together a less expensive, more comfortable vacation.

Suite Hotels

Once a rarity, suite hotels are one of the lodging industry's hottest trends. A suite hotel, at its best, is a cross between a hotel and an apartment. Visitors have many of the traditional hotel amenities like a pool, maid service, and more, but have larger living spaces and kitchens.

Prices vary widely here, too, from very reasonable to nobody's-got-that-much-money. Vacationers will want to be sure of what they're getting. Standard hotel rooms fitted with microwaves, coffee makers, and refrigerators are not suites. If there are not at least two rooms, a dining table, and a small stove, you're not really any better off than you would be in a hotel, and you're probably paying way too much. But you can find some good values, too, and there's usually no minimum stay in a suite hotel as there can be in an apartment.

Your Shopping List

Before most of us go to the grocery store, we make a list of what we want to buy, so we don't forget something really important, or so we don't get a lot of unnecessary items. Shopping for accommodations is exactly the same, only you don't get to bring your purchases home with you.

When you book accommodations for your family in a city you don't know very well, you're in the same position as a grocery shopper. You want to make sure you get all the essentials, but you know it's pointless to pay for things you don't use. Every family will differ on what it considers the essentials.

For example, in all the traveling our family did together, I can remember us using a swimming pool exactly once. But if my brother tried to stop someplace without a pool, his daughters would probably start planning a mutiny before the bags were out of the van. Here's a list of things to investigate wherever you stay. Decide whether each of these is a must-have item, and whether you're willing to pay extra for the ones that aren't.

Make Yourself at Home

One room or multiple rooms: If you're only taking a couple of preschoolers to Washington (I certainly wouldn't, but that's up to you), a single room might be enough. But the more people you've got, the older they are, and the longer you stay, the more you'll crave extra space. Adjoining motel rooms, an apartment, or a suite are your best bets, unless you can get a single very large room.

Extra beds: Do you need a crib for a little one or a rollaway bed? Most places will provide those at little or no additional charge, but you have to ask. Even where there's a charge, asking the manager to waive it if you bring your own linens will often get a positive response.

Meal options: Do you want a full kitchen? That will save you the most money and make better meals possible. Unless you're

No matter what you forget to pack, you can buy it in Washington

doing the eat-every-meal-at-a-restaurant thing, a refrigerator and microwave are the minimum. At the very least, look into the availability of a complimentary continental breakfast. Room service? Forget it. Those are the most expensive meals on the planet. Restaurants that are part of large hotels are usually very expensive, too, although diners and coffee shops attached to motels can be comparatively good value, although not as cheap as cooking yourself.

Accessibility: If a member of your family has mobility problems, make sure an elevator or ground-floor rooms are available, and that the bathroom is accessible. That's usually not a problem in a hotel or motel, but might be in a private apartment.

Air conditioning: Make sure apartments are air conditioned if you'll be visiting in the summer. Washington, D.C., sometimes gets temperatures of over 100°F (38°C) in July and August, and humidity is high as well. In less expensive motels, make sure you can control the temperature in your own room. We've stayed in a few places where the manager set the thermostat for the entire building ... and didn't want to run the a/c any more than absolutely necessary.

Other amenities: Do you, like my nieces, insist on a swimming pool? Few people want to pay extra for a hotel health club on a family vacation, but if that matters to you, find out how it's equipped. I've been in hotels that called one treadmill and one set of free weights a health club. If you're staying more than a week, ask whether you have access to laundry facilities. Do you require a non-smoking room or apartment?

Location and transportation: Do you want to be close to a specific attraction or neighborhood? D.C. is easy to get around in but if you want to stay near a particular site or near family or friends, you'll want to know how far away you are from your target. Know where the nearest Metro station is; you'll want to be within walking distance. Are you bringing a car? Then free parking will save you lots of money. Flying in? Some places provide free or inexpensive airport transfers.

Chapter 20 includes easy-to-use forms that incorporate all these points and more. Fill them out as you investigate accommodations and you'll soon have all the information you need to make a decision about what's best for your family. In no time at all, you'll be ready to unpack your luggage in your comfortable Washington home away from home and begin to Live Like a Local Washingtonian.

Recommendations

✔ Consider renting an apartment. Preparing your own meals is a great way to save money.

✔ Always speak directly to the manager in getting the best price for your accommodations.

✔ Adjoining motel rooms can be a realistic option to an apartment, providing at least one has cooking facilities.

4. Travel Ins and Outs

I suppose we have it easy. If we wanted to take a long trip in an earlier age, we'd have had to spend weeks in a sailing ship, pushed about by fickle winds on a rolling ocean, or weeks in a wagon pulled by a team of surly horses while being trampled by bison and pursued by angry people who, with considerable justification, didn't want us traipsing through their land. No wonder the vast majority of people never traveled more than 50 miles from the spot they were born.

Now all we have to do is spend untold hours cooped up in a rolling metal box about the size of two bathtubs while other speeding metal boxes buzz around us like gnats, trying to see how close they can come without actually hitting us, or else allowing ourselves to be bolted into an oversized soda pop can and flung toward our destination at an altitude at which human life is impossible outside our soda can's thin metal skin, and at a speed approaching that of a bullet.

Yes, things are much better in our modern world.

Obviously I'm not a person who has ever believed that "getting there is half the fun." But I hope you've figured out that I wouldn't be encouraging your family to take this trip if travel were really as bad as all that. In fact, we travel as much as our time and money will allow us to, and few things we've ever done have been as much fun.

Still, it's the being in a place, not getting there, that's the best part. So in this chapter, we'll talk about how to make the actual traveling part of your trip go as smoothly as possible so you arrive relaxed and excited when you get to the good parts of the holiday.

Getting Ready

In Chapter 8 is a little homily on the virtues of spontaneity, but unless you live very close indeed to Washington, you're not going to just take off for a family trip to the city on the spur of the moment. It takes a bit of planning—the sort of thing you're doing right now, learning all about your destination.

We've already talked about how to find comfortable and affordable accommodations. You've probably also already decided how to get there. Most people will either drive or fly, although if you live along the Eastern seaboard or near one of the relatively few other places in the United States where rail service is available, the train is a possibility. That's actually my favorite way to travel, but since the nearest Washington-bound train to my home is 50 miles away, and that one comes in the middle of the night just three days a week, it's not very practical for us.

If you're driving, your plans for getting to Washington can be fairly simple. You can easily drive 400 to 500 miles a day with little strain on Interstate highways, and if you come through the Appalachian Mountains, you'll see some beautiful scenery. Packing as much as you want is no problem, although overdoing it creates more problems than it solves. You'll have no trouble finding a comfortable and inexpensive motel along the way if your drive stretches beyond a single day.

Trains are easy, too, and take roughly as long as driving. They're more expensive, but you're paying for the convenience of not having to spend eye-glazing hours of staring at a ribbon of concrete. Reservations are a good idea for a whole family traveling together, especially in the summer.

That leaves flying.

Traveling with Reservations

You can go to the university nearest you and sign up for graduate classes in astronomy where they'll teach you how to calculate the position of any star for any hour of any day in the past or future, or where you learn to perform complicated statistical tests that will baffle a high-speed computer. Those are much easier tasks than trying to make sense out of the way airlines price their seats.

I used to recommend travel agents enthusiastically and I still do, especially for international travel. But the fees many agencies have imposed as airlines have cut their commissions now can increase the cost of a low-fare domestic ticket by 10 to 20 percent. When you're buying tickets for four or five people, that can add up. Check with your agent to see how much, if anything, the agency charges for domestic bookings. If it's too

*The plane you flew in on was much better than the
Wright Brothers' first one*

much, check individual airlines, airline websites, or one of the travel websites in the back of this book.

You can do some things on your own to keep the price down, however. Here are some things you should know about airfares. They might not get you the lowest fare on the plane, but they'll put you well down the list.

• Prices are often highest in the summer and near holidays when more people want to travel. Wintertime trips can save money, especially if you're coming from abroad.

• Most people know that Saturday night stays are usually mandatory for the lowest fares. But did you know that the lowest fares are usually available only for travel Monday through Thursday?

• Nonstop flights are more convenient but you can often save big bucks if you're willing to make a connection.

• Check the prices from all airports within driving distance of your home. Prices can be greatly different from airports just an hour apart.

• Check prices to all three Washington-area airports—National, Dulles, and Baltimore. Prices will be different.

• There's usually a discount, probably 5 to 10 percent, for booking on the airline's own website.

• Watch for sales. Airlines have them just like other businesses.

• Take advantage of frequent flier deals. Transcontinental or international trips can rack up a lot of miles, and paying the fare with an airline-endorsed credit card can add still more.

Pack Animals

I occasionally travel to weekend conventions with university students, and try as I might, I can't persuade them not to check a suitcase—or two. For a weekend! I've seen individuals travel abroad who have used up their entire carry-on and checked-luggage allowance and pay exorbitant excess baggage fees. Why, oh why?

Customary Procedures

If you're arriving at Dulles or Baltimore from outside North America (visitors from Canada usually take care of these formalities before boarding the plane), your first stop in the U.S. won't be the White House or Capitol Building, but the Immigration and Customs checkpoints. There's no way to avoid the hour-or-so the process takes, so be patient and good-humored and you'll be strolling across the Mall in no time.

On the plane you were given an I-94 form—the landing card. Note that this is free and provided on the plane. Don't fall for the Internet scam of buying one in advance. The I-94 asks a few basic questions (name, flight number, where you're staying and for how long) and the flight attendants are always willing to help if there's anything you don't understand.

When you land you have no decisions to make. Just follow the throng of people to the Immigration Hall. There's one line for holders of U.S. passports and one line for everybody else. The line here is longer than the line for the toilets at a World Cup match, but don't worry, it moves surprisingly fast.

When you finally get to the front of the line, your entire family should go together to the desk. Hand over your passports, I-94, and visas, if you need them. They will be inspected and stamped, and the immigration officer might have a few questions, normally whether you're in the country for business or pleasure, or how long you plan to stay. Despite their reputation for nastiness, I'm never met a rude or unpleasant immigration officer in any country. Don't be intimidated, just answer the questions. Don't make jokes, and smile.

If you're driving to Washington, you don't have to be too rigorous about packing. You can fill the trunk, pile things on your kids' laps, haul a trailer if you want. But a lot of luggage is a pain in the neck (or back) on a train, and a real impediment if you're flying. Here are some packing tips.

Nobody cares what you're wearing, if your clothes are clean, and they won't remember you in five minutes anyway, so it's okay to wear the same clothes two or three times, unless the weather is really hot and humid. You don't need a different ensemble every day. You won't need fancy clothes, just comfortable ones, unless you're dining at the White House.

Take layers, especially in winter when the weather might start out very cold but be quite warm by afternoon. Stick to one basic color and its complements. Then anything can be worn with anything else.

Nothing is more important than comfortable shoes with good support. Everyone will walk a lot more than they usually do and blisters can ruin a day—not just for the Tenderfoot, but for everyone who has to listen to his or her complaints.

> *Next, follow the crowd to the baggage carousels where you can reclaim your luggage. Signs will direct you to the correct carousel for your flight. When you have your luggage, follow the crowd one last time to the Customs checkpoint.*
>
> *You will probably have nothing to declare, so can follow the green "Nothing To Declare" line. Take the red line if you're bringing in fruit or vegetables, unprocessed foods, large quantities of tobacco or alcohol or things you intend to sell— not very likely for a family on holiday. Even passengers following the green line are sometimes spot-checked... even honest-looking people like the Lains. No one will harass you. Just let the inspectors do their work and your vacation will really start in just a few minutes. You're here! Welcome to my country!*

If you're staying for more than a week, don't try to carry enough clothes for the whole trip. Spend one afternoon or evening at the launderette, or wash out a few things by hand every day or two.

If you're coming from outside North America, leave electrical appliances at home unless they're dual voltage. Shave with a blade. Let your hair air-dry. You're tourists, not beauty pageant contestants. (In the interests of full disclosure, your author has thinning hair and a beard, so is less interested in razors and hair driers than many people—but Barb, who has lovely hair and no beard, agrees with me.)

If you forget something you really need, remember that Washington has had stores for several years now. You can buy whatever you need and call it a souvenir.

A good rule of thumb is to take half of what you think you'll need. To check yourself, pack your suitcase and take it for a walk.

If you can carry it for half a mile (about 1km) without setting it down, you are a lean, mean, travelin' machine, ready for the trip.

If you're flying or taking the train, don't take more than one suitcase for every two people. That will keep everybody from overpacking, it will give each person a partner to help carry the bag, and it will make it easier to get around airports and train stations. Soft-sided bags are best unless you're carrying breakables, because they're much lighter than hard-sided luggage. We also have a big nylon tote bag that folds up to practically nothing that we carry in the bottom of a suitcase. If we're coming home with a lot of souvenirs, we have an extra suitcase we can stuff full of dirty clothes.

No matter how you're traveling, have every member of your crew take his or her own carry-on bag. Backpacks, canvas totes that snap or zip shut, small overnight bags—these all serve the purpose admirably. Carry-ons should contain things for their owners to do during the trip—reading matter, snacks, toys, small games, tape or CD players (with headphones, please!). If you're flying, everyone should be sure to take a change of clothes in his or her carry-on, too, in case you're one of the small minority of travelers whose luggage decides to get on a different airplane from its owner. Medicines, film, money, tickets, and other travel documents should never be in checked baggage.

Getting There

Now that your planning is done, you're packed and eager, and you've got your gas tank full or your tickets in hand, let's talk about getting you to the payoff—the capital of the United States! Every big city presents unique challenges to getting around, but with patience and good humor you'll have no trouble. The congestion in Washington is the stuff of legend, but in truth it's no worse than in any other big city.

Travel Ins and Outs

Driving to Washington

If you've never experienced Washington's famous "Beltway," the highway that surrounds the city, think of a circular parking lot a hundred feet wide (30m) and 20 miles (32km) in diameter. Traffic moves so slowly at some times of the day that snails and turtles outpace the cars, laughing at you as they go by. The rest of the time traffic whizzes by fast enough to make an Indy 500 driver nervous. But you're not likely to be traveling far on it anyway. If you're staying in the center city, one of the other highways will take you in close to your destination. If your lodgings are in the suburbs, use the beltway to get close, then take other highways and surface streets.

I have four pieces of advice for drivers new to Washington:
• Don't arrive at rush hour (7 to 10 a.m. or 4 to 7 p.m.) when traffic is at its very worst. Time your arrival for midday or late evening if you possibly can.
• Get a good map and trace your map from the beltway to your accommodations in colored marker. Study the map so you're familiar with the names of roads, towns, and landmarks.
• Have a good navigator who has also studied the map and will let you know what to expect well ahead of time.

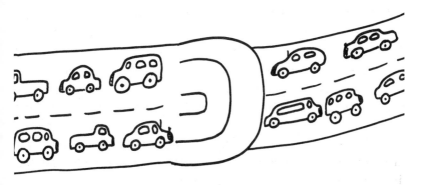

The Beltway is almost always congested

• Be patient. Plan ahead, pick a lane on the highway and stick to it, and anticipate what you're going to do a mile or two down the road. You will get where you're going—everyone always does. Just relax and take your time.

Arriving by Train

If you take Amtrak, the national passenger rail service, you'll arrive in Washington at Union Station, the stunningly renovated terminal modeled after old Roman baths in Italy. Union Station is more than merely a transportation hub, it's a shopping, eating, movie megaplex with dozens of upscale shops and nearly 50 places to eat. You can walk to the Capitol in ten minutes—maybe fifteen if you're weighted down after a visit to the downstairs food court. And there's a Metro station right in the train station, as well as a taxi stand in front, so you can quickly zip away to your accommodations or anywhere else in town.

Flying In

Washington, D.C., is served by three major airports. Reagan National Airport (DCA) is the major destination for domestic flights. Dulles International Airport (IAD) handles most of the international travel and some domestic flights. The third airport, Baltimore-Washington International (BWI) is overlooked by many travelers but may be even more convenient than Dulles because of the availability of rail service into the city. Let's take a look at each.

National Airport (It was renamed for a former U.S. president a number of years ago, but hardly anybody except the airlines calls it "Reagan." Even the airport's own website mostly calls it "National.") is one of the most convenient airports in the United States. It's right across the Potomac River from the city and can offer an exciting view of the major landmarks as you arrive. In fact, it sometimes seems a little scary to land there because you normally come in over the river and passengers just see water below them until an instant before the plane touches down. Don't be alarmed—it's perfectly normal.

More than 13 million passengers a year fly in and out of National. It's a "short haul" airport: with very few exceptions, no nonstop flights come from more than 1,250 miles

> *Tip:* *If you're coming from another country, be certain you have all the proper paperwork. All foreign visitors need passports, of course, and you'll need a visa, too, unless you're from one of the 26 countries that are exempt from that requirement—much of Western Europe, Japan, Australia, and New Zealand. The nearest U.S. embassy, or the INS website in the appendix will give you the information you need.*

(2,025km) away, so if you're coming from further away than that, you'll have to connect or fly into one of the other airports. National's convenience is probably worth a connection.

The best thing about flying into National is that you're just steps from the Metro: There's a station just outside terminals B and C with convenient pedestrian bridges from the terminal to the platform. You might have to walk for ten minutes if you land at Terminal A to get to the bridge in Terminal B.

From the Metro at the airport you can be in the center of Washington in less than fifteen minutes. In fact, we've sometimes scheduled layovers for ourselves at National, just to have a chance to do a little quick sightseeing. If we're on a flight that arrives at noon, for example, we can be in a Smithsonian museum on the Mall by 12:30, and can look at great art or historical flotsam and jetsam until 4 o'clock, making it back comfortably for a 6 o'clock flight home.

If you need a taxi instead, National's close-in status means that fares are low, only about $10 to the downtown area.

The airport went through a major renovation a few years ago and isn't at all like the dark and dowdy place I once flew into. There's lots of glass and natural light, two brand-new terminals that are easy to navigate, and the work of more than 30 artists in glass, sculpture, murals, and other media.

What's more, I once made an informal study of airport chili dogs, and decided that the ones at National were the country's best. I like this airport: close, good transportation links, attractive, easy to use, and good chili dogs—everything you could want.

Dulles International, on the other hand, is much less convenient. It's larger than National, serving about 18 million passengers a year, and is certainly an attractive airport that's easy to navigate and has all the amenities any traveler could want except superior chili dogs. If you're coming from abroad, you'll probably arrive here. The only international flights into National are from Canada.

The problem with Dulles is that it can be time consuming and expensive to get into Washington from here. The airport is 26 miles west of the city, and there's little really convenient public transportation. Taxis are prohibitively expensive at $50 or more, especially if your family is large enough, and carrying enough luggage, to keep from being shoehorned into one taxi for what, at some times of the day, can be an almost hour-long ride.

Tip: Keep an eye on your estimated arrival time. New regulations require that all passengers flying into National must remain in their seats during the last 30 minutes of the flight. Make sure your kids have a last chance to use the restroom before time runs out.

There are shuttle services like Super Shuttle that can take you to your lodgings for much less money, so at least large families won't have trouble staying together. (Super Shuttle charges about $23 for the first person and $10 for each additional one) Another good option is the Washington Flyer bus to the Falls Church Metro for $8 ($14 round trip). Get tickets from Ground Transportation desk on the terminal's lower level for either of these or at the departure point, near the baggage claim area.

Travel Ins and Outs

Buses to the Metro leave every 30 minutes at 15 and 45 minutes after the hour. The trip to the Metro takes 25 minutes, and the train about 20-25 minutes to the center city.

The most economical route is the city bus. Bus 5A runs from Dulles to L'Enfant Plaza once per hour (at 30 to 40 minutes past the hour) for a 50-minute ride. The bus runs 5:30 a.m. to 10:30 p.m. and an hour later on weekends. The fare of just $1.30 makes this the most family-friendly option of all if you don't mind waiting for up to an hour for the bus. Catch the bus outside the baggage claim area.

If you visit in winter, you'll see the National Christmas Tree

BWI (as everyone calls it) is easy to forget, because most people associate it with Baltimore instead of Washington. But it's almost as close to Washington as Dulles is, and is probably easier to get to. Nine international airlines and most domestic carriers fly into BWI, so it's an option that's worth checking for most travelers.

Taxis into Washington from BWI are even more expensive than the ones from Dulles. But the MARC commuter rail line runs two dozen trains on weekdays from BWI to Washington's Union Station, and the fare is just $5. The trip takes 30 to 40 minutes. There's a free shuttle from the baggage claim area to the BWI rail station. For a quicker trip you can board one of the more than 30 daily Amtrak trains from BWI to Union Station. The trip takes from 20 to 30 minutes, depending on the train, but costs $23 to $35 per person. SuperShuttle prices are about $30 for the first passenger and $8 for each additional.

You can also get an inexpensive (about $3.50 round trip) shuttle bus from BWI to the Greenbelt station on the Metro line. Buses run about every 40 minutes from 8 a.m. until 10:50 p.m. Catch the bus from the International Pier (Pier E) or the BWI rail station.

Getting Settled

Once you've arrived at your home away from home, you should take a little time to get organized. Of course everyone is eager to get to the Main Event—the sightseeing you've come here for. Does it make any sense to spend endless hours and great wads of money getting here, and spend your first couple of hours just getting organized? Yes.

Fast forward ahead a few hours. Imagine that you just drop your bags at the hotel or apartment and rush out to see the sights. You get back to your rooms at 10 p.m., crabby and exhausted. Every suitcase, still full, sits where you dumped it. There's nothing to eat or drink except tap water and a nearly-forgotten packet of airplane peanuts. It's too late… and you're too tired… to do anything but flop into bed—if you can find your pajamas.

No, that's not what you want. Take a little time now, as soon as you get in, to do these things:

- Unpack. You'll feel even less like it later.

- Explore your neighborhood. Find the nearest Metro. Look for grocery

Tip: *This will sound like a bizarre thing to do just after you get to the destination you've been anticipating, but if you've arrived on any overnight flight, do it anyway: As soon as you finish unpacking, take a nap. Your internal clock is all messed up and even if you're excited, your body is frazzled. Don't sleep more than two or three hours, though, or it will take you days to get your body clock adjusted. West-to-east travel, as from California or Asia, is especially tough, but a nap is nice even after a daytime flight from Europe. If you haven't made a long air journey today, you can skip this step.*

stores, bakeries, local restaurants, launderette, newspaper vending boxes. While you're out, do the next two items on the list.

- Have a light meal.

- Shop for basics. If you have cooking facilities, get in a few days' worth of groceries and other supplies. If you're not doing any cooking, at least lay in a supply of snacks and beverages.

- Now go begin that sightseeing. The Lain Walk in the next chapter is a good way to begin, and Chapter 19 has more ideas for your first day in the city. But if you spent more than three or four hours in the air today, don't overdo the walking. Your feet swell when you fly, and even now, your shoes are tighter than you're used to. Getting blisters on the very first day of your trip is a miserable way to start one of the greatest family vacations you'll ever have.

Now, unpacked, fed, and rested, you're ready to conquer Washington, D.C. Our family's first evening here was one of the most exciting we ever spent and we all went to bed that night with stiff necks from all the gawking we did. Tomorrow will be your first full day of spectacular sights. All the careful planning you've done has paid off. What a great time you're going to have!

Recommendations

✔ Use every possible resource to get the best airfare—travel agents, general travel websites, airline websites, different airports: there's always a way to lower the price a little more.

✔ Don't overpack. If you can't carry your suitcase for a half-mile without stopping to rest, you're taking too much.

✔ Avoid driving on the Beltway or downtown at rush hour unless you're bringing extra ulcer and blood pressure medicine.

✔ Unpack as soon as you get to your lodgings. You'll hate doing it even more later.

5. Getting Around

Washington isn't a large city at all. Geographically it's only one-fifth the size of New York City. For that matter, it isn't even as large as Fort Wayne, Indiana. That's great for your purposes, because it means things are close together and easy to get to.

No other city in the world has such a large concentration of top-notch attractions packed so densely together. That means you can spend your time seeing them instead of traveling between them. As much as I love places like London and New York, you can spend an hour getting from one site you want to see to the next, if you don't plan carefully. In Washington you're probably just a ten-minute walk from where you want to go next.

While we've taken our car to Washington several times, we haven't used it much once we got to our hotel or apartment. Washington is so walkable, and its subway system so fast and efficient, that battling the horrible traffic is pointless.

Besides—there's no place to park.

I can't prove this, but I suspect that at least 50 percent of the cars on the street are people driving around and around looking for a place to park, and that they do it from 8 o'clock in the morning until 5 in the afternoon, when they finally give up and drive home.

Let's spend the next few pages finding out about the best ways to get where you're going in Washington, finishing with a spectacular stroll your kids will remember for the rest of their lives.

Washington by Car

The first time I used a car to get around inside the city was on our first family trip there. We arrived on a Sunday evening about 7 o'clock and after moving into our apartment near Rock Creek Park, we decided to drive down Connecticut Avenue and see what we could see. In less than ten minutes we were across from Lafayette Park, just a block from the White House, stunned that things were that close and getting there was so easy!

Of course on a Sunday night 20 years ago there was no traffic and plenty of street parking. But even then, if I'd attempted that drive just twelve hours later, it would have taken me a half hour and I couldn't have found a spot anywhere to leave my car. Today? Forget it! Once we discovered how walkable the city was and how easy it was to get around on the Metro, we left our car parked next to the apartment. After that first evening, we didn't get in the car again until it was time to leave for home.

That's been true of the other times we've driven, too. Get to our accommodations, park the car, and forget it. The only exceptions to that have been the times that we're visiting attractions away from the heart of the city that are difficult or impossible to get to via Metro. I'll always point those out in Part II. Most of the time, though, your car will just be a burden, an expense, and an inconvenience.

Besides, even away from the usual tourist areas, driving in Washington is like something out of a Stephen King novel. Washington claims to have a grid system for its streets. Ha, ha, ha. Those neat grids are interrupted every few blocks by streets careening in at odd angles and by other streets that just wander aimlessly wherever they feel like it. Even a good map that has the hundreds of one-way streets marked won't tell you that left turns seem to be prohibited almost everywhere a rational person would need to turn left.

No, thank you. I'll ride the Metro.

A car can be handy for some of the outings in Maryland and Virginia, but even some of those are accessible by Metro, too.

Washington by Public Transportation

If you're going to Live Like a Local, do what the locals do—leave the driving to the professionals. Washington has one of the nicest subway systems in the country—fast, clean, foolproof, safe, and inexpensive. We use it all the time. In the downtown and museum areas, Metro stations are seldom more than 700 or 800 yards apart (640 to 730 meters), and outside the central area are usually located close to the attractions you'll want to visit. The system was carefully set up to be as convenient as possible for both commuters and visitors, and it works well. Supplement the Metro with the Tourmobile, the bus, and if necessary with taxis, and you'll soon see why a car is nothing more than a nuisance.

The Metro is the easiest way to get around

━━━━━━━━━━━━━━━
Being Safe

Washington, D.C., is one of the safest big-city tourist destinations in the United States. Police officers almost outnumber visitors, and there's a large military presence—not surprising in any nation's seat of government. What's more, security has been stepped up to unprecedented levels since September 2001. There's really only one thing you can do that's inherently unsafe.

Cross the street.

Traffic in Central Washington is as fast and furious as anywhere in the country. If you cross in the middle of the block away from the crosswalks or walk against the traffic signals there is a possibility that you won't be run down like a squirrel in the road... but why gamble? Cross at marked intersections, wait for the light to tell you when it's okay to cross, and keep your eyes open for drivers who aren't as conscientious as you are. I want you to get home from your trip safe and sound so you'll be able to buy the rest of my books someday.

Washington does have a few high-crime areas that are best avoided after dark, mostly southeast of the Capitol Building. You won't be going there at night anyway because there's nothing to do or see after the museums close. I won't include any sites that are unsafe for visitors.

Just follow the universal rules of smart travel wherever to go and you'll never have a problem. That means

• Don't flash your cash.

• Don't walk down empty, badly-lit streets at night.

• Keep your wallet in a side pocket, not in the back, to thwart pickpockets.

Using the Metro

Because Washington attracts visitors from all over the country and from around the world, its subway system, called the Metro, is often the first subway people have ever ridden. If that's the case with your family, don't be intimidated by it: It's very easy to use. The Washington Metropolitan Area Transit Authority seems committed, in a way I've never seen anywhere else, to making the experience simple and fun.

On a recent trip I was gathering up brochures and maps from the station at National Airport and watched the most helpful public transportation employee I've ever seen anywhere in the world. Whenever any potential user looked uncertain about how to read the system map, use the farecard machine, or find a destination, he fairly leaped out of his booth, gave them a friendly tutorial on the Metro system, helped them through their trans-actions, and sent them off with a cheerful wave. It was a remarkable performance. Transport employees the world 'round have a reputation

> • *Use a purse with a strap that goes over your shoulder, not dangling from your hand.*
> • *Never leave cameras, daypacks, purses, or bags unattended for even a moment.*
> • *If you find yourself in a place that doesn't "feel" right, leave.*
> • *Keep most of your money and a spare credit card out of sight and reach in a money belt or neck pouch under your clothes.*
>
> *Bad things seldom happen to tourists, and almost never to travelers who are careful, who have planned ahead, and who walk and act safely.*

for being sour and uncommunicative. Not in Washington!

The Metro consists of 80 stations on five interlocking, color-coded lines that cover most (but not all) of the city and run out into the Virginia and Maryland suburbs, as well as to National Airport. The central city is very well served, and that's mostly how you'll use the system anyway. The lines intersect in convenient places, making it easy to transfer (free!) from one line to another to get to your destination easily.

To ride the Metro, check the system map at the entrance to the station or, better yet, pick up the free, pocket-sized maps from the station and give one to every member of your family. Note where you are, what station you want to travel to, and see how many stops to go. If your destination is on a different line, take note of which station to use to transfer from one line to the other; they're clearly marked.

Be sure you get on a train going the right direction. Each train is marked with the name of its end-point, and a quick glance at the map will tell you what direction you want to go. Escalators down to the tracks are marked with the same names, so it's hard to go astray. If you transfer, just follow the signs to the color line you want, and find the correct direction by looking for the right end-point. There are plenty of signs and maps everywhere. If you should happen to end up going the wrong direction, don't worry: Just get off at the next stop, cross to the other side of the station, and head back the other way. We've all suffered from brain lock and done that at one time or another.

Stand on the platform and your train will be along in minutes. Because many stations have multiple lines using the same tracks, make sure you get on a train of the right color. They're clearly identified by signs in the front and at each door on the train. When a train is approaching, the lights built into the platform edge begin to blink.

Here's something that veterans of other underground rail systems will refuse to believe until they experience it for themselves. Once you're aboard, you'll hear announcements from the driver that are loud, clear, and easy to understand. I'm always amazed. When the doors are about to close, passengers are warned by a female voice that says "Doors closing" followed by a double chime.

Paying Your Fare: The Metrorail system uses farecards, credit-card-size tickets that slide into the slot at the front of the turnstile and pop out another slot on top. When you get to your destination you repeat the process to exit the station.

The fare you pay depends on the distance you're going and the time of day. Minimum one-way charge is $1.20, and riding to the end of the line (something you're unlikely to do) can cost up to $4.00. The fare to each station in the network is posted at the information kiosk at the turnstiles of every Metro station. If you travel outside rush hour (5:30 to 9:30 a.m. and 3 to 7 p.m. weekdays), fares are reduced on longer trips. Kids under age 5 ride free. The Metro runs from 5:30 a.m. until about midnight on weekdays, 8 a.m. until midnight on weekends.

Buying a farecard is easy and doesn't really require those pathologically helpful Metro attendants. Just put money into one of the machines located at each station entrance, and punch in the value you want on the farecard. You can put as much money on your pass as you want. The appro-

> *Tip:* Use change or small bills in the farecard machines, if you can. Machines will return change, but only up to a maximum of $5—and all of it in coins!

priate amount will be deducted when you reach your destination and your card returned to you to use on your next trip. Nothing could be easier.

If you plan to do a lot of riding, an even better choice might be to buy one of the Metro passes available. You can get a 1-day pass good for unlimited rides from 9:30 a.m. until closing for about $5. A 7-day pass costs about $18.00, although it's limited to the central area during rush hours; you have to pay a small supplement for longer trips. An unlimited 7-day pass costs about $25.

Don't worry about mistakenly taking a trip that exceeds the value left on your farecard. In some places (like London), doing that would make you subject to a heavy fine. In Washington just put your card in an Exitfare machine in each station, pay the excess charge, and use your card normally.

For most families an economical solution is probably to get a farecard for each family member with enough money on itfor several trips, and to add more money to the cards as needed, something that's easy to do at the machines in any station. Because things are so close together in central Washington, you might ride the Metro less than you expect. The Metro website listed in the back of this book has extensive information on all your options.

Riding the Bus

Washington has an extensive Metrobus system that's easy to use. Unlike some other big cities like New York or London, however,

> *Tip:* Make sure everyone in the family knows how to use the Metro. Have the kids take turns planning the day's route by looking at the Metro map, figuring out what stations to use, and where to transfer. Then let them lead the way through the stations. That way, if you get separated, or the older ones are off on their own, Mom and Dad will worry less.

it's hard to find a single map that covers all bus lines, making it less accessible to the visitor. You can buy bus maps from a few major Metro stations or on line. Every Metro station, though, has maps of the bus lines that serve its immediate area, so just stop in at your neighbor-hood station and pick up maps for the nearby bus lines. The attendant in the information kiosk can also advise you about which lines run to what parts of the city.

Bus stops are designated by red, white, and blue signs, and often have shelters where timetables and route maps are posted. You can board only at designated bus stops (usually every two or three blocks), but on most buses after 9 p.m. the driver will let you off anywhere along the route, even between stops.

Bus fare is $1.30, which you must pay with exact change or by using a Metrobus pass. A 1-day pass costs about $3.00 and a 7-day pass costs about $10. You can buy bus passes at major Metro stations, hundreds of merchants, and online through the Metro website. Drivers can also sell you the 1-day pass on the bus. Kids under 5 ride free.

You can't use your Metrorail farecard on the bus system yet, although plans are in the works for an integrated farecard system. But you can transfer between the Metrorail and Metrobus systems for 25 cents, and transfers between buses are free. Just ask the driver for a transfer; it's good for two hours.

The Tourmobile
One of the handiest ways to get around Washington is the Tourmobile, cool little buses that run a constant loop from

attraction to attraction, all day long. The Tourmobile will take you to about 25 of Washington's most famous sights, saving you time and energy. You can get on and off the buses as often as you want, and a ticket is good for all day. The Tourmobile is great for a sightseeing overview. You can take the complete loop to get a look at everything, then, on your next pass, get off at your favorite attraction, reboarding later to go to the next place on your list.

Guides provide a informative and supposedly witty commentary (the "witty" is in the ear of the beholder) as you roll along. You can buy tickets from kiosks near the Washington Monument, Lincoln Memorial, or Arlington Cemetery, or from the driver at any stop. Cost is less than $20 per person (about half that for kids 3–11). That can be expensive for a large family, so if you use the Tourmobile, plan ahead and use it for a day when all you want to do is visit attractions on the list (available on the company's website). The Tourmobile runs from 9 a.m. until 6:30 p.m. in the

Tip: For an extra $2 per person, you can buy a ticket after 2 p.m. that's good for the rest of the day and all of the following day.

summer, and 9:30 to 4:30 the rest of the year. The company also runs separate tours inside Arlington National Cemetery and to Mount Vernon.

Taxis

I occasionally use a taxi when I'm doing research for a book, have been walking for miles, and am too exhausted to move another step. But otherwise they're an expensive luxury I ignore, and use my money for a little nicer meal that evening, or on an extra chili dog at the airport when I leave. Taxis can be handy, though, when you're going someplace that's otherwise hard to get to or have gotten yourself hopelessly lost. I've never been lost that badly... but they're a good emergency rescue system for an older kid, off alone in the "big city" for the first time, who goes astray. They can also be useful if you've been out very late and the Metro has closed. Few families are out that late, however, unless they enjoy having crabby kids (or parents) the next day.

Taxis in Washington aren't metered, but work on a zone system. The minimum charge is $4 for the first person and can be as high as $12.50, depending on how far you're going. There's an additional charge of $1.50 per person, an additional $1 during rush hour, and an extra $1.50 if you phone for a taxi instead of hailing it in the street. That's a lot compared to the Metro fare of $1.30 to about $4.00.

> *Tip:* Everyone should know the address of your apartment or hotel and carry enough money to take a taxi back there. It's the ultimate solution for someone who's utterly lost.

On Foot

Here's the Lains' favorite way to travel. First of all, it's cheap, and we're known for that. But more important, it's the very best way to get to know a place, to see things up close, to be spontaneous—to stop for ice cream! When you walk, you see a place like the locals do, as a connected whole, instead as just a flashing series of images like a sports highlight film. You see how one part of town blends into another, how small a carefully-preserved famous building sometimes looks as its neighborhood has changed and grown around it. You're aware of how sightseeing attractions and the houses and apartments of ordinary people share the same street, and the city suddenly seems like less of a historical theme park and more like a real city inhabited by real people.

Even when our kids were small, we were relentless walkers. In fact, on our first family trip here, we created one of those little inside jokes every family has. Our kids tended to spread out and charge down the sidewalk three abreast, sweeping all other pedestrians before them like a six-legged snowplow, and we did what we could to rein in their enthusiasm. To this day, the phrase "Keep to the right" at a family get-together will produce groans and rolled eyes—and fond smiles.

Walk as much as you can! You'll feel a part of the city, which is central to the idea of Living Like a Local. You'll notice more interesting architecture, more little parks, more quiet side streets. You'll stumble across things you've heard about or recognize. In Washington, especially, where historic buildings and museums are packed together, you'll be amazed that things on your to-do list that you thought were blocks apart are right across the street from each other. It's one of the most amazing things about Washington.

The Lain Walk Through Central Washington

It's become a tradition in the Family Travel series for me to take you on a first-day walk past some of the finest eye candy in whatever city we're visiting together, to show you some of the things you've come here to see and to tell you a few stories along the way. Today's stroll is through the heart of Washington, D.C., past some of the world's most recognizable structures. It's a perfect way to start your first day in this great city, hitting the highlights and making note of some places you want to return to later for a closer look.

This is a stroll, remember, not a forced march. We'll wander along for about four miles altogether, about a two-hour walk if we just take our time, maybe three if we linger somewhere occasionally. But you don't have to do it all at once. If someplace catches your interest and you want to visit it now, feel free to turn aside. It's your holiday, after all. If you decide to relax for awhile and let your feet rest, do it. If you get tired or it gets dark and you want to go back to the hotel and finish the walk another time, that's fine. We'll be within a block or two of six or seven different Metro stations, so you can opt out at any time.

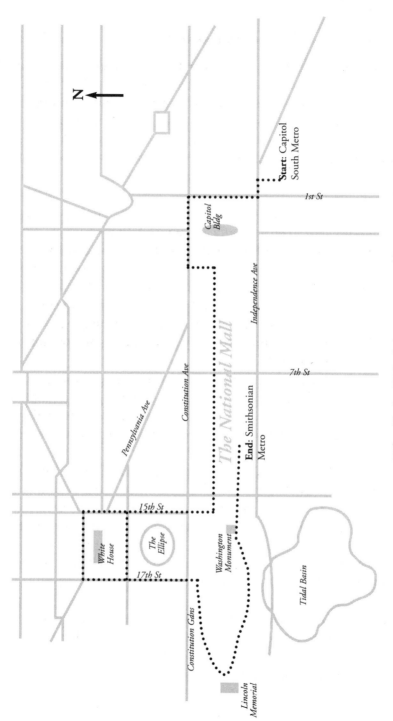

The Lain Washington Walk

Getting Around

But along the way, you'll see the Washington of your imagination, just as ornate and majestic as it is in the pictures you've always seen. This walk will make everyone's eyes light up. And one of the kids is bound to say, "Wow! Now I know we're really here!" So—are you ready? Then tighten the laces on your shoes and we'll get going.

The Capitol Area

If you're visiting the nation's capital, what could be more appropriate than to begin with the Capitol Building itself? Take the Metro to the Capitol South station on the Blue and Orange lines. When you get to the top of the escalator, you'll see it straight ahead. I remember my first sight of it. I was overwhelmed! I knew from photos and movies what it looked like, but it was so huge! It was far larger than I'd imagined, and gleaming a brilliant white in the sun. For one of the few times in my life, I was speechless

Walk straight ahead, north up 1st Street, toward the Capitol. The buildings of the Library of Congress are on your right. Only the British Library can begin to rival the size and scope of this collection, begun when Thomas Jefferson donated his personal library to the nation. Cross Independence Avenue (Wait for the light, please!) and continue straight ahead. The Capitol will be on your left and you'll soon see the Supreme Court Building on your right. The spot where you're standing, between the headquarters of the Congress and the courts, is in the middle of the greatest concentration of power and authority on the planet.

When you get to Constitution Avenue, turn left, along the north side of the Capitol. This wing houses the Senate chamber. The House of Representatives meets in the corresponding wing on the south end of the building. You'll see Congressional office buildings named for influential (or merely long-lived) legislators of the past, and if you make arrangements ahead of time, you can visit your own representative, if you live in the U.S.

Continue your walk along Constitution until you get to 3rd Street and turn left again. On your left is the Capitol Reflecting Pool, and the view of the building here is nothing less than spectacular. Now turn around and look straight west along that huge grassy park in front of you. This is the National Mall, almost a mile long, with the towering Washington Monument near the other end. Ah, yes! This is the view your kids will remember for the rest of their lives.

The Mall
Cross the street (Wait for the light!) and we'll stroll down the Mall. Mostly administered by the Smithsonian Institution, this is the greatest collection of world-class museums on earth, and we'll be visiting these in detail in Part II. You can walk along

The walk takes you past the National Gallery of Art

Madison Drive, but I think it's nicer to take one of the graveled walkways that run down the center of the Mall.

On your right, the angular, modern building is the National Gallery of Art East Building, which houses modern and contemporary art. Next on the right is the domed-and-columned National Gallery of Art West Building with its collection of older works, including one of the world's few paintings by Leonardo. Across the Mall, on your left, is the National Air and Space Museum, the world's greatest aviation museum, where you can see everything from the Wright Brothers' first airplane to rocks brought back from the Moon.

We once had timed tickets to see a special exhibition at the National Gallery West, and while we were waiting for our assigned time to enter, some of us wandered over to Air and Space and National Gallery East. We've never been anywhere that had more convenient sightseeing than Washington.

After you cross 7th Street, you're in a real sculpture-lover's paradise. On the left is the sculpture garden of the Hirshhorn Museum, the wonderful round building behind it, an unforgettable museum of contemporary art. On the right is the sculpture garden of the National Gallery. In its center is a fountain that becomes an ice rink in the winter, and beyond that is the National Archives, the building that houses the original drafts of the Declaration of Independence, the Constitution, and much more.

On the left now are some of the oldest and newest parts of the Smithsonian. First is the Arts and Industries Building, which now hosts a wide variety of temporary exhibits but which held the backbone of the Smithsonian collection early in the 20th century. Next is the unmistakable Castle, the Smithsonian's headquarters. You'll want to stop here and pick up maps, guides, and sacks of information about the museums.

Just behind those two old buildings are two remarkable newer ones, the National Museum of African Art and the Sackler Gallery,

---

Paraphernalia

Here are three things to think about as you're sitting at home, thinking about how to outfit your expedition: shoes, daypacks, and maps.

Unless you're a family that takes daily ten-mile hikes together, you're probably going to be doing a lot more walking than usual, and you're going to be paying more attention to your feet in a week than you do during an average six months. Almost nothing has more power to create a miserable holiday than sore, blistered feet. Fortunately, those sores and blisters are easy to avoid.

Take at least two pairs of shoes that are comfortable and well broken-in. Alternate pairs of shoes each day, or change shoes before you go out in the evening and your feet will be happier. Slap a plastic bandage on any sore spot right away. Sometimes two pairs of thinner socks will provide more comfort and protection against rubbing than one pair of thick ones. If you treat your feet kindly, they'll thank you for it by not blistering up, and your traveling companions will thank you for it because you won't be a grouch.

The other thing everyone ought to have is some sort of daypack to carry the little necessities of life as you go through your day. A daypack might be a small backpack, a lightweight nylon briefcase with a shoulder strap (what I carry), a large purse (Barb's choice), a small tote bag that will snap or zip closed, or something similar. If it's something with separate compartments, that's even better.

In your daypack you can carry a snack, water bottle, camera, spare film, map, guidebook, umbrella, sunglasses, reading glasses, travel journal—whatever you need for

which specializes in Asian art. Both collections are stunning. Just past the Castle is the Freer Gallery of Art with its vast collection of American and Asian works.

The huge building with the tall columns on your right is a place your kids won't let you miss, and I wouldn't be surprised if you stopped off now to visit a dinosaur or two. This is the wonderful National Museum of Natural History, jam-packed with bones, fossils, gems (including the enormous Hope Diamond), animals, and more than I have time to tell you about here. We'll come back to it in Chapter 12.

The next museum on your right is one of my favorites. (I have about 50 favorite places in Washington, to tell the truth.) It's the National Museum of American

History. The original Star Spangled Banner sung about in the National Anthem hangs here, together with everything from old movie props and sets to the ball gowns worn by the wives of the presidents.

This would be a good time to mention that there are places to buy inexpensive snacks, sandwiches, and drinks all along the Mall and adjacent streets, and if anybody needs to stop for a bathroom break, all the museums are free. Just walk into the nearest one and ask at the desk or follow the signs.

The Presidential Quarter

The Washington Monument lies straight ahead, but we're saving that for later. For the moment, let's cross busy

your day of charging about. The bag with all your gear will weigh just three or four pounds, so each person can carry his or her own, much better than expecting Mom or Dad to lug everything along that might be needed. Most school-age kids are used to wearing backpacks crammed with enough stuff to supply an Everest expedition, so they shouldn't complain about carrying their own gear around Washington. Altogether it will weigh less than an algebra and literature book.

You'll find perfectly good free maps of central Washington available everywhere. The National Park Service publishes one called Seeing Washington *that's available at just about every official building. You should be able to pick up several from the Pavilion on the Ellipse, from the White House Visitor Center, from information kiosks near the Lincoln, Jefferson, or Roosevelt memorials, or from many other places.*

If you subscribe to Smithsonian magazine, take your membership card to The Castle and pick up a packet of information from the members' desk, including a first-class map of the area. Auto clubs offer free maps to members and most are very good. I also like the Washington version of Fodor's slim, portable Flashmaps for more street-by-street detail, although there are a few inaccuracies.

Every family member ought to have his or her own maps of the city and the Metro system. Carry them in your daypacks.

15th Street and turn right, walking north on 15th. After we cross Constitution Avenue, there will be a large park on our left. This is the Ellipse, the park the President can see from his windows. The National Christmas Tree is placed here in the winter, along with trees for each of the states, and there are monuments and fountains galore. At the northeast corner of the Ellipse is the Pavilion with public toilets, an above-average snack bar, and an office for National Park Service rangers. The building across the street on your right is the Department of Commerce. There's the small National Aquarium in the basement and, at the north end of the building, the White House Visitor Center, which will tell you more than you ever wanted to know about the presidential mansion except how to get invited to dinner there.

You've got a choice here, depending on how long a walk you'd like. We're about halfway once we reach this point. For a slightly shorter walk, turn left here on Pennsylvania Avenue South, and walk west. You'll get a great view of the south front of the White House. If you'd like to be just a bit closer to the White House and don't mind walking an extra couple of blocks, just keep walking straight up 15th, passing the massive Department of the Treasury on your left, and turn left at the next street.

Now you can walk along with the White House on your left and Lafayette Park (traditionally a popular place for picketers and protestors) on your right, perhaps stopping to chat with White House guards. It's also interesting to chat with a protestor or two (there are always some around) and ask about the causes they're promoting. Kids need to know that it's interesting and stimulating (and sometimes entertaining) to listen to other people's views, even if they're different from their own.

You'll pass the opulent Eisenhower Executive Office Building on the left and the Renwick Gallery and Blair-Lee House on the right. Blair House became the presidential residence from 1948 to 1951 when President Truman lived here while the White House was being refurbished. In this house, Robert E. Lee was offered command of the Union army at the request of President Lincoln. Lee refused, and took command of the Confederate army instead.

Foggy Bottom

Turn left again and you can meet any members of your group who took the shortcut at 17th and E streets, near the Corcoran Gallery of Art. As we walk south on 17th, now, we'll see more impressive buildings, especially the DAR Building and the headquarters of the Organization of American States on our right. But let's cross Constitution Avenue again and walk through the park on our right. This is Constitution Gardens. We can stroll along the pond toward the large white building we see in the distance. We'll pass a memorial to the signers of the Declaration of Independence and, at the west end of the pond, convenient public restrooms. Next we'll come to the somber Vietnam Veterans Memorial and the Vietnam Women's Memorial, places of quiet pilgrimage for men and women who served in that divisive war.

This whole area was once a mosquito-infested swamp and still carries the none-too-promising name of "Foggy Bottom." The Potomac River used to flood the area repeatedly, and summers

Stop and rest whenever you walk—it's a walk, not a race

with high heat and humidity were especially awful. The floods are gone now, but they haven't been able to figure out what to do about the summer humidity.

The area was drained early in the 20th century to build the gleaming white temple in front of us, the Lincoln Memorial. This is one of Washington's most revered places. The view eastward from its steps—the Reflecting Pool, the Washington Monument, and, more than a mile in the distance the Capitol Building—is awe-inspiring, especially in the afternoon with the sun behind you. Fittingly, this site dedicated to the Great Emancipator has been the scene of other hallmarks of racial progress (see Chapter 11 for more).

Walk through the south side of the park as you make your way back toward the Capitol, bearing a bit to the right. you'll pass the haunting statuary of the Korean War Veterans Memorial, more public restrooms, and arrive in a couple of minutes at the picturesque Tidal Basin. If you're visiting in early spring, this whole area is a sensory cacophony of color and fragrance as the hundreds of cherry trees that ring the water and fill the park are in full bloom. (It's also famous as being the place a drunken congressman once drove his car into. He was with a local exotic dancer at the time. Of course no current members of Congress would do such a thing.) Across the water you can see the classic elegance of the Jefferson Memorial, and can make out the low rooms of the FDR Memorial off to the right. We'll return here to visit them another time.

Right now, though, we'll turn around and head up the hill to the Washington Monument, passing a Park Service ranger station on the way. The theater on our right is the Sylvan Theater, scene of free band concerts and theatrical performances during the warm months. (There are public restrooms here, too.)

You can linger at the Washington Monument for as long as you'd like. You don't even have to go to the top for a spectacular view (although I recommend it, and the kids will absolutely insist) because even from the top of this hill, you have an amazing prospect. Close your eyes, point your camera in any random direction, and push the button—you'll have a memorable photograph. To the north is the White House; to the east is the Capitol Building; to the south is the Tidal Basin; to the west is the Lincoln Memorial. If eye candy was as fattening as the sort of candy you eat, everyone who walked up this hill would walk down again weighing 500 pounds.

We're finished with our walk now. The handiest Metro station is Smithsonian, straight ahead toward the Capitol Building, right on the Mall near the Castle. But the two or three hours we've spent strolling this part of the city has already made the planning, the cost, even the discomfort of being cooped up in a plane or automobile absolutely worth the effort. If you take this walk on your first day in Washington, you can be forgiven for wondering how this trip can possibly get any better. You'll just have to read the rest of the book to find out.

Recommendations

✔ Use the Metro to get quickly from one part of the city to another, but walk as much as you can. Washington is surprisingly compact.

✔ Make sure every member of your group has a Metro map and a farecard and knows how to use them.

✔ Everyone should carry his or her own supplies in a daypack. There's no reason for Mom or Dad to be the family pack mule.

✔ Never ever wear brand new shoes on a trip! You'll walk yourself into blisters in an hour.

6. Life in the Big City

If you didn't like big city life—at least in the small doses you get as a traveler—you probably wouldn't have picked up this book in the first place. Sometime perhaps I should add a title like *Boring Empty Places for Families* to my list for the rest of the market.

But while our family always liked tramping through the woods, and even tried its hand at camping (without notable success), it was almost always the urban destinations with their incessant bustle, their unending variety of things to do, and their 24-hour-a-day lifestyle that lured us. Washington has all the bustle and variety you want.

In planning for a trip like this, though, we always tend to think mostly about the attractions, museums, parks, and neighborhoods we want to visit. Sometimes the smaller details get left aside until the last minute. But let's take a few pages now, before we get to all those attractions, to deal with a couple more necessities of the trip—how you'll handle the issues of money and food.

Money Management

It's a shame that commonplace issues like money can get in the way of having a good time, and it's why the books in this series show you, as one of their central purposes, numerous ways to cut back on expenses without cutting back an iota on fun. It should not surprise you that Washington can suck money straight out of your wallet so effectively that you're hardly aware of it. After all, if you're an American, you've seen just how much of your paycheck gets waylaid by taxes on its way to your bank account. And if you're not an American, I'll bet you've got some stories from home to tell on that subject, too! Governments are good at separating us from our money.

So while almost every chapter of this book has plenty of ideas for saving money, and lists of free and inexpensive attractions, right now we're going to talk for a few minutes about managing that money most effectively.

Four Types of Money

When you travel, you have a choice of four different sorts of money to use, and most of us use a mix of at least two or three of them. Let's discuss each.

Cash: This is the easiest and most reliable sort of money to use. Almost everyone except rental car companies is happy to take cash for any transaction. Many small purchases can be made only in cash, of course. The only way to use a credit card to get a newspaper out of a corner vending box is to use it to pry open the door. Small snack bars and many taxies aren't equipped for anything but cash. But only American dollars will do the job. There are places in the world that are willing to accept foreign currency, especially from neighboring countries. But not here. Not even Canadian dollars will be accepted, the long, cordial relationship between the U.S. and Canada notwithstanding.

Please don't bring your entire travel budget in cash, though!

Bad things can happen. All the parts of Washington you'll be visiting are perfectly safe, but it's silly to take chances. Never carry more cash than you'll spend in a day or two.

People traveling to another country frequently ask me whether they get a better exchange rate at home or at their destination. I can't honestly answer that because it varies from country to country and week to week, and every experienced traveler has a different view. The difference will probably be small, and the convenience of arriving in a country with a quantity of local cash already in hand almost certainly outweighs any minuscule difference in exchange rates. I vote for changing your money into U.S. dollars before you arrive here.

If you do need to exchange your own currency for U.S. dollars, you'll have no trouble finding a bank that will do it. But never exchange money at your hotel! The rates are by far the worst in town. If you're from outside the United States, the sidebar will review the currency and coinage for you.

ATMs are everywhere you turn

Credit Cards: We've been putting as much as we can on a credit card in the past several years because our card gives us frequent flier miles, and we've earned a number of free plane trips that way. But we pay off the full balance each month. Our card company hates us for that because we don't pay interest on anything and we cut into their profits. Are we not playing fair? But interest payments on a large balance would quickly amount to far more than plane tickets would cost, and somehow I just can't find it in my heart to feel sorry for the multinational bank that issued the card. Maybe I'm just a bad person.

Credit cards are a great convenience in

Money Matters

Visitors to Washington from outside North America should remember that only U.S. dollars can be used. You can use credit cards without any trouble, but only American cash is accepted. Here's a quick guide to the money system.

Paper money (called "bills" in the U.S., rather than "notes," which is the more common term elsewhere) is all the same size and color, regardless of value. Bills come in denominations of $1, $2, $5, $10, $20, $50, and $100, although the $2 bill is very rare. You might still come across older bills issued before a revised design incorporated anti-counterfeiting devices. Those older bills are still perfectly acceptable.

Coinage, at 100 cents to the dollar, most often comes in denominations of 1 cent, (written 1¢)—a copper-colored coin called a penny, and in silver-colored coins of 5, 10, and 25 cents, called a nickel, dime, and quarter respectively. The dime (10¢) is the smallest size of the three coins, the quarter (25¢) the largest. There is also a very large, silver-colored 50¢ coin, but it is very uncommon.

You might also see occasionally the new $1 coin, about the same size as a 25¢ piece but copper-colored. Despite an enormous effort by the government to introduce the coin, it's still uncommon and probably doomed to remain so until the government follows the example of most other countries and withdraws $1 bills from circulation.

---

other ways. All your transactions are carefully documented. Lost cards can be replaced easily with just a phone call, while the only way to replace lost cash is to go back to work. If you use a credit card, you can carry less cash and feel a bit safer.

Almost everywhere in Washington accepts a wide variety of credit cards.

The chief problem with credit cards is that it's easy to spend more than you intended—much more. When we're traveling, I write down every purchase in a notebook and keep a running total of expenses so credit card bills don't sneak up on us with a nasty surprise when we get home.

Never use your credit card to get a cash advance, except in the most dire emergency. The interest rate and fees make it a very expensive loan. If possible, use a debit or ATM card (see below) instead.

Visitors from abroad have one additional problem. You don't know exactly how much things cost until you get home. Your credit card company will charge your account based on the exchange rate on the day the charge is posted, not on the day you made the transaction. That means $250 shopping spree could cost a visitor from Britain, for example £156 if the exchange rate is £1=$1.60, but twelve pounds more if the rate drops to £1=$1.50. Of course you could end up paying less than you expect, too.

Debit and ATM Cards: These look like credit cards, but you never get a bill. Now that's an idea that could really catch on. Of course that sounds too good to be true, and it is—the money is just immediately withdrawn from your bank account back home. We use these machines a lot, both in the United States and abroad. They allow us to carry less cash, which gives us more peace of mind, and let us avoid larger credit card bills later, which makes us happy weeks after the trip is over. You'll find ATMs (Automated Teller Machines, also called bank machines or cashpoints in other places) everywhere you go. You just have to make sure you've got enough money in your bank account back home! That's another reason we keep track of our spending when we travel.

There are few draw-backs. Your bank will certainly impose a fee for the transaction, which will increase your costs a bit, but machines will remind you of the fee and give you a chance to cancel it you

Tip: ATM and credit card transactions save foreign visitors in another way. The exchange rate is usually the best you can get, the international bank rate, instead of the higher consumer rate.

think it's excessive. Foreign visitors will have the same uncertainty about exactly how much they're being charged as they will when they use credit cards: There's no way to know until you get your next statement. Remember, too, that you're normally limited to how much money you can withdraw from your account each day, typically $200 to $300. Know what that limit is and plan accordingly so you don't run out. Washington doesn't have debtors' prisons, but police do take an unsympathetic view of people who don't pay their restaurant bills.

Traveler's Checks: We haven't used these for domestic travel since ATMs became common, although we still sometimes use them abroad. Traveler's checks are safer than cash because if they're lost or stolen they can be replaced easily. Most businesses will take them as readily as cash, although you'll occasionally find a place that will refuse them. Remember, though, since traveler's checks are treated like cash, foreign visitors should make sure they're in U.S. dollars. Banks will change them, but you'll usually be charged an additional fee.

What's more, there is never a surprise about how much something costs. You pay up front for the traveler's checks. It's just like spending cash.

Tip: If you buy traveler's checks from a bank, you'll usually be charged a service fee of 1 to 2 percent. But some auto clubs and credit unions sell them to members for no additional fee. Be sure to ask.

Strapped for Cash

That headline has a nasty ring to it, doesn't it? Sounds like I'm about to plead poverty and ask you to send me money. I'm not— but it's okay if you want to do it. No, I'm referring to strapping on a money belt.

It's a bad idea to carry all your eggs in one basket... or all your money in one place. People leave their wallets on counters next to cash registers hundreds of times a day; billfolds drop out of pockets with dismaying frequency; purses get left in restrooms, on subways, and under restaurant tables more often then you'd think. And once in awhile—much less often than any of the above—pockets get picked.

There are ways to protect yourself, and you must. Split up the money between Mom and Dad. If you're in a hotel room or suite with an in-room safe, put enough cash for a day or two, plus an extra credit card, in there—never just in a desk drawer or cleverly hidden in a place you're sure no one will ever think of. Almost all hotel employees are as honest as you are, but if you have the bad luck to encounter one who isn't, he or she will know about that "secret" place.

And here's an idea that most people never think about, but that experienced travelers do all the time: Strap on that money belt I mentioned.

I'm not referring to the sort of belt that looks like the one that holds your trousers up but has a zipper in the back. Those aren't much use. A money belt is a lightweight nylon pouch that ties around your waist, and goes under your slacks, invisible but accessible. It's large enough to hold all the extra money and traveler's checks you want, a spare credit card for emergencies, even your passport, if you're coming from another country. It's impossible to lose or forget, impossible to burgle, and provides more security and peace of mind than a full tank of gas in the desert. Barb and I wear them on every long trip and recommend them. If you prefer, you can get a pouch that hangs on a cord around your neck and under your shirt or blouse, inaccessible to everyone but you. They're easy to find in travel departments for about $15. That's a mighty inexpensive insurance policy.

Paying Off the Kids

Every parent has been tempted to bribe the kids to stop whining, eat their peas, go to bed, get out of bed—a million reasons. It doesn't work. Besides, in a neat place like Washington, D.C., there's never a reason for it. Everyone will be so busy taking in all the memorable sites that the general mood and level of cooperation is likely to rival the run-up to Christmas.

But kids older than 6 or 7 will want to have money of their own to spend—that's what I mean. If kids have their own money from allowances, paper routes, yard work, or elsewhere (Grandma is usually a good source...), let them bring a reasonable amount to spend as they wish. Or you can give each child a set amount. Let that be their own money to spend however they want.

If kids know they have their own money, and they know what it's limited to, they're less likely to pester Mom and Dad for more; they'll spend more wisely. Some will buy souvenirs. (I suppose ten million little plastic Washington Monuments are sold here every year.) Some will buy tee-shirts. Some will buy extra snacks. But whatever it is, let them use their money for it. Kids and parents aren't likely to value the same things, and what seems like a worthless piece of junk to Dad might be what the 8-year-old sleeps with under her pillow for the next six months.

If kids are small, dole out the money a little at a time. But unless your kids are taking their own earnings, give them some to use however they like and build it into your budget. It will be money well spent.

Food, Washington Style

New York has its pastrami, Chicago its pizza, Boston its clam chowder, London its "pub grub," Paris its snails, San Francisco almost anything that was swimming around a couple of hours ago. What is Washington's trademark cuisine?

Hmm. Tough question. Some epicures will argue for the crab cakes, but the good people of Baltimore perhaps have a better claim on those. Unless you cast a vote for the Congressional Bean Soup (which is not as good as Barb's), Washington doesn't really have a signature dish.

But that doesn't mean you won't eat heartily in Washington. This is an international city, after all, with embassies, consulates, trade missions, industry groups, and whatnot from 200 or more countries around the world. Perhaps Washington's culinary trademark is the wide variety of food available here.

That really works to the advantage of a family on vacation, because it means there are lots of options, and that makes it easy to be as elegant or as economical as you want to be. And vacationing with a family usually means you're looking for more economical alternatives than elegant ones. You've come to the right place!

Strategic Eating
One of the reasons the books in this series urge you to consider

Get a snack from a street vendor, or take your own

an apartment or hotel with cooking facilities is because it's a terrific money-saving strategy at mealtime. In a regular hotel you might feel (wrongly, as we'll see in a moment) that you have little choice but to dine out at every meal. That can be expensive—at least $20 per person/per day, and that's pretty Spartan. Unless your kids are small, you could easily spend $30 or more. For a family of four, that's getting close to $1,000 per week! Just the thought of that is enough to ruin my appetite.

There are ways to cut costs whether you have an apartment or an ordinary hotel room, and we'll outline both approaches here.

If You Have Your Own Kitchen: If you have a kitchen available, you can fix your own breakfast and supper for a fraction of what restaurant meals would cost. You won't be far from a grocery store, small market, or convenience store where you can stock up on basics, the same sort of things you eat at home for quick, filling

Ben's Chili Bowl has been a Washington institution for half a century

meals: cereal, milk, eggs, bread, pasta, ground beef, maybe a boneless ham you can serve for a meal and then slice for sandwiches—things that are easy to prepare in less than a half hour and that your family enjoys.

> *Tip:* Plan your menus before you go. You can always change your minds once you get there, but if you have a plan to start with, you'll know what to take along or to buy at the market and won't have to try to think of something to fix when you're hot and tired from a busy day.

Your most economical approach is to have breakfast before you go out in the morning—whatever you'd eat at home, whether it's just a bowl of cereal or something more elaborate. Eat lunch in the city as a break from sightseeing. Getting off your feet for a half hour in an air-conditioned restaurant or kicking off your shoes under a shady tree with a sandwich from a nearby fast-food deli is an absolute joy after a busy morning. Or you can save a few more dollars and take along a picnic lunch to eat along the Mall or in a handy park. Sandwiches and fruit are just right and allow you to bypass restaurants and sidewalk vendors altogether. If you fancy an elaborate meal, on the other hand, lunches are less expensive than dinners in most restaurants, even for exactly the same food.

When you finish your afternoon attractions, you can go back to your apartment and most of your group can flop on a bed or sprawl on the floor, behavior that few Washington restaurants encourage from their patrons. Meanwhile, one person can cook, one can set the table, and a third can watch the evening news to try to figure out who was in that motorcade you saw pulling up to the White House this morning.

In the morning you can fix eggs, bacon, and toast, with milk, juice and coffee for a family of four or five for well under $10. Exactly that same meal in the coffee shop around the street will be more than $30, and it will probably be $50 in a hotel restaurant—plus tip! In the evening a home-cooked meal of spaghetti with a meat sauce, bread, and a salad will cost less for the entire family than the restaurant down the street will charge per person!

Tip: *If you're on a tight budget, never eat in your hotel restaurant. Prices are usually wildly inflated. A nearby coffee shop or diner will serve up large, tasty meals for less than half the price. All you'll give up is fine china and a waitress who calls you "Sir" or "Madam." You'll probably get called "Hon" instead.*

Of course somebody has to do the cooking and washing up. Be fair. This is supposed to he a holiday for everybody. Everyone who is able takes equal turns at kitchen duties... not just Mom and Dad! In fact, that can be a fun part of the planning. Maybe all the 13-year-old knows how to do is microwave some hot dogs and baked beans and open a can of peaches. Plan it! That will be a fine supper one night. The fixings are cheap, the preparation easy. You'll have a youngster who feels like he's made a contribution to the success of the trip, and everybody's happy. Tomorrow night it will be Dad's turn to fix a pot of chili. On your last night in Washington, use a little of what you've saved to take everybody to a nice restaurant for a dinner cooked by somebody else.

If You Don't Have a Kitchen: If you've decided that the best accommodation solution for your family is to stay in a hotel or motel without cooking facilities, you can still economize on food by doing what the Lains have done many times. If you're driving, bring some dishes, silverware, and a cooler with you. It doesn't have to be the sturdy insulated sort, although that's best. An inexpensive foam cooler will work just fine. If you're not driving, you ought to be able to find cheap coolers at grocery stores, convenience stores, and large drug stores for less than five dollars. You can also buy plastic utensils and paper dishes there.

Add ice to your cooler from the machine in your hotel or motel and you have a place to keep milk and yogurt for breakfast, and sliced sandwich meats for a light supper in the evening.

Now the strategy is to have breakfast in your room in the morning. Cereal, bread and jam, peanut butter, and fresh fruit need no refrigeration, and with your milk and perhaps some yogurt you'll have plenty of choices to get everyone's engine running.

Have your main meal of the day at lunchtime, when prices in restaurants are lower, and back in your room in the evening, finish off the day with sandwiches, fruit, and munchies. You will have had three more-than-adequate meals for little more than the price of one and you can use a little bit of your savings to take everyone out for ice cream later.

Refueling at Midday: No matter how much we're enjoying ourselves when we travel, we're always glad to get off our feet for a few minutes at lunchtime—having fun can be hard work! By 12 or 1 o'clock, we've been sightseeing for several hours and have already visited a historic house and a museum, or toured an ornate cathedral and taken a long walk through a fascinating neighborhood. It's time to re-stoke those furnaces!

With a family in tow, it's important to have lunch planned before the kids get hungry. Hungry kids, as all parents know, get grumpy and whiny and cross. Come to think of it, that describes me when I get hungry. And hungry, crabby people don't always make good choices when it's time to eat. Here's a can't-miss plan.

When you reach your last stop before lunchtime—before you enter that museum, park, or church—take a look around. This is the time, while everybody's still fresh, to decide where you'll eat later. Is there someplace near the attraction you want to stop at? Is there a food court, diner, or pizza place within a short walk? Did you pass a nice-looking restaurant on the way here? Decide now where you'll have lunch, because if stomachs are really rumbling later, there's a danger you'll just wind up going to the closest place, even if it's a bit beyond your budget or someplace nobody really wants, just because it seems easier than looking around and delaying lunch even more.

Life in the Big City

One place you probably shouldn't eat, though, is in the restaurants you'll find inside many museums and art galleries. Food there is usually overpriced and often of mediocre quality. There are a few exceptions, but few enough that avoiding them is usually a good rule to follow. But the cafeterias at the Library of Congress and the Air and Space Museum are known for their cheap prices and tasty lunches. The premier food courts in Washington, with endless choices, are on the lower level of Union Station, a few blocks north of the Capitol, and in the Old Post Office Pavilion just up 12th Street from the Natural History and American History museums. If you want to hang out with congressional staffers, try the cafeteria at the Dirksen Senate Office Building a block from the Capitol. It's only open for lunch Monday through Friday, but you can sample some of that Congressional Bean Soup.

You'll experience new tastes at a dinner in Chinatown

Tip: The Ellipse Visitors Pavilion between the White House and the Washington Monument has food, film, rangers, and bathrooms. Sandwiches, although of the generic pre-made sort, are better than average and piled high with meat.

For a quick and inexpensive lunch or snack, stop at one of the countless snack bars, pushcarts, and lunch wagons you'll find about every 30 yards in central Washington. The food is pretty indifferent in quality and there's not nearly as much selection as you'll find someplace like New York. You're limited mostly to hot dogs, sausages, pre-made sandwiches, giant chewy pretzels, and nachos, but the price is low, the service is quick, the food is hot—and soon the stomach is full.

Recommendations

✔ Don't carry more cash than you'll need for a day or two in your wallet or purse. Keep your reserves, and a spare credit card, in a money belt or neck pouch.

✔ Let your kids manage their own money, unless they're very young. Nobody ever said you can't use a holiday for teaching valuable lessons.

✔ Save money by visiting restaurants as seldom as possible. Simple meals, even without benefit of a kitchen, are easy and economical.

✔ Small ethnic restaurants away from obvious tourist areas often have above-average food and below-average prices.

7. Living Like a Local

I used to claim that there were two kinds of tourists. The first were the Cliché Tourists, the sort we see in cartoons all the time, walking around with their video cameras glued to their eyes, staying at famous chain hotels for way too much money, going only from museum to museum, never noticing what lay between them, treating every destination as a trip to the zoo with all the buildings and people placed there on exhibit for them to photograph and comment loudly about, then moving on to the next thing on their checklist.

The other sort I called the Stealth Tourist, seeing many of the same attractions but never asking questions, never probing, perhaps never speaking to another living soul except to order food, afraid of making a dreadful faux pas that will cause him or her to look foolish in front of strangers. I have a friend who actually avoids going to wonderful attractions because he's afraid people will know he's a tourist! Aargh!

I've tried, in the Family Travel Series, to promote a third approach: Living Like a Local. This doesn't imply that you're trying to conceal the fact that you're a tourist. Heck, there are a lot of advantages to being a tourist that I really enjoy: Freedom from alarm clocks, the right to wear comfortable clothes, occasional meals and snacks with little or no actual nutritional value but great taste, feeling like I don't have to check my e-mail five times a day—being a tourist is a great way to live!

(Not freedom from everything, though. Our youngest son was excited about a September weekend trip while he was in high school. A free weekend, and in Washington! He was disgusted to discover, though, that we still planned to made him take along his algebra homework. But he was living like a local. All over Washington, kids were doing algebra homework that night.)

To Live Like a Local means you get more of the authentic flavor of the place you're visiting, one reason I encourage people to rent an apartment, when that's possible, instead of staying in a hotel or motel. In an apartment you're living in a neighborhood, surrounded by local people instead of other tourists. You'll shop for food at local stores, relax in local parks, read the local paper in the morning, live a life that gives you a much more genuine feel for your temporary home than any hotel ever could.

Living Like a Local means talking to people at bus stops and stores and Metro stations just the way you would at home. How would you feel if you were back at home and a friendly family from out of town asked your opinion on what to see and where to shop or eat in your home town? I'll bet you'd be pleased, and try to be as helpful as possible. That's just what will happen to you in Washington when you Live Like a Local.

You might need to do laundry once

Living Like a Local

Even if you're not in an apartment, the idea of Living Like a Local is still possible. Get into the neighborhoods and chat with people, eat at off-the-beaten-track restaurants, ask advice of people walking their dogs or pushing baby strollers. Whenever I travel I ask museum staff members, waitresses, police officers, gas station attendants, and passers-by where they think out-of-towners ought to go, what they ought to see, where they should eat. I meet a lot of nice people that way and get some great insider information. It's exactly what I do back home in Ohio.

I've found Washingtonians to be more conversational and friendly than people in almost any other big city I've been in. You're unlikely to find any of the rudeness people fear (unjustifiably so, in my experience) in New Yorkers and Parisians. Maybe it's partly because visitors are so pervasive here; maybe it's simply because Washingtonians are just nice people.

D.C. Life

Let's spend just a few pages talking about what you'll want to know about the little details of life in Washington. This might be especially helpful for visitors from abroad making their first trip to the United States, but there's useful information here for anybody coming for the first time.

Getting Around

We talked more about this in Chapter 5, but it's worth noting again that in central D.C., it makes no sense at all to try to drive. Parking is expensive enough to make even a member of the Senate twitch, and those folks spend billions of dollars every morning before breakfast. Besides, there will probably be a Metro station closer than you could park anyway. Remember, too, that many prime attractions are just a few steps apart. Washingtonians walk a lot, because this is a city built for convenience.

Washington D.C. for Families

Weather

I don't know what kind of weather you like, but you're sure to find it in D.C. Of course it might last for only twenty minutes before it morphs into something quite different. Ask a Washingtonian about the weather and this is what you'll be told: Washington can experience dreadful heat and humidity in the summer (which can begin as early as May and can linger into October), gets hit with the occasional blizzard in winter (paralyzing a city that's not really equipped for it), is popped with an autumn hurricane every decade or so (because it's near the Atlantic coast), and sometimes has spring rains that would make a Philippine jungle jealous. And sometimes the weather really gets nasty....

Remember that everybody complains about their weather, though. While Washington does have its share of unpleasant weather, it's no worse than it is where you live. Winter is usually mild, with less snow than I'm used to in Ohio. Spring can be delightful with the cherry trees blooming in Potomac Park. Summer can be very hot, it's true, but the heat isn't unremitting and you'll seldom have plans interrupted by rain. Autumn is a delight and can last deep into November.

There's weather everywhere you go. It will slow you down only if you let it. Roughly speaking, here's what you can expect in Washington:

	Day	Night
Winter	35–55°F/2–13°C	20–40°F/-7–4°C
Spring and Autumn	55–75°F/13–24°C	45–65°F/7–18°C
Summer	80–100°F/27–38°C	60–75°F/16–24°C

Living Like a Local

You're more likely to have rain in the winter than snow, but you won't see much precipitation at all in the summer. That doesn't mean there's no moisture: Washington is notoriously humid. Fortunately, almost everywhere you'll be is air conditioned. I've been in Washington in almost every month of the year and have never had anything I wanted to do curtailed by the weather.

What to Wear

I said in Chapter 2 that there were only two industries that matter in Washington—government and tourism—and their mode of dress is very different. Fortunately you don't have to dress up in your power suit and burgundy tie, fill a briefcase with pointless paperwork, and go everywhere with a cell phone glued to your ear. That's the government uniform just as surely as baggy shorts are for a basketball player.

Tourists are exempt from dress codes. Washington certainly has restaurants where jackets and ties are required, but you're a normal person and can't afford to eat there anyway—especially with a family! Some churches and the Islamic Center ask

Explore your new neighborhood, like Georgetown's M Street

women to dress modestly, but that's just politeness and common sense. Otherwise, be comfortable. Any clean clothes are fine, although everybody appreciates visitors who leave tee-shirts with offensive slogans at home.

You'll find a lot more people wearing red, white, and blue in Washington, or shirts with American flag motifs. But last time I checked, it wasn't required.

The Media

Washington is one of the world's major press centers. Every important newspaper, news agency, television and radio network, and serious magazine in the world has a correspondent here... or maybe dozens. If there's a third major industry in this city after government and tourism, it would have to be journalism. The sheer number of news stories that comes out of Washington is so vast that almost once a week a story is written that is completely accurate. (I can make snide comments like that about journalists. I teach journalism and some of my former students work in D.C.)

Surprisingly... and sadly... Washington is different from the other major journalistic centers of the world in one important

Washington is one of the country's media capitals

respect: There's only one newspaper. The *Washington Post* is one of the great newspapers of the world, but it's the only local daily paper in Washington, D.C.—unless you count the tiny *Washington Times*, which lacks influence and can be hard to find.

Other newspapers are available. *The New York Times* is almost as easy to find as the *Post*, and Washington's international population ensures that major newspapers arrive here from all over the world. But a city like Washington deserves more than a single viable local daily paper.

The Baltimore-Washington area is served by more than a dozen television stations and radio stations of every description and format. Virtually all hotels and motels, and most apartments, have cable TV, offering from 20 to 200 channels for those evenings you just want to stay in and rest your weary feet.

In an Emergency

If you're confronted with any sort of emergency, call 911 from any telephone, either standard or cellular. A dispatcher will quickly send the proper medical, police, or fire department assistance.

In a city that houses the President of the United States, the Congress, and all the top judicial officials, you'd expect top-notch medical facilities, and you'd be right. Washington is one of the best places in the world to be taken ill.

United States residents are covered by the same health insurance they have at home, although you should review the procedures you need to follow if someone gets sick. Hospitals and emergency facilities are available everywhere you turn.

If you're coming from abroad, be aware that the United States is one of the few countries on the planet without a national health program, and medical care here is unbelievably expensive. Hospital emergency departments will usually treat visitors with life-threatening conditions without charge, but payment for other care normally will have to be arranged in advance through a credit card or evidence of insurance. Please protect yourself by making sure you have some sort of insurance coverage that will be accepted in the United States before you come. Short-term policies are not expensive, especially when compared with the cost of medical care in the U.S., where a single day in a hospital can easily cost $5,000.

Shopping

Every residential area has small markets and specialty stores where you can buy whatever you need for the cooking you do, and larger grocery stores won't be far away. People in big cities tend to buy food in smaller quantities and more often because apartments usually have less room for storing things than houses. Locate two or three places between your accommodations and nearest Metro that you can visit for what you need. You'll also find large drug stores like CVS or convenience stores like 7-Eleven that carry a good range of snacks and staples, but watch prices. You can often get the same things cheaper elsewhere.

Laundry

You'll be able to find a self-service laundry in any residential area of the city, but it will cost up to $2 a load for your wash. If you're just staying a week or so, you shouldn't need to do laundry, but if you're traveling for two weeks or more, you'll probably need to wash clothes at least once. But after you've run through your wardrobe several times and are out of underwear, a price of $2 per load will seem insignificant indeed compared with the luxury of clean clothes.

If you Live Like a Local, you'll get more out of your trip and meet a lot of nice people in the process. Washington isn't just a vast historical and governmental theme park; it's filled with genuine people who have real lives just like yours, something that's worth reminding your kids about. If they haven't traveled much before, stress that the people you meet aren't just exhibits or costumed historical interpreters. They have homes and families. They go to work every day. Their kids go to school. Washington is home, not a tourist attraction like Disney World or Six Flags, for more than a half million people. That just makes it even more fascinating, as far as I'm concerned. I can't connect with living in some sort of theme-park fairyland castle, but I can feel at home in Washington… like a local.

Recommendations

✔ Talk to people, ask questions, and smile! Be the sort of neighbor you wish you had at home.

✔ Read a local paper or watch local news on TV regularly—the local news as well as national and international. Look on a map to see where local events have taken place. You'll feel more a part of the community.

✔ Think of yourselves as temporary Washingtonians, not just tourists. Feeling like you have a stake in a community makes you want to get more out of it. Encourage your kids, especially, to think of Washington as their city while you're here.

II

The Washington of Your Imagination

Now you know how to thrive in Washington. In Part II, we'll talk about what to do while you're there. Before you read on, though, I want to remind you again that you can't do it all, no matter how much you want to. Chapters 9 to 17 contain about 130 places to go, things to do, and sights to see—Washington's very best, and taken from a much longer list of possibilities.

Encourage everyone in your family who's old enough to read this section of the book, at least, so you can have some good family discussions about how you'll spend your time. I've tried to show you how to get to the head of the line at popular attractions and to give you enough information about each place to allow you to determine how badly you want to go there, because you'll certainly have to leave out things you'd like to do. This section will help you decide what will go at the top of your list, and what will have to wait for next time.

Now, on with the planning!

8. Making Choices

The seven chapters before this one were all about preparing for your trip—getting to Washington, finding a place to stay, eating well for little money, getting around... I don't have to tell you—you've just read them: They're all about how to live in Washington, like a local.

The nine chapters after this one introduce you to more than a hundred places to see and things to do—the very best the Washington, D.C., area has to offer to a family. Oh, there are plenty of things that aren't listed: romantic walks, exhilarating nightlife, erudite lectures on important subjects. But those probably won't be the best choices for most families, and I want to keep this book practical... not to mention affordable! So the next chapters are all about what a family can see and do here.

In this chapter, however, we're going to talk about how to use what follows, how to put together a can't-miss family trip that will keep everybody enthusiastic and excited. Everyone in the family will want to read the other chapters in Part II to get an idea of what the possibilities are, but first spend some time with this one. Pay attention, now. Some of my very best family travel advice is in this chapter, and there may be a quiz later. Take notes if you like.

Mapping Out a Plan

Planning is critical to the success of a family vacation. If you arrive in a place as large, as historic, as complex, and as packed with attractions as the Washington, D.C., area without a pretty clear approach in mind, you'll see some of the big-name attractions, but will probably miss the lesser-known ones just nearby—one of which would have been the highlight of the trip for somebody in your family... if only you'd known about it.

On the other hand, a holiday that's planned out to the minute isn't a holiday at all, it's a marathon. There's nothing more discouraging than setting out with a massive checklist in hand, doggedly going from one place to the next to the next, dashing through museums, staring glassy-eyed at monuments, squeezing in two more attractions after dinner each night so you'll remember you've been there after you get your pictures developed. The Geneva Convention forbids prisoners of war to be tortured as cruelly as that. Why would you want to do it to your own family? (Besides, I do a lot of that when I'm traveling by myself to work on a book—all so that you don't have to. Don't make me waste all that effort!)

So start the sightseeing plan by having everybody read Chapters 9 through 17, making lists of what each person really wants to do. Chapter 18 provides a handy checklist of all the attractions in the book. Make a copy of that chapter for each person to rank or check off the attractions they want to see. (Or if you'd like to buy each person his or her own copy of the book, Interlink Books and I would not object. No? I didn't think you'd fall for that.)

Don't think for a minute, though, that you'll get to every place on everybody's list, unless you're actually going to live in Washington from now on. The lists really have two purposes: to find out what you can safely leave out, and to find out what each person's Number 1 attraction is.

Next step is to move to Chapter 19 and see just how to put together a workable itinerary for your trip. The chapter provides possible blueprints for up to two weeks worth of fun, and shows you some realistic ways to pace a trip like this.

I have to warn you, though, (and now is a good time to take notes) that overplanning is just as bad as underplanning. I've never been on a trip to Washington or anywhere else where one of the real highlights didn't come from a spur-of-the-moment decision to ditch my original plan and do something spontaneously. Does it work every time? Of course not. But I see things I never expected to see—that I didn't even know existed—that turn into memorable experiences with surprising regularity.

For example, in Washington working on this book, I spotted the National Building Museum across the street from a memorial I was visiting. I hadn't planned to go there, thinking to myself, "A building museum would have to be the most boring place imaginable. Why would anybody care?" But even though I felt pressed for time, I decided to stick my head in.

*The National Building Museum is a spectacular
and overlooked surprise*

Wow! I stuck my head in—then wasn't able to drag my body out for almost an hour. I had stumbled across the most spectacular indoor space in Washington. My jaw dropped, my eyes popped, and with that probably disgusting expression on my face, I spent more time than I could afford gawking at the building—and wouldn't have missed it for anything. Would everybody react the same way? Almost certainly not. But I left myself open to being spontaneous, to being surprised, and I was.

This happens to experienced travelers all the time. One of the many wonderful things about travel is that you can never be certain what's down that little side street you just passed, what that puzzling building up ahead is, why a small crowd has gathered on a street corner. Maybe you'll investigate a knot of men in suits early on a Sunday morning and come across the President of the United States going to church. Maybe you'll look behind a church and find a tiny, perfect park that's not on any map, an island of serenity just yards from a traffic-choked street. Maybe you'll turn down a street and recognize it from a scene in your favorite movie. Those things have all happened to me.

Plan carefully... but sometimes change those plans.

Three Rules of Family Travel

Whenever a new acquaintance discovers I write books about family travel, I inevitably get asked for the "secret" to a successful vacation. Think about that. If it were a secret, I couldn't tell you! Fortunately, there is no secret. If you travel enough with kids, you'll figure out these things without having to ask somebody to break a confidence. But just so it's all laid out clearly, here are three things you can do to practically guarantee that everybody in your brood will have a good time.

1. Make sure everybody gets their first choice
When you plan your itinerary, ask every member of the family (including Mom and Dad), "If you could only see or do one

single thing on this trip, what would it be?"

Now you've got a short list of the experiences that will "make" the trip for each person. This is the starting point in your planning, because you want to make sure that everybody gets his or her first choice. The kids will know right away that they're not just tag-alongs on a family vacation, but that their feelings and preferences are an important part of the trip. It's the best guarantee you can get for having agreeable traveling companions, because everybody has a stake in the success of the trip.

Tip: *It's important to put these "first-choice" attractions early in the trip. You don't want to save something a person is really looking forward to until the last day—then find it closed that day for the visit of some international dignitary. How sad and disappointing for the person who's been anticipating it as the highlight of the trip!*

This also means that in exchange for getting to have their first choice at the top of the family list, everyone agrees to be tolerant of everyone else's first-choice attractions. If everyone goes to a Wizards' basketball game with big brother, he won't grumble about going to the Dolls' House Museum tomorrow with little sister. (And trust me, Brother—it's really a pretty cool place. Your buddies back home will never have to know you went there.) We've already talked about how important the planning and anticipation are before you travel, so you encourage that involvement from everybody by making an absolute commitment to do everybody's No. 1 activity. Just remind the kids that they have to be reasonable: Lunch with the President, or a basketball game in July, is probably not going to work out.

Warning! What follows is the most difficult advice in the book—and some of the most important!

Making Choices

2. Plan free time

Whatever you do, don't try to be on the go all the time. Schedule a whole afternoon just to picnic and relax in Rock Creek Park. Spend some evenings just playing games or watching TV in your apartment or hotel room. Sleep late occasionally and don't start your sightseeing until after lunch sometimes. Don't try to fill every available minute.

Whenever I give this advice to people, they respond with a look of absolute incredulity. Then, with a shrill, almost hysterical voice, they say something like, "You mean we're flying halfway across the country (or world) and spending goodness-knows-how-much money on this trip and you want us to sit around watching television?" Right.

Not all the time, obviously. But occasionally. Having fun is hard work. People who do hard work get tired. Tired people get crabby. Crabby people make other people cross. Cross people do not have fun.

If there really is a "secret" to successful family travel, this might be it, because I've heard from a lot of readers who said they hadn't thought of it before, and it made their vacation

Make your choices and away you go!

Using This Section

The next nine chapters contain more than a hundred places to go. Let's see—if you're staying for a week, that's about 15 attractions a day. Sure! You can do that!

I don't think so.

But the descriptions will help your family sort out what's most important to them on this trip, and will provide practical information for getting there.

All the information was accurate when this book went to press. I wish I could promise that museums will never change anything I've written, but I can guarantee that they will. One reason listings usually do not include exact admission prices or opening hours is because those are the things that change most often. Check the Web page for this book before your trip for updated information. The page is at: www.interlinkbooks.com/dcforfamilies.html

There is also an e-mail link on that page for you to contact me with any needed updates you discover on your trip. You can also get up-to-date information from attractions' own websites listed at the end of this book, or in the Links section of my page.

Attractions in the chapters that follow are listed like this:

Anderson House *[2118 Massachusetts Ave. NW. Metro: Dupont Circle. Open 1–4 p.m. Closed Sun–Mon. Free.]*

In brackets after the name of the attraction (or at the end of a lengthy entry) is its address or location. That is followed by the nearest Metro stations. After that the entry lists days the attraction is closed, or unusual hours of operation. Unless specified otherwise, most attractions open between 9 and 10 a.m. and close between 4 and 6 p.m. Hours may be

much less stressful. I'll admit that it took the Lains awhile to figure it out, too, and we often still have to remind ourselves to slow down a bit when we travel. When you've spend weeks or months planning an exciting trip, you don't want to waste a minute of it.

But slowing down and recharging your batteries isn't wasted time; it's just as important as stopping to eat. If you try to have fun all the time, you won't have fun at all. And if you pick your spots to rest carefully—well, you have fun doing that, too. An impromptu picnic anywhere along the Mall is a wonderful, relaxing way to spend a couple of hours resting, people-watching, and maybe throwing or kicking a ball around. Rock Creek Park is lovely and quiet.

3. Maintain your regular schedule of eating and sleeping

One of the first things every parent learns is that kids need a routine. When mealtimes and bedtimes get very far off schedule, children's dispositions suffer. (And not only children's—I'm certainly no kid any more, but any member of my family can tell you

longer in the summer and shorter in the winter. But these can change frequently, so only hours that vary significantly from the norm are specified. Finally, free attractions are specified, or the age under which admission is free.

Note, too, that because of security concerns, sometimes buildings that are usually open to the public may be closed—either for the day or, sometimes, indefinitely. But at the same time, buildings that have been closed may be reopened for public tours. I'll try to keep current information on the website, but if you find more up-to-date information than I have, please e-mail me so I can post it for the benefit of others.

what I'm like when I'm bumped out of my rut.) While everyone will have to show a little flexibility as you all adjust to a holiday routine, having meals at close to your normal time and getting to bed about when you usually do will go far toward keeping everybody content.

That doesn't mean that you should forego occasional special activities at night. It's absolutely worth an evening of walking or riding around central Washington to see the spectacularly lit buildings and monuments. You'll enjoy going to a play at Ford's Theatre, if there's a suitable show there. The nighttime view from the top of the Washington Monument or the Old Post Office Tower is one you'll never forget.

Most nights, though, especially if your kids are small, regular bedtimes are your best bet. Remember the travel maxim: The mood of a group is determined by its most tired member. If everybody is well-fed and well-rested enough to get through all the day's activities, the whole group will enjoy the trip more. Far better to eat a half hour too early, or stop a half hour too soon than to create a bad mood that will spoil the rest of the day.

The Smithsonian

I only use adjectives like terrific, wonderful, or spectacular when they're warranted, but because I only write about things I truly like, those words do turn up often in my work. The Smithsonian, however, goes far beyond those petty accolades. This must be the most phenomenal complex of museums in the world. While the libraries and research facilities of the Smithsonian span the globe, the fourteen (soon to be fifteen) museums and the National Zoo that are located here in Washington are more than enough to keep you busy for your entire holiday.

And it got its start from the bequest of a man who wouldn't arrive in the United States until three-quarters of a century after his death!

James Smithson was an English scientist of modest repute who left his fortune to his nephew in 1829 with the provision that if the nephew died without heirs, the fortune was to be given to the United States (a place he'd never even visited) to found an institution to increase and disseminate knowledge. And that's exactly what happened. The nephew died childless just six years after his uncle and the Smithsonian Institution was created with his money by an act of Congress in 1846.

No one has any idea why Smithson left his fortune to the United States, but visitors to Washington are his real heirs now. The museums are free for everyone and open every day of the year except Dec. 25. Most are clustered on or near the National Mall and are within easy walking distance of each other. What's more, all are air-conditioned and have plenty of public rest rooms.

Each of the museums is covered in the appropriate chapters that follow, but here's a quick summary. Starred museums are on the National Mall.

*The Castle—The original 1855 building, now an information center for the complex. Smithson's remains were moved here in 1904. See Chapter 11 for more information

*Arts and Industries Building—Used mostly for offices and special exhibitions.

*National Museum of Natural History—From insects to dinosaurs, meteorites to the Hope Diamond.

*National Museum of American History—The original Star Spangled Banner, Oscar the Grouch, Dorothy's ruby slippers and more: America's attic!

*National Air and Space Museum—The Wright Brothers' first airplane, moon rocks, and everything in between.

Anacostia Museum for African American History and Culture—The history and achievements of America's black families from slavery to the present.

National Postal Museum—Much more than stamps, a journey through the growth of public communication.

*Freer Gallery of Art—Asian and American art.

*Arthur M. Sackler Gallery—Asian art.

National Museum of African Art—From around the continent, but mostly sub-Saharan.

National Museum of American Art—American fine art, folk art, and sculpture.

Renwick Gallery—American art and crafts.

National Portrait Gallery—paintings, photos, and other images of famous Americans.

*Hirshhorn Museum—Modern art and sculpture.

*National Museum of the American Indian—now under construction.

National Zoo—One of the leading zoos of the world.

I do hope you won't confine yourself only to the Smithsonian, however, no matter how great its museums are; Washington has much else worth seeing, too. But many of these are certain to be on everybody's A-list, and for good reason. These are some of the most terrific, wonderful, and spectacular museums in the world.

Tip: While there are free guides available to each museum, pick up a free copy of the booklet "My Smithsonian" at any Smithsonian facility. It has floor plans, information on special exhibits, highlights, suggestions for how to get the most out of each museum, and special ideas for kids.

The crypt of James Smithson, who never saw the institute he founded, is in the Castle

A Few More Suggestions

The previous three ideas are laws... rules... commandments. Violate them only if you want the Travel Fairy to show up at your hotel and sprinkle Grumpy Dust on your kids. I have a few more suggestions for you to think about, though, all things that have worked well for us and others we've compared travel notes with. They don't have the force of law, but they are wonderful—and perhaps surprising—pieces of advice that have stood up to countless family trips, including many by the Lains.

The Two-Hour Rule

Kids have short attention spans, unless they're playing video games, in which case they can sit unblinking for weeks, moving only one hand for the game and the other to shovel potato chips into their mouths. While most adults can spend endless hours in a museum as large and complex as the National Museum of American History or Natural History (even without benefit of potato chips), kids will eventually become impatient with what they see as too slow a pace.

Anticipate that, and avoid the restlessness by declaring a two-hour rule: You will never stay in a museum for more than two hours. If everyone knows that when they enter, they are more likely to be patient even if they get a little bored before the time is up—at least they know the rest of the group doesn't plan to spend all eternity there. And if everyone is really fascinated with a place and isn't ready to leave in two hours, you can stretch the time limit by another 30 minutes... if everyone agrees.

Usually the two-hour rule won't apply to large, varied attractions like zoos and theme parks, or to sporting events where everyone knows how long it's going to take. But indoor spaces with hard floors—that's where people begin to get restless, even parents. Put a time limit on them. If a place is so fascinating that some of your group just can't bear to leave, come back another time, or agree to split up for awhile.

And that leads straight into the next point:

Making Choices

Divide and Conquer

Here's a bit of advice that often catches people by surprise: It's okay to split up sometimes.

Just because you're taking a family vacation doesn't mean that you spend 24 hours a day glued to each other. Not everyone will enjoy the same things equally. It really is fine to go your separate ways for awhile occasionally. If Mom and Little Sister want to visit the Dolls' House Museum while Dad and Big Brother sneak over to the Spy Museum, there's nothing at all wrong with that. It's fun to do things as a family, but it can also be fun to cover twice as much territory in groups just half as large some afternoon. It will give everyone lots to talk about at dinner tonight, and everyone will be happier at being allowed to concentrate on what they like best and avoid things they're certain they'll hate.

It's even okay (and, parents, this might be hard for you the first time) to let the older kids head off on their own sometimes. They will be able to see what interests them and gain the confidence that comes from knowing they can manage on their own for a little while in the big city. They'll see things you would never have noticed, including, maybe, something special to lead everyone back to later, and be much more agreeable to full-family outings later.

Washington is easy to get around in and they'll have no trouble managing, especially in the central tourist areas. How old should they be? You know your kids best, but 12 to 14 is old enough if they're staying in the Mall area, or a little older if they're going further afield. Make sure you have a meeting time and place, and that the kids know how to use the Metro and how to get to your lodgings. A kid who is hopelessly lost can get help from anyone in a uniform.

Variety is the Spice

With so many museums in Washington and not nearly enough time to see everything you want, you're going to have to make hard choices. This next bit of advice is going to make your situation even more desperate: Limit yourself to one of each type of activity per day.

To get the most out of everything you see, try to vary your pursuits. If you visit the National Archives and the Museum of American History back to back, neither will seem quite as wonderful as it would alone. A trip to the Jefferson Memorial followed by the Lincoln Memorial will dilute each. Stops at the National Gallery of Art and the Hirshhorn on the same afternoon can leave you feeling like you merely saw a bunch of miscellaneous pictures. Just as you probably wouldn't have pork chops, pork cutlets, and a pork roast all at the same meal (although that might be our youngest son's ultimate fantasy), you should vary your intellectual palate, too.

If that means that you won't get to both National Cathedral and the Basilica of the Immaculate Conception, at least you have one truly spectacular church to look forward to on your next visit, whichever one you choose. The church you do visit will stay sharp in your mind, undiluted by one that's different, but equally grand. I've seen far too many people return from a trip they've planned for years, unsure of just what they saw where. That's a shame.

Recommendations

✔ Make certain that everybody gets his or her first choice, no matter what.

✔ Plan a late-morning sleep-in, a free afternoon, or a TV or game evening every few days.

✔ Don't be afraid to split up sometimes, even to the point of letting older kids set off on their own.

✔ Plan all you want, but don't overlook the joys of spontaneity once you're in Washington.

9. Three Branches of Government

Every American kid has to memorize the three branches of government that create the checks and balances that make their political system work—at least insofar as it does. So what better place to start our tour of Washington sites than with the key Legislative, Executive, and Judicial temples of the nation.

Here are the halls where many of the most famous and influential Americans (at least those who weren't movie stars or professional athletes) have done their best work, where billions of tax dollars are spent, where the future of the country and, to a large extent the world, is decided.

Sorry to be so depressing like that, right at the beginning of a chapter.

No, that's unfair. The U.S. government is the largest, most complicated organization on earth, and the most amazing thing about it is that it works as well as it does, and has for more than two centuries. Your family is coming here to learn about it, so we'll start with perhaps the three most important places in Washington.

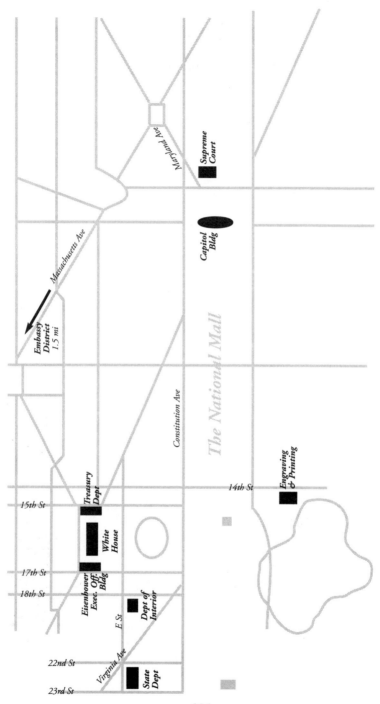

The Capitol Building

Tip: Travel light. Some government buildings no longer permit visitors to bring in large backpacks, food and liquids (even bottled water), or infant strollers.

The Lains were lucky. We went to Washington in a more innocent age, and were able to stroll around the city, going in and out of almost everywhere we wished as much as we wanted. Unfortunately, that's no longer the case. Security concerns have meant bag searches, x-ray machines, metal detectors, and limited access to places where we used to wander freely, including the Capitol. It's been very obvious to me on recent visits, however, that even at the frenzied height of the tourist season, security guards are making a real effort to be cheerful, upbeat, encouraging, and friendly.

At the moment, you can only visit the U.S. Capitol Building as part of an official tour. These tours, limited to 40 people each, are conducted every half-hour Monday through Saturday from

Going to the Capitol is a capital idea

9 a.m. to 4:30 p.m. Tickets are required; you can get them at the Capitol Guide Service kiosk located on the curving sidewalk in front of the building on the right-hand side as you face it from the Mall. Tickets are given free on a first-come, first-served basis beginning at 8:15 a.m. But you need to be there very early because there are only 640 spots available each day and they're gone by 8:30. Each person, even infants, must have a ticket, and each person taking the tour must wait in the line; Dad can't pick up the tickets for everybody while the rest of the family visits another attraction.

Tip: *It's possible to beat the lines here and at other attractions, but you have to plan well in advance. Congressional offices can arrange special tours of many popular attractions. Read the sidebar "Go to the Head of the Line" in this chapter.*

Still, it's worth all the hassle. It's easy to make the case that this is the most important building in the country (except the ones where my grandchildren live), and one of the most impressive. It looks just like a nation's capitol should look, overpoweringly tall and sturdy, gleaming white, topped by an enormous dome, with massive columns everywhere. Just the site of it is humbling and inspiring all at once.

How can I pick out a few highlights of what you'll see when *everything* will leave you agog? George Washington himself laid the cornerstone of this building in 1793, and Congress has met here since 1800. There's nothing about this building—its size, its importance, its history, its furnishings, its physical features—that doesn't boggle the mind. Your kids will never forget their first visit here.

Walking through the 180-foot-high (55m) rotunda is the ultimate test of your neck muscles as you crane your neck to see the fresco of George Washington painted there. You can visit the original Senate and Supreme Court chambers, or walk through the Statuary Hall with sculptures of the most famous residents of every state in the country. You can be dazzled by the artwork, by the sheer opulence of the building, even by its gargantuan bronze doors.

Yes, getting in is a nuisance at the moment (unless you can get yourself elected to Congress). But that's all forgotten as soon as you're here.

If possible, try to attend a session of the Senate or House of Representatives. Everyone will be fascinated (and, if it's a bad day, maybe a little disillusioned) by seeing the lawmakers at work. Your Congressional representative, U.S. senator, or the U.S. embassy in your home country can provide free tickets for your family. It's fun for everyone to see their representatives at work, and maybe see in person the faces they've only seen on the evening news. *[Capitol St. Metro: Capitol South or Union Station. Closed Sun. Open for guided tours only. Free, but tickets required.]*

The White House

Unfortunately, the only way to tour the White House at the moment is to be part of a school group, military, or veterans' organization tour. There's no other way to get in (unless you're a big enough campaign contributor to get invited to a state banquet). Eventually this will probably change, and if you're planning a trip to Washington, you should keep an eye on the White House website, and on mine.

It's certainly worth walking around. The White House is a historic and familiar sight and the kids will be impressed to see it in person. After all, every president of the United States has lived here... except George Washington himself. As a kid I always thought it was a strange idea that somebody actually lived in such a famous building, and I tried to envision what it would be like. Would the President take out the trash? Fix a dripping faucet? Help the first lady move the furniture around in the living room? Well, walk past. Maybe you'll see the President outside weeding the garden. *[1600 Pennsylvania Ave.*

Go to the Head of the Line

Tickets for Washington's most popular attractions are very difficult to get. Lines are long and there's always more demand than there are tickets. But if you can plan several months in advance, it's possible to beat the crowd and get a free V.I.P. tour arranged by your Congressional representative, U.S. senator, or a U.S. embassy overseas. Here's how it works.

Months before your trip, write to your representative, senator, or the embassy in your own country and request tickets for the attractions you want to visit. Request specific dates or a range of dates, and if it's possible, the staff of that office will make the arrangements and send you the tickets (or, in some cases, will make a Congressional request to another agency, which will contact you directly itself).

This won't work if you call two weeks before your trip, one Congressional staff member told me. Each office has only a very limited number of tickets, and they go quickly. If you're planning a visit during the summer, for example, request tickets at least six months before your trip—more, if possible.

These tickets may be for special tours before or after the regular public tours, and are the best way to beat the long first-come, first-served lines. Tours can be arranged for

*The Capitol Building
*Supreme Court
*Bureau of Engraving and Printing
*FBI Building
*Library of Congress
*State Department Reception Rooms

Metro: Metro Center or McPherson Square. Open only for pre-arranged tours by school, military, and veterans' groups]

You can get closer to the building on the north side, but you're not likely to catch a glimpse of the President no matter where you stand. But as you walk down Pennsylvania Avenue, look for the camera and light setups at the side of the White House, where TV reporters tape their stories with the building in the background. Be sure to walk past the White House appointment gates. This is where you'll go to be escorted in if you're having dinner with the President.

Since the White House itself is closed, the next best thing might be the **White House Visitor Center** [1450 Pennsylvania Ave. NW. Metro: Metro Center, Federal Triangle. Opens at 7:30

a.m. Free.] on Pennsylvania Avenue at the back of the Department of Commerce Building. It's worth a stop for three reasons: First, you'll learn a lot. Second, even if it tells you way more than you want to know, it's free and has public toilets. And finally, it opens at 7:30 every morning when not much else is going on. Exhibits are mostly photographs and text, with some furniture and artifacts, and a few videos and dioramas.

Coolest thing in my opinion is the silver centerpiece "Hiawatha's Boat." I don't think you'd want to put gravy

In addition, that's the source you need for gaining admission to the Visitors' Galleries of the Senate and House of Representatives. Unfortunately, tours of the White House cannot presently be arranged this way as they used to be.

Here's one more strategy: If you come from a heavily-populated area like we do, you might find that your senator or representative is out of some tickets for the days you want, even if you request them early. Don't despair. The principle of "Congressional Courtesy" means that legislators who haven't used up their allotment of tickets will provide tickets for the constituents of other legislators, if they're asked. The first time we took our kids to Washington, our local congressman from Ohio was out of tickets for all the days we planned to be in the city. So we wrote to an obscure congressman from the thinly-populated, far-away state of Wyoming, figuring few of his constituents would be making such a long trip at the same time we were.

Sure enough, the obscure congressman quickly sent the tickets we wanted. By the way, that congressman, a young fellow named Dick Cheney, became Vice President of the United States sixteen years later.

in that one! Older kids will get more out of this than younger ones because there's a lot of reading. But the exhibits do a great job of explaining the history of the White House, how it's changed over the years, how it's used, how it entertains the bigwigs of the world, and much more.

Supreme Court Building

This is the least well known of the Big Three buildings in Washington, but the men and women who work here have the

Don't expect to see the President out mowing the White House Lawn

final say on what the Congress and President do. This court never convicts or acquits a defendant, never passes sentence, never questions a criminal. The nine justices of the Supreme Court decide whether trials have been conducted fairly, according to law, and judge whether laws and regulations are legal according to the Constitution. Racial segregation in America's schools was banned in this courtroom, countless laws overturned, the death penalty limited, and U.S. presidents held to the same rules of law that govern other citizens.

The building itself is impressive, suitably monumental for the grave purposes it serves. It's not hard to get in, since access isn't restricted here as much as it is in some other places. But there's less to see. There is a museum containing court artifacts, judges' robes from other countries, and impressive statues. If you like, the sidebar on page 120 tells you how to arrange a personal tour.

The best part, though, is being able to watch the court in session.

If you're visiting between October and April, you can line up outside to be admitted to the courtroom where the country's most distinguished judges are hearing arguments before the court. Admission is free and on a first-come, first-served basis. When the court is not in session, brief lectures about the work of the court, about 20 minutes long, are presented in the court-room at 30 minutes after the hour from 9:30 a.m. to 3:30 p.m. You won't see the court at work, but you'll sit in the same room where the great issues facing the country have

You'd have to be nuts not to visit the Supreme Court

been decided. *[1 First St. NE. Metro: Capitol South or Union Station. Closed Sat–Sun. Free.]*

Government at Work

These were the out-in-front, high-profile, make-the-news-every-night forms of government—Congress, the President, and the Supreme Court. But most of the real business of running the country is done at a much lower level... by normal people. There are a few places you can go to see what makes some parts of the Executive Branch tick. The first one, especially, is popular with families because who, after all, isn't interested in money!

Bureau of Engraving and Printing

I don't care how good your job is—you'll never make more money than the people who work here... because they make it all. Every dollar in your wallet came from the Bureau of Engraving and Printing here on C Street SW, and one of the most popular tours in Washington lets you watch printers manufacturing the country's currency and postage stamps.

It's another tough ticket to get because lines extend down the street. The 40-minute tours run Monday through Friday from 9 a.m. to 2 p.m. and sometimes summer weekday evenings from 5 to 7 p.m. The ticket booth opens at 8 a.m. and tickets for the day usually are gone by 8:30. (Evening tickets are issued at 3:30.) But the sidebar tells you how to sidestep that endless line.

Once inside, you'll be shown how money is designed, how it incorporates features to thwart counterfeiters, and you'll be able to watch endless streams of money rolling through the presses, possibly more during your tour than you're likely to earn in a lifetime! That is such a depressing thought! You'll see postage stamps being printed, too, as the government gets geared up for the next big postal rate increase. I feel safe writing that, because a rate increase is always right around the corner.

There's even a gift shop! What can you buy at the BEP gift shop? Since the BEP destroys worn-out currency by shredding it, how about a 5-pound bag of shredded money, guaranteed to contain the shards of at least $10,000. The price? A very reasonable $45. Fortunately, smaller quantities are available. You also can get uncut sheets of genuine money, suitable for framing, and lots of collectibles. It's one of the most unusual shops in Washington. *[1400 C St. SW. Metro: Smithsonian. Closed Sat–Sun. Free, but tickets required.]*

Department of the Interior

If you ask ten people at random what the Department of the Interior does, you'll get eleven wrong answers. Here's a chance to find out, from what may be Washington's most overlooked small museum.

Three Branches of Government

Most importantly, perhaps, Interior runs the country's National Park Service, and this is a good place to get information about the parks. The Department is also responsible for the Department of Indian Affairs and has nice exhibits about a Cherokee classroom and a tribal council. The Fish and Wildlife Service section describes the agency's conservation efforts. There are exhibits and videos about coal mine rescues, fighting forest fires, and plane crash rescue work. It's a pleasant museum about a little-known agency, and a good place to stop if you'd like to know more. *[1849 C St. NW. Metro: Farragut West. Closed Sat–Sun. Free.]*

Some Impressive Architecture

If you're interested in architecture or the decorative arts, here are a few more places that might be worth a look, just to prove that a government agency can actually have an aesthetic sense. These aren't high on the list for most families, but you'll walk past the first two of them anyway. They are not usually open for public tours, but your senator or representative can probably arrange a tour, if you're interested.

The **Eisenhower Executive Office Building** *[1700 Pennsylvania Ave. NW. Metro: Farragut West.]* was known until recently as the Old Executive Office Building. In 2002 it was renamed for the former president. It's the ornate building right next door to the White House, and holds the offices of the Vice President and many White House officials and agencies. It was built in 1888.

On the east side of the White House is another grand building, one most people think looks like an especially grand bank building. Close. That's the **Treasury Building** *[Pennsylvania Ave. and 15th St. NW. Metro: Metro Center.]*, one of the oldest buildings in the city. At one time, the country's money was printed here, but it no longer contains stacks of cash, even in its famous central "burglar-proof room." Now it's mostly office space for the Department of the Treasury.

Visiting foreign dignitaries are normally received formally at the **State Department Reception Rooms** *[2201 C St. NW. Metro: Foggy Bottom]* Free tours are available here Monday through Friday, if you make arrangements in advance, but the State Department discourages children under 12 from touring because they are less likely to be interested in the lavish decoration, antiques, and furniture that form the majority of the visit. The idea, after all, is to impress visiting heads of state, not kids.

Other Governments

When they're not being fawned over at the State Department Reception Rooms, where do all those visiting foreign big shots

hang out? Probably at their own embassies. One of the neatest walks in Washington is through the **Embassy District** *[Massachusetts Ave. and surrounding area, especially New Hampshire NW. Metro: Dupont Circle.]*, where you'll pass street after street of opulent buildings flying the flags of every country you've ever heard of, and many you haven't.

And if you're a visitor from abroad, it's nice to know where your countrymen are, just in case

A walk through the Embassy District goes past dozens of palatial buildings

you lose your passport or have another problem you can't resolve. Our family has enjoyed walking the streets of the district, looking at the grand houses, and I still stroll through parts of the area: It's quiet, it's pretty, and it connects me to the wider world.

If you take the Metro to Dupont Circle and walk north, up Massachusetts Avenue, you'll pass more than 25 embassies before you get to Rock Creek Park a half-hour's walk away, including those of India, Ireland, Japan, Pakistan, Thailand, Turkey, and Venezuela. Beyond the park on Massachusetts Avenue are Bolivia, Great Britain, South Africa, the Vatican, and several others. A large cluster of embassies on New Hampshire Avenue includes Argentina, Indonesia, Namibia, Zimbabwe, and many more. It's a relaxing and educational place to walk.

Recommendations

✔ Above all else, write your Congressional representative, U.S. senator, or local U.S. embassy months in advance of your trip for free tickets to some of Washington's prime attractions, especially the Capitol Building.

✔ Read about different architectural styles with your kids before you come. The spectacular buildings will mean even more to you if you know the difference between Federal and Greek Revival styles.

✔ Attend a session of Congress or sit in on arguments at the Supreme Court. Your kids will be the class hot-shots in social studies next year.

10. Surrounded by History

When I was a kid I wanted to be a history teacher. Everyone advised me, though, that history teachers were a dime a dozen and it was a certain ticket to slow starvation. So I went into journalism and mass communication instead, but I never lost my fascination with history. Everything worked out eventually, though: Now one of the things I teach is the history of journalism and mass communication. And I've learned that the reason so many people claim to find history boring is because it's taught from dry books that make little effort to show how people of the past were living, breathing human beings. It's all dates and lists to memorize.

In Washington, though, history can come alive for your family like never before. You're surrounded by it! You can sit in the very same pew where Abraham Lincoln sat when he went to church. You can walk up the very same steps into the Capitol as dozens of American presidents. You can see for yourself one-of-a-kind documents written personally, pen on paper, by the scientists, the philosophers, the poets whose names are household names the world 'round. All the things you've read about in your schoolbooks, seen on television, and heard talked about are laid out before you in Washington.

Woodrow
Wilson
House

S St

Q St

Anderson
House

Rhode Island Ave

Dupont
Circle

St. Matthew
Cathedral

Massachusetts Ave

Connecticut Ave

16th St

M St

K St

NY Ave
Presbyterian
Church

New York Ave

H St

10th St

Petersen House

F St

Ford's
Theatre

E St

DAR
Museum

National
Archives

Constitution Ave

Museum of
American History

The National Mall

It was difficult to know just what to include in this chapter. So many places in other chapters could as easily go here as where they ended up. But in this chapter, I'll show you my very favorite historical corners of the city and surrounding area. Every one is guaranteed to please someone—or everyone!—in your family. Our kids claimed I enjoy history the way I do because I'd seen so much of it. But even if you didn't come west in a Conestoga wagon the way they apparently believe I did, you'll find a lot here to connect with.

The National Museum of American History (Smithsonian)

In many ways the Museum of American History is like your Aunt Agatha's attic—so jam-packed with wonderful and curious and mysterious things that you're never sure what you'll find, and every visit is an adventure. The museum has an incredible

Washington never wore a toga, despite this statue in the American History Museum

variety of artifacts among its exhibits, sometimes making its collection difficult to categorize. On various visits I've seen Judy Garland's ruby slippers from *The Wizard of Oz*, sets from the television show M*A*S*H, a lunch counter from the racial integration sit-ins of the 1960s, a stunning model of the U.S. Capitol Building made entirely of crystal, Muhammad Ali's boxing gloves, the sweater and sneakers of beloved children's TV host Mr. Rogers—it's an amazing list.

Even though it's the Museum of *American* History, don't avoid it if you're visiting from abroad. You'll see much here that's meaningful to you too, and you're bound to see some exhibits that will help you understand us a little better—or else give up on us altogether.

Some people come just to see the gowns worn to inaugural balls by America's First Ladies. Some come to marvel at the unexpected size of the country's original Star Spangled Banner—the American flag that flew above Fort McHenry in 1812 and inspired Francis Scott Key to write the poem that became the words to the country's National Anthem. Some focus on the fascinating history of communication or technology, from colonial printing presses to modern computers. Kids love the huge John Bull steam locomotive. There's no way to list it all, and no way for you to see it all.

There are two things you won't want to miss, though, and both are on the first floor. (If you enter from the Mall, you're on the second floor. If you enter from Constitution Avenue, you're on the first floor.) One is a visit to the *Hands On Science Center.* Here you can use lasers, test DNA, measure radioactivity, measure water pollution levels now... and from more than a hundred years ago, and much more. There are dozens of activities for visitors from age 3 to 103, and everybody goes away fascinated by science. The lab is closed on Mondays.

The other first-floor stop? A perfect piece of Americana—an ice cream parlor, open 11–4 daily. *[Constitution Ave. and 12th St. NW. Metro: Federal Triangle or Smithsonian. Free.]*

Three Abraham Lincoln Sites

Lincoln is considered by almost every historian to have been one of America's two or three greatest presidents, and you'll be reminded of his achievements everywhere you go. He is probably the president most foreign visitors are familiar with.

He guided the country through its most tragic period, the Civil War, and was the first U.S. president—although unfortunately not the last—to die from an assassin's bullet. We'll visit the Lincoln Memorial in the next chapter, but first, we'll go to places that Lincoln actually visited himself.

Ford's Theatre

Lincoln was a big fan of the theater and attended performances at Ford's as many as 40 times during his presidency. The final time, however, was April 14, 1865, to see a popular comedy, *Our American Cousin.* He was accompanied by his wife Mary and by an Army major and his girlfriend. About an hour after the play began, John Wilkes Booth, a Southerner bitter about the South's recent surrender after four years of Civil War, slipped up to the Presidential Box just to the right of the stage, sneaked past a guard who was watching the play instead of the door, crept into the box, and shot Lincoln once, just behind the left ear.

You can visit the theater yourself now, and even attend performances there. It still looks very much as it did on the

Lincoln was shot while attending a play at Ford's Theatre

terrible day Lincoln was shot, although it is probably more comfortable for modern audiences than it was in Lincoln's day. In Abe's day, 1,700 people would pack the place; now there are only about 700 seats.

A National Park Service ranger will give you a minute-by-minute account of the evening as you sit in the theater beneath the Presidential Box, then will allow you to go upstairs for a closer look inside the box. Follow that with a visit to the basement museum, where you can see the clothes, overcoat, and size-14 boots Lincoln was wearing on his last night (but not his famous stovepipe hat, which is in the Henry Ford Museum in Dearborn, Michigan), the assassin's gun, Mrs. Lincoln's opera glasses and gloves, and much more. By the way, those size-14 boots would be size 13½ in the U.K., size 46 in the rest of Europe, and size 33 in Japan. Those are big feet in any language. *[Ford's Theatre and Petersen House. 511 W. 10th St. MW. Metro: Metro Center. Free.]*

Petersen House

Doctors who entered Lincoln's box realized at once that the President was in mortal danger. They had to find somewhere nearby to treat him. Across the street from Ford's Theatre was a small boarding house owned by William Petersen, a tailor. The Petersens were not at home that evening but one of the lodgers, hearing the commotion, shouted at the doctors to bring Lincoln into the house. It was already apparent that Lincoln's wound was mortal, and that a carriage ride through the rough streets to a hospital or back to the White House would kill him almost immediately. So the doctors carried the president as gently as they could to the back bedroom of the house across the street, laying him diagonally across a bed that was too short to accommodate Lincoln's 6-ft-4-in (1.93m) height. While Mrs. Lincoln waited in the front parlor for the inevitable, the doctors made the president as comfortable as possible. At 7:22 the next morning, he died.

You can see the first floor of Petersen House now with some of its original furnishings. Just walk to the red brick house directly across the street from the theater. Admission is free.

If you're ready for lunch after your visit, the Hard Rock Café is on the corner. Everyone in the neighborhood tries to capitalize on the area's history, so don't be surprised to see places like Honest Abe Souvenirs and Lincoln House Pizza. Abe would have been embarrassed.

New York Avenue Presbyterian Church

Visitors flock to Ford's Theatre and Petersen House to learn of Lincoln's death, but very few find the remarkable celebration of his life just minutes away. (Possibly that's because a map in another popular guidebook places it miles east of here.) **The New York Avenue Presbyterian Church** is a hidden gem that even at the height of tourist season you'll probably have all to yourself.

Tip: *Most historical places sell inexpensive booklets that are filled with facts, pictures, and background material. If you buy a nice selection of them, you'll be able to relive this trip for years to come and have great source material for school reports and papers.*

This church, just a few blocks from the White House, is where President Lincoln often attended church on Sundays. There are two things very much worth seeing here. But first you'll have to get in. The church is kept locked because of problems with transients in the neighborhood, but visitors are welcomed any time just by going to the office at the side. I always feel a little intrusive doing something like that, but being a bit pushy, I did it anyway, and the welcome I received early one Monday afternoon was one of the warmest I've ever had anywhere. A staff member opened the quiet sanctuary for me and turned on the lights. This was Lincoln's own church, and his regular pew has been preserved and been kept in place throughout several renovations of the sanctuary. Look for the dark wood pew amidst the blond and white-painted ones elsewhere in the church. (It's pew B14—second from the front on the right side of the main aisle.) Visitors are welcome to sit in it, and it's the unusual kid (or travel writer, which is practically the same thing) who doesn't think it's pretty neat to do so.

After you've finished in the sanctuary, ask to see the church's greatest treasure—the original manuscript, in Lincoln's own hand, of the Emancipation Proclamation. Few people realize that this document, which was the first step in ending the shame of slavery in the

Abraham Lincoln often attended the New York Avenue Presbyterian Church

United States, is not kept in the National Archives or in some museum, but here, in this historic church. It is the most important document of the Lincoln presidency. It's kept in the first-floor Lincoln Parlor behind a yellow filter to protect it from light, in a case on the wall above a blue settee Lincoln used on his visits to the minister here. This is another room that's kept locked most of the time, and few signs guide the visitor to its location. But staff members are delighted to have you visit and see this piece of history. *[1313 New York Ave. NW. Metro: Metro Center. Free.]*

Two More Lain Favorites

If you have an appetite for seeing original documents and artifacts—the things written, signed, created, and used by the people who fill the pages of your kids' history books, Washington is a smorgasbord of possibilities. It has always thrilled me to see the actual letters written by famous people of the past, to look at the very clothes they wore, the chairs they sat in, the books they'd held in their hands. It made them come alive for me in a way that just reading about them never did—it made them seem real. That attitude rubbed off on our own kids, apparently. One of them even majored in history in college.

There should really be *three* places in this section, but the **National Archives** *[800 Constitution Ave. NW. Metro: Archives.]*, which houses the original Declaration of Independence, the U.S. Constitution, and the Bill of Rights, is closed for renovation until late 2003. But it will have a prominent place in the next edition of this book, and I'll include information about in on my website.

The other two places below, however, are almost always overlooked, a real shame, because they're fascinating and historic places where you can see things you'll find nowhere else.

Anderson House

Not very many people find this elegant building. It's a short stroll from the Dupont Circle Metro, up Massachusetts Avenue. Once the home of U.S. diplomat Larz Anderson, the house is now a fascinating look at what gracious and wealthy living was like early in the 20th century. More importantly, however, are the exhibits, including a sizable collection from the Revolutionary War. There's a noticeable emphasis on George Washington artifacts, and the belongings of many of his officers.

The museum is open only for three hours at a time on five afternoons a week, so plan ahead. You'll probably enjoy visiting the neighborhood anyway, just to walk through the opulent embassy district, trying to imagine what it would be like to live in such high-toned surroundings. It's an unusual museum in other ways, too: There's not even a gift shop!

One of the most interesting aspects of Anderson House is that it's the headquarters of the Society of the Cincinnati. The society began as a fraternity of American and French officers who had served in the Revolutionary War, and General Washington was its first president. There was some concern at the time that Washington might set himself up as king, with his brother officers as the new aristocracy. The fears were unfounded except, perhaps, in the imaginations of a handful of ambitious ex-officers, and Washington quashed the idea firmly. Indeed, the society was named for the Roman general Quinctius Cincinnatus, a farmer-soldier who twice came out of retirement to help protect Rome, and each time returned afterward to his farm, refusing all offers of power and leadership. Membership in the society is still limited to descendents of Revolutionary officers, normally in the direct male line. *[2118 Massachusetts Ave. NW. Metro: Dupont Circle. Open 1–4 p.m. Closed Sun–Mon. Free.]*

DAR Museum

The Society of the Cincinnati, open to male descendents of Revolutionary officers, has its close counterpart in the Daughters of the American Revolution. The DAR is open to women whose ancestors served in the Continental Army during the Revolution (making it a little less picky than the Society of the Cincinnati, which is only interested in the army's officers). The organization promotes a variety of historical, educational, and patriotic programs, although it has skeletons in its closet, too, having refused the use of its facilities in 1939 for a concert by the great African-American opera star Marian Anderson because of her race.

But that's long past, and everyone is welcomed warmly in this fabulous complex of buildings just down the street from the White House. Most visitors come to do historical or genealogical research in the organization's extensive library, but kids will find the museum much more interesting, for it's a little-known treasure trove that opens earlier than most things around here—8:30 a.m. every day but Saturday, when it's closed.

You'll find a painting and furniture gallery in the basement, and the first-floor museum has a gallery of textiles and ceramics, as well as a large space for changing exhibitions. On one visit I had a wonderful look at childhood through the centuries, with hundreds of examples of children's clothes, toys, and furniture, and lots of carriages, sleds, prams, rocking horses, tea sets, and more. You have to sign in and get a badge to see the museum, but there's no charge.

You can also visit many of the 33 rooms furnished with period furniture and artifacts to see how people of an earlier age lived. There are 17 rooms accessible on the self-guided tour, but to see the others on the third floor (including the New Hampshire room with a wonderful collection of historic dolls the girls will *ooh* and *ah* over), you'll need to be taken by a docent. That's a good idea anyway, since they've got thousands of facts about the rooms at their fingertips and in the little notebooks they carry.

Tip: Visit the DAR first thing in the morning. While most of the Smithsonian museums don't open until 10 a.m., this museum is perfect for people who want to get a jump on the day.

Outside the New Hampshire room is a play area with reproductions of toys of earlier ages that will delight your small children. On the first and third Sunday of every month, the museum sponsors a Colonial Adventures Tour for kids 5 to 7, where they can dress in costume and learn what it was like to be a child more than 200 years ago. Reservations are necessary, but are free.

You'll find lots of historical musical instruments, especially pianos, but my favorite is the harmonicon, or glass harmonica, which is a set of glasses played by filling the glasses with varying amounts of water and rubbing a wetted finger around the rims. Once your kids see this, dinnertime will never be the same at your house!

A word about that library: The DAR has one of the country's

best genealogical libraries, as well, which visitors can use for a small fee most afternoons. You can get a good view of the library from the second floor gallery. The room is vast, having started life as an assembly hall/theater: Notice the old theater boxes above the reference desk. Now meetings and concerts are held in adjacent Constitution Hall. There's also the old kitchen in the Oklahoma Room, the Audubon bird paintings in the Kentucky room, and, oh so much more. It's another of the capital's unknown treasures. *[1776 D St. NW. Metro: Farragut West. Closed Sat. Free.]*

History Everywhere You Turn

This could easily become the basis for some literary horror movie, something like *The Chapter That Wouldn't Die*. There's no end of wonderful historical places to go in this town. Here are more can't-miss places.

If you want to see how a president lives after *leaving* the White House, stop at the **Woodrow Wilson House** *[2340 S St. NW. Metro: Dupont Circle. Closed Mon. Adm. for tours but special exhibits are free.]* Staff members there might talk your ear off as they show you around. I've never met more enthusiastic people anywhere. My favorite spot was the room Wilson called "The Dugout." Wilson was a big baseball fan and the room contains, on the mantelpiece, the most unusual baseball I've ever seen—signed by King George V of England! Until late 2001, when former president Bill Clinton bought a house about a mile from here, Wilson was the only ex-president to remain in Washington after his retirement. Staff members report that Clinton often jogs by the Wilson house on his morning run.

Beside a wealth of Wilson memorabilia, the museum sponsors special exhibits. I spent lots more time than I'd planned in their temporary exhibition on toys and dolls of the 1920s. It was exceedingly well done, with dolls and playsets of all sorts, an early Raggedy Ann book, baseball games, Lincoln logs, and other building sets, and much more. Everyone in the family will find something to like here.

St. Matthew's Cathedral *[1725 Rhode Island NW. Metro: Dupont or Farragut North. Free.]* is where President Kennedy's funeral was held on November 25, 1963, following his assassination three days earlier. In 1979, Pope John Paul II celebrated Mass here. The cathedral is undergoing major renovation now, since the church is more than a hundred years old, but you can still gaze up at the inspiring 190-foot-high dome and admire the beautiful mosaics in the Blessed Sacrament chapel and baptistery. Don't miss the great lamps hanging in the transept. This has been called one of the most beautiful church interiors in America, and you're unlikely to disagree.

The Historical Society of Washington, D.C., located in a beautiful historic mansion *[1307 New Hampshire Ave. NW. Metro: Dupont Circle. Closed Sun. Adm.]*, will open the new City Museum soon in the old downtown public library. The society's website, listed in the appendix, provides details of the museum, which will tell the story of the city and area from prehistoric times to the present.

Virginia is for *History* Lovers

I've made the point that you'll find some of your trip's most memorable attractions *outside* of Washington. In no other field is that more true than in history, and a selection of Virginia's remarkable historical sites is virtually required in this chapter. The first one is easily accessible by either car or Tourmobile bus, but the others really do require a car. But they will more than repay the extra time it takes to visit them.

A President's Home

The home and burial place of George Washington, America's Revolutionary War commander and first president, is **Mount**

Vernon [*Fairfax County, VA at the end of George Washington Memorial Pkwy. Adm.*]. Washington inherited the estate when his brother's widow died, and it was his home for more than 40 years. He enlarged it from a modest-size farm with a four-room house to an 8,000 acre estate with an elegant mansion overlooking the Potomac River.

Getting to Mount Vernon is easy if you're driving. Just cross the Potomac on the Arlington Memorial Bridge near the Lincoln Memorial and take the George Washington Memorial Parkway south just across the river. It will lead you right to the gate. The drive is only a half hour. If you don't have a car, numerous bus tours are available at information kiosks everywhere. The best bet might be the bus trip run by the Tourmobile company, which leaves from near the Washington Monument at 10, 12, and 2 every day from March through November 11.

Plan on spending at least two to three hours at Mount Vernon. There's a lot to see. The grounds are lush and a pleasure to stroll through. After spending days in bustling Washington, here you will get the feel for what the area might have been like 250 years ago.

You'll want to tour the house, of course. Most visitors expect it to be larger, but it was more than adequate for Washington,

Get acquainted with George Washington at his Mount Vernon home

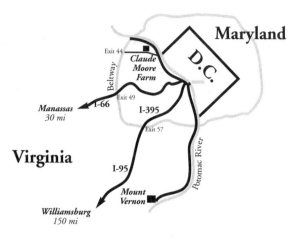

Virginia Attractions

who had no children of his own to gallop through the place. The central hall that divides the two wings of the house was more than just a passage, it was a place for entertaining visitors, especially in the hot, humid Virginia summer, because the cross-ventilation kept the space cool on even the muggiest of days. There is much else: the elegant banquet hall, the parlors, and the bedroom where Washington died, just two years after finishing his terms as the nation's first president. The rooms are preserved just as they were more than two centuries ago, when Washington lived there, and entertained the most notable men of the age, including others of America's "Founding Fathers" and the French hero Lafayette.

You'll certainly spend as much time outside the house as inside. Sit on the East Portico, watching the Potomac roll quietly past. I could relax there for hours, as Washington must have—but the Lain boys were rambunctious and would never let me sit for long. Visit the slave quarters. It comes as a shock to many

The Claude Moore Farm provides an authentic look at life in the 1770s

people that the "Father of his country" was a slaveholder, like most of his contemporary plantation owners. And you won't want to miss the tomb, where he and Martha, his wife of 40 years, have lain for two centuries. This is a wonderful outing, as rich in history as anything in the city itself, and more carefully preserved than most.

A Colonial Farm

Few people were wealthy enough to live like George Washington. If you'd like a look at what life was like for *normal* people in Washington's day, an even shorter drive from central Washington, D.C., will take you to the **Claude Moore Colonial Farm** in a pretty rural area just outside the capital.

The farm is frozen in time in 1771 and shows how a poor family living on a tenant farm in northern Virginia would have lived on the eve of the American Revolution. Twelve acres of the 100-acre farm is cultivated using only the equipment and techniques available more than 230 years ago, and the crops are the same varieties as the ones raised then. Even the few farm animals such a poor family were able to keep are the same breeds. The one-room house shows how the family would have lived, and employees and volunteers, in clothes of the period, cook, work the farm, and answer your questions just as they would have done in 1771. Kids will inevitably try to trip them up with questions like "What's your favorite television show?" And the answer will always be something like a confused "Telly-Vision? What's that?"

Unlike some of the other historical re-creations we've visited, the Claude Moore Farm is compact and extremely accessible to children, who can pet the pigs and horses, and maybe see a deer, as we did, wandering through the wooded surroundings. It won't take you more than an hour to visit, unless you're picnicking nearby, but it's a pleasant stop and both the pace of life and the admission price are low. If you're lucky, you might

The first major battle of the Civil War was on this field at Manassas

hit the one weekend each season (usually in May, July, and October) when a market fair is held on the grounds. *[6310 Georgetown Pike, McLean, VA. Closed Jan-Mar. Adm. Georgetown Pike is also VA Highway 193. From the Beltway, use Exit 44 and take Georgetown Pike east for 2 miles. At the sign, turn left and follow the road ½ mile to the farm. You can also take the George Washington Parkway north from Arlington to the Route 123 exit and go 1 mile west on 123. Where it meets highway 193, watch for the sign, turn right, and follow the road ½ mile to the farm.]*

Bloody Ground

The most tragic chapter of American history was undoubtedly its four-year Civil War in the 1860s. A number of important battles were fought in the area between Washington, D.C., and Richmond, Va., capital of the Confederacy. Two of the bloodiest were at Manassas, also known as the battles of Bull Run.

Manassas National Battlefield Park is just off Interstate Highway 66, about 30 miles (50km) west of central Washington, D.C., less than an hour away. If you have a car, it's worth a morning or an afternoon of your trip. The park is very accessible and presents a moving look at the days in July 1861 and 1862 when thousands of young American men of both the North and South met their deaths at each others' hands.

An easy, 1-mile walk takes visitors around the key sites of the first battle, among the cannon that still mark the positions of the Union battery; past the house where an infirm, elderly woman, unable to evacuate, was killed in her own home by artillery fire; across the field where Union soldiers could see Confederate troops bearing down on them. On the sort of sweltering, hazy July day that we visited, you can almost hear the cannons roaring.

Rangers do a good job of explaining the battles, the tactics, the blood and fear of the troops. And the site is well marked with signposts (some of which play audio descriptions) that graphically describe the events, as this one:

Shells were exploding overhead as Ricketts' men dueled Stonewall Jackson's artillery, directly across the field. Sharpshooters' bullets thumped into the wooden limber chests. On the rear slope horses were screaming, dying. Suddenly from the far woods came an eerie, blood-chilling cry—the rebel yell. Through dense smoke, Ricketts could see the Confederate infantry starting across the field.

A 12-mile driving tour takes visitors past the key sites of the 1862 battle, although maps of walking trails of varying lengths are available in the Visitor Center. The Stone House, used as a field hospital by both sides in the battles, survives and is open daily. Perhaps most poignant is the Groveton Confederate Cemetery, where the remains of 260 Southern soldiers, left decaying in the July sun, were buried in mass graves. Only two were ever identified. *[Manassas, VA. Adm. Take I-66 to Exit 47. The park and Visitor Center are 1.2 miles (2km) north on Route 234.]*

Williamsburg, Virginia

A trip to Williamsburg isn't a daytrip; you'll need to add at least one additional day to your holiday, and honestly, a week won't be too much. But if you're really a history junkie, a trip to Williamsburg isn't just a trip in the car… it's a trip in a time machine.

Williamsburg is about 150 miles (250km) south of Washington, D.C., near Interstate 64, about a three-hour drive. The showpiece, the reason most people make the trek, is Colonial Williamsburg, the country's most comprehensive Living History site.

Williamsburg was the capital of Virginia from its days as a British colony in 1688 until after the dawn of American independence in 1780. Now the city looks just the way it did in 1774, on the eve of the Revolutionary War. More than 400 buildings have been reconstructed, many on their original foundations, and 88 authentic buildings survive. You can see realistic portrayals of everyday life in 18th century Virginia, with scores of costumed interpreters, actors portraying genuine

Surrounded by History

Williamsburg residents of the era, and tradesmen and women, practicing their crafts just as they would have done almost 250 years ago.

It's not cheap. A one-day adult pass is about $35, and kids 6 to 17 pay almost $20. But there are three things to consider about the price:

• It's no more expensive than tickets to a major league baseball game or big national amusement park;

• Add a five or six dollars and you can get a ticket that's good for an entire year;

• The best bargain: If you arrive at 2 p.m. or later and buy a one-day pass, your ticket is good for the remainder of that day plus all of the next day. (Plus: ticket lines are very short then.)

You'll park at the visitor center, can watch a film orienting you to the site, and climb aboard a shuttle bus that will take you a few hundred yards to the historic area. Remember: This is an entire Colonial town. Be prepared to do a lot of walking, although there are shuttles that run around the perimeter of the site and can take you quickly from one side of the city to the other. The town is about a mile long by a half-mile wide (1.6km by .8km).

If you don't have your tickets, get to the visitor center very early. It opens at 8:30 a.m. and lines are extremely long by 9 o'clock. If you're only there for the day, there's little point in wasting

Tip: Numerous accommodations packages are also available on the website and they are terrific places, but expensive ones. You don't have to stay in the village, if you don't want to, though. There are countless inexpensive motels within a 10-minute drive.

much of it standing in line. But you can order tickets on-line through Colonial Williamsburg's website, so if you're better-organized than I am, that's what you'll probably do. The address is in the appendix at the end of the book.

Once you're in the historic area, there are dozens of things to see and do. You can start with a half-hour orientation walk or just plunge right in. The guide and map you got with your ticket has things of special interest to kids highlighted in yellow.

They might like taking part in authentic 18th-century games like trap ball (a very early cousin of baseball) or rolling a barrel hoop down the street with a stick, or learning to juggle. March with the fife and drum corps from the Governor's Palace to the Capitol, watch members of the Virginia militia compete in a tomahawk-throwing contest, or attend a witch trial. Kids can even rent costumes by the day and feel part of the town themselves.

You might meet people like Thomas Jefferson, Martha Washington, and Patrick Henry walking the streets of the town. All of them lived, worked, or visited here often in the 1700s, and you can discuss the issues of the day with them. (That's the issues of their day! They won't understand your 21st century world at all.)

In front of the Court House it's hard to resist putting somebody in the pillory for a memorable photo. The elegant Wythe house is open for tours to get a glimpse of what the upper class lived like; Mr. Wythe was a signer of the Declaration of Independence. And the far simpler Tenant House will show you how people like you and I lived. Guided walks abound on subjects ranging from the role of women in the city to archeology to the place of religion in the society. You can even take wagon and stagecoach rides. Many activities, like the walks and rides, have limited availability and, even though they're free, you have to make reservations early in the day.

You'll notice that many houses are not open to visits. That's because authentic 21st-century people live in them. Williamsburg is a real community (you don't need a ticket just to walk around the town) and people live here. In the historic area some homes are inhabited by park workers, some by private individuals, and some rented by tourists. For a price, you can stay here.

If there's a downside to all this, it's that Colonial Williamsburg is rather commercial. Many buildings are open, but often it's just to sell things (beautiful, expensive things) to visitors. The park does have to make money—it's not a part of the national or state park system but a private, not-for-profit foundation. Sometimes the history does get rather submerged in the commerce. But if there's a determined shopper in your group... and a credit card with a high melt-down level... then there's certainly something for everyone here!

I could yammer on lots more about Colonial Williamsburg— but the material you receive when you go in, the people at the information counter in the visitor center, and the people who live and work here do a wonderful job of helping you enjoy your day and pointing you in the direction of things you'll like. However, Colonial Williamsburg is only the tip of the local entertainment iceberg. Just 12 miles away is Jamestown, site of the first successful English settlement in America. Located on the original site first inhabited by the colonists in 1607, the park now includes full-scale replicas of the three ships that landed here and the buildings the settlers lived in. An Indian village and fort like those located here in the early 1600s take you back to that earlier time.

The third point in this marvelous historic triangle is Historic Yorktown. George Washington and French ally General Rochambeau battled the British commander General Cornwallis here in October 1781. The surrender of Cornwallis effectively ended the American Revolution and gave this country its freedom. Here you can walk that battlefield, see the monument begun after the victory, and inspect reproductions of Colonial buildings and military encampments. America's story truly begins here.

There's a plethora of other activities in the area.
• Busch Gardens with terrific amusement park rides and entertainment from around the world
• Water Country USA, a big water park
• Go Karts Plus, for racing fans
• Shopping, shopping, shopping, shopping....
• Wineries
• Virginia Beach, just an hour further down the highway.
Brochures and booklets available everywhere describe the area's countless attractions. So if you want to extend your holiday beyond Washington, you'll have no trouble at all doing it in Virginia.

Recommendations

✔ If you're an American, many of Washington's historic associations will be familiar to you. If you're coming from abroad, however, you might want to read a little about George Washington and Abraham Lincoln, probably the country's two greatest presidents, and focus on them.

✔ If possible, visit some of the Virginia sites for an especially vivid look into other parts of the nation's history.

✔ These are not, of course, the city's only historical sites. Be on the lookout as you walk, or as you visit other museums, for exhibits that could just as easily have gone into this chapter. If you find something really special, let me know!

11. Monumental Monuments and Buildings

WThat would tourists visiting Paris do if they couldn't look down at the city from the Eiffel Tower? It's the most visible structure in the city. The same is true of New York and its Empire State Building, of San Francisco and the Coit Tower, of Toronto and the CN Tower, of Seattle and the Space Needle. If visitors couldn't make the obligatory pilgrimages to the tops of those wonderful buildings, the most touristy thing they could do is just sit around eating baguettes, pastrami sandwiches, Dungeness crab, Tim Horton donuts, or drinking Starbuck's coffee.

Washington, D.C., doesn't have a special cuisine like those other places, so it had better have a signature building for its skyline. Fortunately, it does. The gleaming white Washington Monument, the tallest freestanding stone structure in the world, is one of the country's most familiar edifices. The sight of it as you land at nearby National Airport is unforgettable.

But Washington is a city of notable monuments and buildings. You can't avoid them even if you want to—and why would you want to? They're fabulous. Your kids won't tolerate a trip to Washington, D.C., without a visit to the memorials they've only seen in books and movies, and they're absolutely

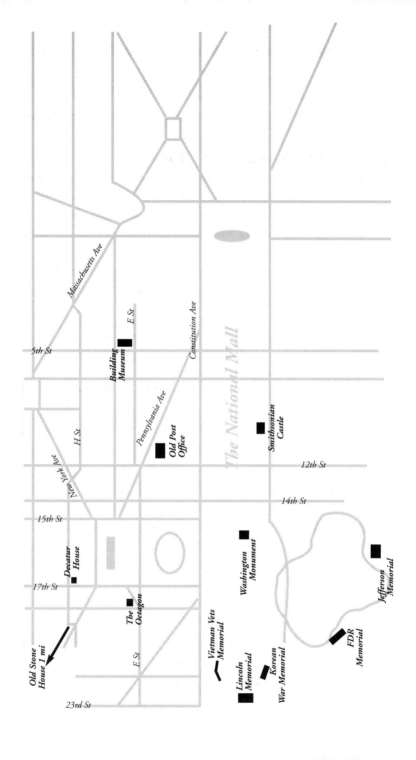

right. If Washington's eye candy were as sweet as regular candy millions of visitors a year would go home with no teeth. Let's take a tour of some of the city's best buildings and monuments.

The Washington Monument

We're in Washington, so we pretty much want to start either here or at the Capitol, don't you think? The Lains stopped here first on our first visit to Washington, and I think it's a good approach—the first morning of the first day we went straight to the top and had a wonderful panoramic view of what awaited us for the rest of the week. Our kids referred again and again to the view they had seen from the top as they went into the ground-level attractions.

You might be surprised by what a huge structure the Monument is, as we were. Photographs in books make it look very tall and slender, and considering its great height (twice as tall as the dome of the Capitol Building), I suppose it is. But it was much larger and more massive than we

Tip: *If you haven't reserved tickets by phone or over the Web, your visit here should come very early in the day. Get up early, have a quick breakfast, and head straight for the Monument. Lines (and waits!) get very long by mid-morning. It's also worth coming back one night after dark in the summer (when the Monument is open until midnight), when the view of the brilliantly lit Capitol and buildings on the Mall is unforgettable.*

were prepared for, with walls 15 feet (4.6m) thick at the base. Even a teenager who has already decided never again to be impressed by anything will be impressed.

The monument has just undergone an extensive restoration, which included replacing the elevator that will whisk you to the top of the 555-foot-tall (170m) monolith. In the viewing room at the top, everyone will enjoy picking out familiar buildings and trying to get their bearings. Plaques beneath each window will help you identify what you see. It's no longer possible to climb the stairs to the top; they were closed to the public in 1976. However, rangers sometimes lead walks *down* the stairs (897 of them) Saturdays at 10 a.m. and 2 p.m. These are on a first-come, first-served basis and are your only way to see the almost 200 memorial stones inside that come from every state and many foreign nations.

While you're waiting in line to get into the Monument, take a good look at the outside. See where the stone changes color about one-third of the way up? That's because when work on the

Monument began in 1848, construction was being financed by private donations, which had been accumulating for 15 years. The project started well, and the cornerstone was laid using the same trowel that George Washington himself had used to lay the cornerstone of the Capitol Building. Things went downhill from there, however. Political wrangling over the design and internal tensions among the states made it increasingly difficult to raise money.

In 1854, the money ran out, and the stump-like structure sat there, a national embarrassment,

The Washington Monument is the city's most prominent landmark

for 24 years, just 150 feet (45.9m) tall. Finally in 1876 President Grant authorized the federal government to finish the work. By then, though, stone from the original quarry was no longer available, and the closest match the engineers could find was just a shade darker than the original stone. So even though the work was completed at last in 1885, the change is stone color serves as a constant reminder of just how slowly the wheels of any bureaucracy can turn... making it perhaps a more apt government memorial than even its designers had in mind. *[The Mall at 14th St. Metro: Smithsonian. Obtain ticket from kiosk at 15th and Madison. See the website for obtaining reserved tickets by phone or over the Web. 9 a.m.–4:45 p.m.(8 a.m.–midnight in the summer) Free, but a small charge for advance tickets.]*

Presidential Memorials

You can't buy lunch in Washington without being reminded of the city's countless political figures. Anyone for an LBJ steakburger or a plate of Hoover Hash? There are much better memorials to America's presidents, though, and three of the best are near the National Mall. Don't expect them to be like museums, though. That's what we thought they would be before we went. They're just large building-sculpture combinations with inscriptions discussing the accomplishments of each man. It probably won't take very small kids long to get bored by them, but by all means visit at least one.

Lincoln Memorial

If you only visit one presidential memorial, this will probably be the one. First, it's the easiest to get to. It's on the far west end of the Mall, but you'll see the lovely setting when you visit the Washington Monument and probably will be tempted beyond your resistance to go. It's worth the easy walk across grassy Constitution Gardens and along the serene Reflecting Pool. The view from its steps is memorable, straight east through the

Washington Monument, down the center of the Mall, all the way to the U.S. Capitol.

Inside the memorial, built in 1914, is a massive statue of the seated Lincoln, with the words of his famous Gettysburg Address inscribed on the wall behind him and murals depicting his greatest achievements on the walls nearby. The most difficult photograph in Washington to take—harder that getting a picture of the President, harder than getting a picture of snow on the White House lawn in August—is getting a picture of this statue without a pigeon sitting on Abe's head. So much for the majesty of the presidency.

The memorial has important connections with the civil rights movement in the United States. Marian Anderson was invited by First Lady Eleanor Roosevelt to sing from its steps to a crowd of 75,000 people on Easter Sunday, 1939, when she was denied the right to sing at Constitution Hall (operated by the Daughters of the American Revolution) because she was black. And in 1963, Dr. Martin Luther King delivered his famous "I Have a Dream" speech to a quarter million people from the same place. These are reasons enough to visit and let your children stand on the same steps where others have made history. *[W. Potomac Place & 23rd St NW. Metro: Foggy Bottom. 8 a.m.–midnight. Free.]*

Jefferson Memorial

It's a long walk from anywhere else, but you'll find no more serene setting in Washington. The Jefferson Memorial sits on the south side of the Tidal Basin, looking out over the water, and the Washington Monument and Lincoln Memorial beyond. When the cherry blossoms bloom here in the early spring, the beauty of the place is indescribable. But that's the one time of the year, alas, that it's not peaceful, since the tourists descend on the area like a Biblical plague.

The panels behind the great bronze statue of Jefferson contain excerpts from his writing, including the Declaration of

The Jefferson Memorial sits beside the serene Tidal Basin

Independence. This 1943 structure is a fitting tribute to a public man who relished his privacy and the peace of his country estate. Even if you don't get to the memorial, you'll see it in the distance, standing like a Greek temple reflecting in the Tidal Basin. *[15th St. at the Tidal Basin NW. Metro: Smithsonian. 8 a.m.–midnight. Free.]*

Franklin D. Roosevelt Memorial

This unusual memorial is not a building like the others, but a series of four open-air rooms, each one symbolizing one term of office for the country's longest-serving president. It's about halfway between the Lincoln and Jefferson memorials along the Tidal Basin, but it's worth the stroll, in my opinion. It's very quiet here, with great views of the Jefferson Memorial and Washington Monument.

The outdoor "rooms" are larger than other guidebooks led me to expect. Walls are covered with FDR quotes, and there are waterfalls everywhere. There are life-size bronze sculptures that reflect his presidency. A man listening to his radio commemorates Roosevelt's radio "Fireside Chats." Weary people standing in a breadline recall the Great Depression. Be sure to see the larger-than-life sculptures of Roosevelt and his dog Fala. Kids must love the dog. The monument has been open only since 1997 and already Fala's ears and nose have been petted shiny. (And a shiny spot on FDR's trousers suggests that a lot of people have been dandled on his knee, too.)

This memorial has an interesting and very different feel from the other presidential monuments, though, more accessible and personal—less monumental, somehow—and is a pleasant and picturesque stroll from either the Lincoln or Jefferson memorials. [*900 Ohio Dr. SW. Metro: Smithsonian or Foggy Bottom are the closest, a 20- to 30-minute walk. 8 a.m.–midnight. Free.*]

Men and Women in Uniform

Not all memorials in Washington are to presidents. Some are to ordinary men and women who did extraordinary things, even to giving up their own lives for their fellow citizens. They are some of the most moving places in the capital. A family trip to this city should touch as much as possible on what has gone into the making of this country, and a stop at one of the memorials in this section will inspire your kids in very different ways from the presidential monuments. Even visitors from abroad will see how these places celebrate what is best about the United States—ordinary people shouldering far more than ordinary burdens.

Vietnam Veterans Memorial
The period of the Vietnam War was a highly controversial and extremely divisive time in America, and emotions on the subject still run high. But whether people supported the war or opposed it, all are saddened by the agonizing cost of more than 58,000 American lives that this memorial recalls. Just a short walk

northeast of the Lincoln Memorial, this is a somber and emotional place. The name of each deceased American serviceman or woman is inscribed into this low, angular wall and you can't visit without seeing comrades and family members of those who lost their lives searching the wall for their names, then tearfully tracing the letters with their fingers, or just standing there gazing and remembering.

On the west end, closest to Lincoln, are several books that list all the American men and women killed in the war, and direct visitors to the proper panel and line number to find their names. I found the names of a couple of neighborhood and high school friends of mine who died there. Almost every American visitor looks up someone. A ranger is always around to help and answer questions. On the east end of the Memorial there is just one book of names.

Why visit such an emotionally wrenching place on what's supposed to be a joyful family trip? If you have lost a loved one to war or disaster yourself, you know the answer, and it's one of

The Vietnam Veterans Memorial is a stark and somber place

the reasons you're taking your family to Washington. Kids mustn't lose touch with the past. That's what went into making them who they are, and will influence who they become. This stark monument, a low, dark granite wall inscribed not with patriotic phrases but merely with name after name after name, is a more poignant reminder of human sacrifice than any gleaming, soaring alabaster monolith could be. The Vietnam Women's Memorial is just to the south. *[West end of the Mall north of the Reflecting Pool. Metro: Foggy Bottom. Open 24 hours. Free.]*

Korean War Veterans Memorial
The 19 statues that make up the weary-looking platoon are a reminder of the hardship of war in the way the Vietnam Memorial is a reminder of its cost. Coming between the national support for World War II in the 1940s and the divisiveness of the Vietnam War of the 1960s, Korea is often considered America's "Forgotten War." But the sacrifices of its combatants were just as real and its losses just as tragic. The etchings of the faces and privations of its soldiers fill the adjacent black granite wall, and the central inscription reminds every visitor that "Freedom is not Free." *[West end of the Mall south of the Reflecting Pool. Metro: Foggy Bottom. Open 24 hours. Free.]*

More Sites to Sight

We're not nearly finished yet. Washington has more eye candy than any city in the country. We've got six more memorable places to visit before we can get to the next chapter, and you won't want to miss any of them.

Two Cool Buildings

The Castle: What kid doesn't like a castle? The United States is too young a nation to have the stone fortresses that dot Europe, but if you can't travel that far on this vacation, you can get the general idea from the **Smithsonian Institution "Castle"** *[on the Mall at 1000 Jefferson Dr. SW. Metro: Smithsonian. Free.]*. This is the headquarters of the wonderful series of national museums. Make this 1855 landmark one of your first stops to pick up all sorts of maps and information about the Smithsonian and to view the short film about the museums. And if you're a member of the Smithsonian (all you have to do is subscribe to its colorful and inexpensive monthly magazine), there's a members' desk with even more special goodies.

The Castle also has a couple of large three-dimensional models of the Mall and Downtown areas to help you get oriented to central Washington, and you'll find computer kiosks with touch-screens that will provide all the information you need about the world's largest museum complex—and provide it not only in English, but also in Chinese, French, German, Japanese, and Spanish. Everybody is friendly and helpful here. In fact, on my last visit even the maintenance man, about to scurry up a ladder to change a light in the ceiling, greeted me, asked where I was from, shook my hand, and wished me a pleasant stay.

Get information about D.C. at the Smithsonian Castle

The Tower: Let me take you to one of my favorite Washington secrets, another of those tourists usually miss. To begin with, if you're looking for lots of lunch choices near the Mall, you'll find a large food court ... and lots of other shopping ... at the **Old Post Office** [*1100 Pennsylvania Ave. NW. Metro: Federal Triangle. Free.*] The best part, though, is taking the elevator to the top of the 270-foot-tall Tower, the second tallest building in Washington. It offers a terrific free view of the city and while it's only half at tall as the Washington Monument, the lines are much, much shorter and even during the height of the tourist season, waits of more than fifteen minutes, even at midday, are rare. What's more, the Tower contains the official bells of Congress, which are rung 60 to 70 times a year—on national holidays, for the opening of Congress, that sort of thing. But you don't have to wait for a holiday. Just be around about 7 p.m. Thursday evenings when the bell ringers have practice. If the weather is cold or wet take a jacket, because while you'll have a roof over your head at the top, the sides are open to the elements. The protective wires up there are not electrified, a ranger reassured me, but please don't touch them.

Three Cool Houses

We like to poke into old homes and see how people used to live. We enjoy pioneer homes, the homes of famous people, the lavish homes of the wealthy of bygone years. And some kids like that too, although usually their tolerance for historic homes is exactly one home only. If you like that sort of thing, here are a few of Washington's many possibilities. Pick the one that's the nearest or that sounds the most interesting. If you let the kids decide which one to visit, their attention spans might stretch another fifteen minutes or so, always a good thing.

Probably the most interesting is the **Octagon** [*1799 New York Ave. NW. Metro: Farragut North or West. closed Mon. Adm.*] Built in 1801, this six-sided building was the grandest house in

Washington when it was completed. (Yes, I know. Octagons are supposed to have eight sides. I didn't name the house and it's not my fault. Actually it does have eight if you count the round entry and two adjacent short walls as three sides instead of as one. The origin of its name is a mystery even to its staff. But the builder's uncertain grasp of geometry shouldn't keep you away.) The Octagon was built as a country residence by John Tatloe, who hoped (in vain, as it turned out) that the cream of Washington society would eventually settle in that area. But here you can get a good look at an authentic early 19th century house. See the servants' hall and indoor kitchen, something very unusual for the time. Follow the winding staircases from the basement to the second floor (the third floor is all office space and off limits to visitors). The basement and first floor are best, and have excellent signs that will answer all the questions you have and many you wouldn't think about—unless you want to know why it was called the Octagon.

When the British army burned down the White House in 1814, President James Madison and his wife Dolley lived here for six months. Madison signed the treaty that ended the war on a desk you can see upstairs. Later the building was used for a school and for government offices before its restoration to its original 19th century grandeur in 1955. Be sure to notice the chandeliers and spend some time in the second-floor round room with its big curved windows letting in the sunshine. And be sure to stand at the base of the winding staircase and look up at it twisting its way to the top.

Just a few blocks away is **Decatur House** *[748 Jackson Pl. NW. Metro: Farragut West or Farragut North. closed Mon. Adm.]*, an elegant 1819 home built by Stephen Decatur, an American naval hero, with money from the prizes he earned capturing British ships during the War of 1812. Guides will take you around the first two floors of the house and explain how people lived in the 1820s, and how the house has been restored. This was a private

The Old Stone House in Georgetown predates the Revolution

house from the time it was built until 1956, when it became a museum. As you go through the rooms, have the kids look for an ordinary chair that unfolds into a set of steps, find the portraits of the 15 principal residents of the house (including one U.S. president—Martin Van Buren), and talk about what it must have been like for a maid to have to clean the ornate chandeliers in the second-floor parlors.

If you visit the refined neighborhoods of Georgetown, a wonderful place to walk, by the way, you might stop at the **Old Stone House** [*3051 M St. Georgetown. Metro: Foggy Bottom. afternoons only. Closed Mon–Tues. Free.*], the oldest dwelling in Washington. It dates from 1765 and has a small but fascinating museum of colonial life.

One Beyond-Cool Interior

What's going to be the reaction if you suggest going to the National Building Museum? [*401 F. St. NW. Metro: Judicial Square. Free but donation requested.*] Probably either a yawn or a cringe. Wrong answer! Even by lofty Washington standards, the inside of this building is eye-popping! In fact, I would call it the most spectacular interior space in Washington, and that's saying a lot! The enormous red brick building (more than 15 million bricks, as a matter of fact) was built in 1887 to serve as the U.S. Pension Bureau. Its breathtaking interior is larger than a football field and is a single vast open space 15 stories tall with massive columns and a large central fountain.

Exhibitions at the museum are ever changing, and cover all sorts of building, from skyscrapers to dams to bridges to landscaping, to air conditioning to mass transit. One recent exhibition told the story of the building of many Washington, D.C., monuments you'll see throughout the rest of your trip. The museum sponsors hands-on workshops for kids, like flying model airplanes inside the Great Hall on Sunday afternoon, or building a geodesic dome. Guides conduct fascinating tours at 12:30 each day, starting from the fountain, and you might even find concerts on weekend afternoons. This is one of the grandest interior spaces in the world and has even been the site of inaugural balls. Because few tourists have ever heard of it, sometimes you'll have practically the whole place to yourselves. This isn't a stop that's on most people's "A" list—but it's now on mine!

Recommendations

✔ Get to the Washington Monument early—both early in the day and early in the trip.

✔ Don't forget the Old Post Office Tower. Most visitors miss it, but it has a fabulous view.

✔ See things, but see their surroundings, too. The Lincoln and Jefferson memorials are examples of buildings really enhanced by their settings.

✔ Talk about architecture with your kids. Ask them what they like and don't like about the buildings and monuments they see, and study the small details.

✔ Remember that even on a pleasure trip, it's OK to look at and talk about memorials that make us feel sad about something.

12. Science and Technology

Wherever families travel, the first museums they seek out often focus on some branch of science. Kids are fascinated by things that fly, by things that can destroy half a state, by things too tiny to see with the eye, and by things that come crashing down out of the sky.

Kids' eyes goggle at the bones of ancient monsters, at diamonds as big as fists, at how people live in bizarre habitats like deserts and arctic regions, at critters of almost any sort. If it's very old, very new, very large, very small, very fast, very furry, or very loud it's probably going to interest most kids. Science and technology often deal with things like that. And if those are the sorts of things that turn your kids on, they will be very, very happy in Washington and the surrounding area.

Because James Smithson was a scientist himself, many of the museums that grew from his bequest to the United States deal with the major branches of science. These Smithsonian sites are a good place to start. But they will be only a start. We've struck an especially rich lode of attractions in this chapter.

National Air and Space Museum

Welcome to one of our favorite places in Washington. We can't help but be fascinated by flight, because, after all, we come from Dayton, Ohio, home of the Wright Brothers and the birthplace of aviation. Besides, when we go to Washington, it's often on an airplane. But even if you come from Idaho and arrived by train, or from Venezuela and arrived by ship, you'll be amazed by this place.

The excitement begins as soon as you step through the door. High overhead are some of the most famous airplanes ever made. See the very first airplane ever flown, the Wright Brothers' plane (designed and built in a bicycle shop in Dayton!) from 1903. See *The Spirit of St. Louis* that carried Charles Lindbergh on the first solo transatlantic flight in 1927. See the Apollo 11 Command Module that carried astronauts Neil Armstrong and Buzz Aldrin on their flight into history in 1969 when they became the first men to walk on the moon. Touch an actual moon rock, brought back from the lunar surface by other astronauts.

And this is just the first room!

Kids will love going into the cockpit of a genuine DC7, walking through the Skylab space station, learning how things fly, seeing an airplane that uses human legs instead of an engine to fly, or looking at the evolution of the space suit.

Because it's part of the Smithsonian, there is no charge for the museum. If you're interested, both the Einstein Planetarium and the Imax Theater present several shows a day (for an admission charge). If you've never been to an Imax movie, you'll find it an incredible experience, watching films shot from hot air balloons, jet planes, and spacecraft, sometimes in 3D, on a screen 50 feet high by 75 feet wide

Tip: This is one of the most popular museums in the world and millions of people visit every year. Get here when the museum opens at 9:30 or earlier. With increased security at museum entrances, the line to get in quickly extends down the street.

(15.25 by 23 meters). Buy your tickets in advance or as soon as you arrive; they sell out quickly. *[Independence Ave. & 7th St. SW. Metro: L'Enfant. Free, but adm. for theater and planetarium.]*

National Museum of Natural History

Entering a museum for the first time is always exciting, because there's almost always something just inside the entrance that will get a visitor's heart pounding. In Air and Space, it's all the famous airplanes soaring above. In American History it's the enormous Star Spangled Banner. And at the Museum of Natural History you're greeted up close by a colossal African Elephant that seems almost to fill the huge rotunda. It's just the first of the museum's many wonders.

Turn into the galleries on the right and you're among the dinosaurs, mastodons, and other great fossils, provided you're in the mood for life on a gargantuan scale. But if it's tiny living things you want, go up the stairs on the back left of the elephant, follow the corridor on your right, and spend some time in the insect zoo. If you're there in late morning or early afternoon, you'll be around for the tarantula feeding.

Also on the second floor, on the other side of the balcony, is another of the museum's biggest draws, the Hope Diamond, the largest blue diamond in the world. There are dozens of other spectacular gems in the gallery, but this is the one, with its legendary curse, that draws the attention. Many of its owners, including French Queen Marie Antoinette, have met rather nasty fates. But no evil befalls those who merely look—or fantasize, like the Dad I saw on a recent visit who was listening to his excited 6- to 9-year-olds twitter, "Wouldn't Momma love it if we'd get her something like this for Christmas?"

Probably the answer to that would be Yes.

You can learn about cultures from around the world here. The museum's anthropological displays are hard to beat, even if some of them look a little dated. And there's an Imax Theater here, too, in case you missed the one at Air and Space. There's nothing like sitting in a comfortable seat watching a five-times-larger-than-life rhino bearing down on you, or a 40-foot-tall spider inching its way in your direction!

There are plenty of hands-on experiences for the kids in the Discovery Room and throughout the museum, a place where you'll surely be tempted to violate that two-hour rule we discussed earlier. *[Constitution Ave. and 10th St. NW. Metro: Federal Triangle or Smithsonian. Free, but adm. for theater.]*

National Zoo

There are a few pleasures a person should never outgrow: Going to the circus. Eating popcorn. Watching or reading *The Wizard of Oz.* And visiting the zoo. If you like zoos, Washington has a very nice one, located in Rock Creek Park about two miles northeast of the White House. And because it's part of the Smithsonian, the zoo is free.

Though the Giant Pandas have long been the National Zoo's most famous inhabitants, don't forget all the standard lions and

Take a ride out to the National Zoo

tigers and bears (Oh my!). Kids love the prairie dog town and the amazing Komodo dragons, the closest thing you'll ever see to a living dinosaur. Amazonia, a re-creation of an Amazon rain forest, is complete and authentic, right down to the poison frogs.

Of course it's hard to get your fill of the elephants, giraffes, gorillas, and monkeys. Don't miss the Bird House, where you can see many of the zoo's avian residents gliding happily above you, and the Bat Cave—the sort that houses winged mammals, not superheroes.

And here's something you didn't know, worth thinking about as you look at the elephants: The king of Siam (now Thailand) once made a generous offer to President Buchanan. The United States, he had heard, had no native elephants. In a letter now in the National Archives, he offered to send the President several pairs of elephants so they could populate America's forests, growing someday into large herds.

By the time the letter arrived in Washington, Abraham Lincoln had become president. Lincoln thanked the king but declined his offer, saying that he was afraid the climate of the United States wasn't really suitable for elephants. Good thing, too. Farmers have enough trouble now with large populations of deer. Can you imagine the problems they'd have dealing with enormous herds of free-range elephants? *[3001 Connecticut Ave. NW. Metro: Woodley Park–Zoo. Free.]*

Smaller Spaces

National Aquarium (*Washington*)
Don't confuse this with the much grander National Aquarium in Baltimore (see the sidebar on the next page), but if it's just a quick dose of fish you want, this space in the basement of the Department of Commerce Building will do nicely. There's a small admission charge for this, but it's only a small aquarium, after all. It can provide an interesting 30 to 45 minutes and a chance to cool

Call It BaltiMORE

Baltimore is close (less than an hour by train or automobile), big (larger than Washington), historic (older than Washington), and packed with attractions. You can leave Washington after breakfast, have a full and fascinating day in Baltimore, and be back in D.C. by bedtime, filled with great memories and crab cakes. A sidebar can't do justice to this grand city, but let me whet your appetite by hitting a few highlights.

Driving is easy. Highway 295, the Baltimore–Washington Parkway, (exit 22 on the Beltway) will take you straight to the Inner Harbor, where most of the attractions are. If you don't have a car, or don't want the nuisance of driving, it's even easier. The MARC train from Washington's Union Station will take you there effortlessly. Get on a Camden Line train. It will let you off at Camden Station at Pratt and Eutaw streets, a block from the baseball stadium and a 5-minute walk along Pratt Street from the waterfront attractions.

The National Aquarium

This is not the little one in the Department of Commerce basement: this is one of the great aquariums in the country. It's expensive (more than $17 for adults), but worth it for anybody who likes to have his or her mind boggled. Visitors are guided along a route that takes them through every part of the aquarium, from the entrance up to the fifth level in easy stages, with well-placed computer discovery stations along the way. When you enter, you're met by an enormous tank of rays, those amazing ghosts of the deep. A whale skeleton looms overhead and you can see what commodious lodgings Jonah had.

Kids go crazy for seahorses, and the seahorse exhibition here is the best I've ever seen. It includes real oddities such as pipefish and the leafy seadragon, which looks just like a tree branch.

The rainforest is so realistic the 5-year-old ahead of us was afraid to go in, wailing "But there will be cobras!" Mom reassured him that she'd save him if there were, and all was well.

But kids know who the real stars of the show are: the sharks! As you descend into the middle of the 360-degree shark tank, the lights dim and you hear eerie music in the background. This place feels dangerous. Angry-looking sharks—more than you can count—circle the perimeter on silent patrol. It's scary. And perfectly safe, of course. But the illusion is marvelous.

There's a dolphin show, naturally, and a window into the dolphin pool where you can watch them from below. The Aquarium isn't perfect: It needs seals. But a new 10-story building due in 2006 will house them. [Pier 3, 501 E. Pratt St., Baltimore. Open until 8 p.m. Fri. Adm.]

Science and Technology

The MORE in Baltimore

We're not finished with Baltimore by any means. The Aquarium is on Baltimore's marvelously restored waterfront area, the Inner Harbor, a great collection of places to have fun, to eat, and to shop. Try the observation deck at the Top of the World, go to the Baltimore Civil War Museum, eat and shop in the restored Powerhouse or the new Harborplace indoor mall, rent a dragon paddleboat for an hour and take your own tour of the harbor.

A boat that's a lot less work is the U.S.S. Constellation [Pier 1, 301 Pratt St., Baltimore. Adm.], *the last all-sail warship built by the U.S. Navy. This is the last authentic Civil War naval vessel still afloat. It offers tours, lots of hands-on activities, and cannon firings. Other nautical exhibits are available, too, including a submarine, a maritime museum, and more.*

Down near the entrance to the Harbor is the Maryland Science Center [601 Light St, Baltimore. Open until 7 p.m. Fri–Sat. Adm.], *another great science museum. There's a big emphasis on space here, but kids can learn how paleontologists dig for dinosaur bones, how optical illusions work, and countless other fascinating things. The Science Arcade has dozens of hands-on experiences, there are demonstrations all day long, and a special room for kids 8 and under. There's even a planetarium and an Imax theater.*

From the Inner Harbor you can catch a water taxi for the short ride to Fort McHenry, the bombardment of which Frances Scott Key wrote about in his poem, "The Star Spangled Banner," which became America's National Anthem. And a few blocks from the Harbor you can visit the Star Spangled Banner House, where the historic flag was made.

Also nearby is Port Discovery [35 Market Pl., Baltimore. Adm.], *a museum for kids 6 to 12 where the emphasis is on learning by doing—following clues, time traveling, problem solving, testing senses, inventing. Kids can swing through a tree house, see how television works, create marionettes. Experts from a wide variety of fields are always on hand. This is one of the finest children's museums in the country.*

Adjacent to Port Discovery is the HiFlyer, [Baltimore and President streets, Baltimore. Open until 10 p.m. in the summer. Adm.] *a helium balloon (tethered with a steel cable) that takes up to 25 people at a time 450 feet (138m) above Baltimore for a 15-minute ride.*

There's much more than that in Baltimore—professional sports, quaint old ethnic neighborhoods, walks through historic Federal Hill, even the National Museum of Dentistry (with a juke box that looks like a large open mouth!) if anybody's interested.

Baltimore. Who'd have thought of that?

Sail high above Baltimore in the balloon at Port Discovery

off on a hot day or warm up on a cold one. Kids love to watch fish up close, and they'll enjoy themselves.

Kids will love feeling the sea life in the small touch pool, and the highlights of the exhibits are alligators and sharks. If you're there at 2 o'clock in the afternoon, there are feedings and lectures about the animals. (Best bets: 'gators on Fridays, sharks Monday, Wednesday and Saturday). There are a few interactive exhibits that do things like test your knowledge of alligators, and the research labs are open for you to see marine biologists at work. *[25 Constitution Ave. NW in the Dept. of Commerce basement. Enter on 14th St. Metro: Federal Triangle. Adm.]*

Arts and Industries Building

Probably the most overlooked building on the National Mall is the Smithsonian's second oldest building, the Arts and Industries Building. The interior is beautiful (beautiful enough for President Garfield to hold his Inauguration Ball here in 1881) and its exhibition space has held everything from paintings to rockets. Now it's used as office space and as a gallery for temporary exhibitions, which often touch on the

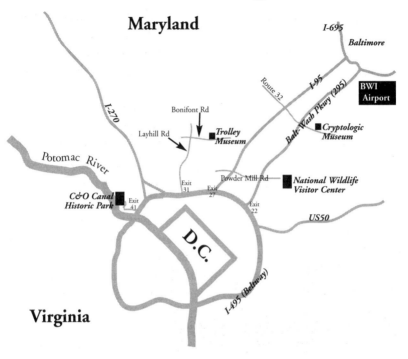

Maryland

Maryland Attractions

natural or social sciences. By all means, check out the temporary exhibit and get a look at this beautiful building, a surviving example of what 19th century museums aspired to be, but rarely were. *[900 Jefferson Dr. SW. Metro: Smithsonian. Free.]*

Out of Town

I keep telling you that some of the Washington area's best attractions aren't in Washington at all. Here are two examples for anyone fond of animals. But you'll need a car to get both places; neither is accessible by public transportation. If you like the sound of them, though, they're more than worth the effort.

National Wildlife Visitor Center

If you're arriving in Washington from the north, or returning from a day or two in Baltimore … and if you love nature and the outdoors… let me lead you to one of the area's best-kept secrets, the National Wildlife Visitor Center, part of the Patuxent Wildlife Research Center, a 12,750-acre research refuge, where scientists study a broad variety of ecological and wildlife issues, just a half hour from busy Washington, D.C.

Follow the directions at the end of the section to get there. The actual address of the place is not helpful because it's really miles from what most maps identify as Laurel, MD.

Just a small caveat—Maryland seems to do a less-than-adequate job in places of making sure foliage is trimmed back from its highway signs. Be on the lookout for signs that are half obscured by tree branches!

Now, about this place. It's gorgeous! The sleek Visitor Center is packed with exhibits on conservation and ecology, all within the context of preserving the habitats of America's native animals. You'll find exhibit areas about habitats, pollution, wetlands, bird migration, and much more. There are few static exhibits. Kids will love all the buttons to push, slides to slide, sounds to hear—and

The National Wildlife Visitor Center is a little-known gem

there are all sorts of 3D displays that teach. They'll learn about endangered species like the whooping crane, one of the great preservation success stories. The entire world population of the species in 1942 was just 16 birds. It's now almost 400 and growing stronger each year.

Spend some time in the "viewing pod," a telescope- and binocular-equipped glass-walled room from which you can spot deer, eagles, ospreys, hawks, heron, and some of the 250 beavers who live nearby. Or take a 40-minute ride on the tram, where a guide will point out local wildlife and habitats. There are 5 miles of trails near the Center as well.

How good is it? One volunteer told me: "I'm retired from the [government] intelligence community, so I've seen my share of waste and fraud. This is the best tax money I have ever seen spent." *[10901 Scarlet Tanager Loop, Laurel, MD. The Visitor Center is just off the Baltimore-Washington Parkway (Maryland 295). Take the Powder Mill Road exit (about 3 miles north of the Beltway) and go east 2 miles. The entrance is on the right side of the road and the Visitor Center is 1½ miles up a quiet wooded drive. Free.]*

Leesburg Animal Park

If you've got kids under age 10 who like to get up close and personal with animals, they'll have a ball at this small gem. About an hour's drive northwest of Washington, this probably isn't worth a special trip, but if you're returning your rental car to Dulles Airport or

You'll meet lots of friendly animals in Leesburg

driving home to Pennsylvania, this would be a fun place to stop for an hour. It's open April to October only.

If your kids like to visit the petting zoo at larger zoos and parks, they'll love this place. In the contact area they can pet and feed deer, llamas, sheep, goats, a great big 80-year-old tortoise, and more. Be careful, though—one sheep seemed determined to eat Barb's straw purse when we stopped by one afternoon. She followed us all over the petting zoo area.

Kids can also get acquainted with pigs, zebras, ponies, calves, emus—an array that would have made Noah proud. Nearly all the animals are accessible to the kids either in the petting area or in their pens, and they almost always seem friendly enough, although I did hear one 7-year squeal, "Oh, shoot! Those things peck!" as she inspected a litter of 6-day-old piglets.

There are colorful parrots and macaws, colorless white doves and a white peacock, monkeys, lemurs, homing pigeons, and a

A handler at the Leesburg Animal Park shows visitors a baby tiger

changing array of more exotic animals, like the baby tiger we saw on loan from a larger zoo. Staff members give regular talks about the animals, and about caring for house pets. Pony rides are available and there are a couple of small playgrounds for kids to burn off a little energy. The park is just south of Leesburg on U.S. 15. It will be on the left-hand side of the road as you head south. Watch for it. The sign is small and it's easy to miss. *[19270 James Monroe Hwy (US15), Leesburg, VA. Closed Nov–Mar. Adm.]*

Recommendations

✔ Get to the big attractions early, especially the Air and Space Museum.

✔ Remember that as great as they are, not all the things worth seeing are on the National Mall, or even in the city. Don't miss what could be a highlight for someone in your family if you have a car available. But in central Washington, take the Metro!

✔ Keep possible school assignments in mind as you visit. Take lots of pictures and pick up every free piece of literature available. They'll come in handy next year. Many places have resource guides for students or teachers on request.

13. Keeping the Peace

Among the many effects of the attacks in September 2001 on the World Trade Center in New York and the Pentagon here in Washington, two still influence most people's experiences in this city.

First of all, you can't miss the heightened sense of security. Places that used to be open to the public now have bag searches and metal detectors, or more restricted entry, or are closed altogether. Uniformed security personnel—military, police, and private—are everywhere and, while unfailingly polite, are very businesslike. Make no mistake: Washington doesn't feel at all unsafe. Quite the opposite. But if you've been here before, you will notice the difference.

The other change is evident more generally across the country. There seems to be more respect for the difficult jobs that men and women in uniform have. Military personnel, police officers, firefighters, park rangers—all seem to be accorded a respect for the danger and difficulty of their jobs that has been missing, probably, since the 1960s. Even people who are sometimes skeptical of the roles in society that uniformed personnel have to play are more willing to acknowledge that they are good people with tough jobs who are doing the best they can in tough conditions.

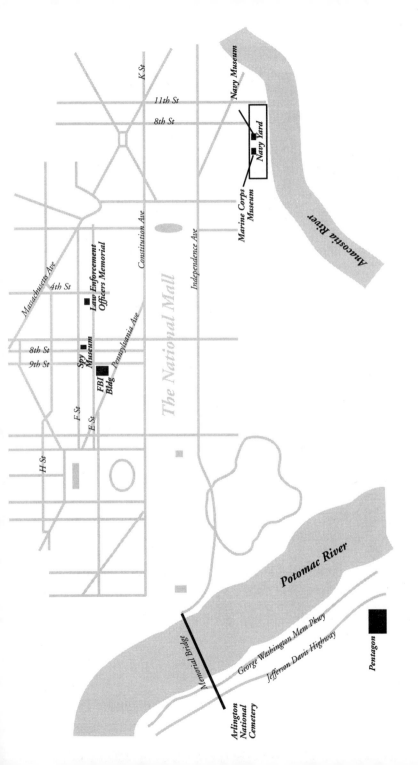

Those are the people who figure most strongly in this chapter. Washington is full of people with difficult jobs that few people want to do, but that are necessary for the rest of us to live in safety and peace. Maybe your family will learn a little more about them while you're here.

Walking Among the Heroes

Arlington National Cemetery is America's most famous burial ground, and the remains and ashes of more than a quarter of a million military veterans and their spouses (including my father, a World War II Air Corps sergeant) lay here. Arlington averages 20 funerals a day, and almost 4 million people walk through its quiet green parkland each year.

Many visitors are family members of the deceased, of course. But most are people who just want to come to see the gravesites and memorials of some of America's most heroic figures. A visit here is easy. The Metro stops just outside the main gate, and there's plenty of inexpensive parking if you're driving.

Arlington National Cemetery can accommodate the ashes of veterans and their families

Keeping the Peace

Although the cemetery was not set up until 1864, during the Civil War, casualties from every war the United States has fought rest here, from the Revolutionary War to the present day. Two U.S. presidents, John Kennedy and William Howard Taft, are buried here, and Robert Todd Lincoln, the great president's oldest son, is also in Arlington.

Astronauts Roger Chaffee and Virgil Grissom, killed in the Apollo I fire, and Dick Scobee and Michael Smith, who died in the Challenger Space Shuttle explosion are here, along with Arctic explorer Robert E. Peary, heavyweight boxing champ Joe Lewis, and too many others to mention. One section contains the graves of 3,800 freed slaves, civilians identified as "Citizen," instead of by military rank.

You'll also see numerous monuments in the cemetery: the mast of the U.S.S. Maine (whose destruction began the Spanish-American War), the Challenger Memorial, memorials to nurses, Confederate soldiers, Canadian allies, and of course, Kennedy's Eternal Flame.

The most visited and most moving memorial, of course, is the Tomb of the Unknowns. The remains of three American soldiers lay here from World War I, World War II, and the Korean War, representing the thousands of their comrades who lost their lives and whose bodies were never identified. (An unknown casualty of the Vietnam War also lay here from 1984 to 1998. But developments in forensic science and DNA typing allowed him to be identified as a young Missouri soldier, and his remains were disinterred and reburied near his family.)

An honor guard is posted at the tomb 24 hours a day and the solemn ceremony of the Changing of the Guard takes place every hour on the hour from October to March, and every half hour the rest of the year. (At night, when the cemetery is closed, the guard changes every two hours.) Since 1948, members of the Army's 3rd Infantry have had the task of guarding the tomb, exhibiting the highest levels of military dignity and discipline.

You can get a map at the visitor center next to the main gate showing the whereabouts of the most famous gravesites and memorials. If you're looking for a family member or specific grave, personnel there can also give you a map that will take you directly to the spot you want. If you're visiting a family member or friend, you can get a pass that will allow you to drive to the gravesite. Otherwise Arlington Cemetery is for pedestrians only, unless you're part of an organized tour. *[Arlington, VA. Metro: Arlington Cemetery. Open until 7 p.m. Apr–Sep; 5 p.m. other months. Free.]*

Arlington House

On the grounds of the cemetery is one of the Washington area's most fascinating houses, Arlington House, also sometimes called the Custis-Lee Mansion. Daniel Parke Custis, who built the house in 1802, was the step-grandson of George Washington, and was raised by Washington after his father's death. In 1831 his only daughter, Mary Anna, married a young Army lieutenant named Robert E. Lee. The Lees moved into the big house with the bride's parents, lived there for 30 years, and inherited the property on the death of Custis and his wife.

Lee, of course, became commander-in-chief of the Confederate Army in its war against the Union, ironic, perhaps, for the husband of the step-great-granddaughter of the man who won the nation its independence in the first place. With the outbreak of the Civil War and her husband in the field, Mrs. Lee fled, and the house became a military headquarters for the Union Army.

The Union confiscated 200 acres of the Lee estate in 1864 for a cemetery for Union war dead, the beginning of today's national cemetery, and after the war, the United States formally purchased the estate from the Lee family for $150,000.

You can tour the house and adjacent museum now to see how a distinguished Virginia family lived in the days before the Civil War, and see many artifacts of the Custis and Lee families. The house is operated by the National Park Service.

First Line of Defense

Whether it's at the local, state, or national level, police forces are the most immediate protection people have against the bad guys. Washington has two unmatched places where you can get a feel for what it takes to work in law enforcement, and of the price some have to pay. These, too, are places I have something of a personal stake in, with a brother who's been in law enforcement since he got out of college, which was back when Aristotle was still a professor.

FBI Headquarters

A tour of the FBI building must be on almost every kid's list of Ten Most Wanted Tours. It's a tough ticket to get because half a million people a year traipse through the building. Better go back and reread the sidebar "Go to the Head of the Line" in Chapter 9 and let your congressman or woman help you. If you rely on just turning up at tour time, about the only way you're going to get into the FBI Building is to finish law school, fill out an application, pass the physical, and join the Bureau—or rob a bank! The FBI suggests contacting your Congressional representative at least three months ahead of time.

Fugitives should not tour the FBI building

But once you're in, you'll see what the notoriety of the FBI is all about. This is one of the world's most highly regarded investigative agencies. Fair warning, though: As good as the FBI undoubtedly is, no one holds them in higher regard than they themselves, and you'll get a good dose of public relations as you go through the tour.

That's fair, though. The agency has pioneered countless investigative and forensic techniques that are standard law enforcement practice. Let them brag a bit; they've probably earned it. Learn the history of its Ten Most Wanted Fugitives list and check to see if anyone you know is on it. See summaries of its most famous cases, from John Dillinger and Ma Barker to foreign spies and the Unabomber. Walk through its crime lab and watch scientists examining evidence in cases they're investigating now.

Unfortunately, the popular conclusion of the tour, a visit to in indoor shooting range for a demonstration of FBI weaponry is not available right now. But the rest of the tour is still on. Tours take about an hour, and you should arrive at least 15 minutes early for the required security check. *[935 Pennsylvania Ave. NW. Metro: Metro Center. Closed Sat–Sun. Free.]*

Tours of the FBI Building are very popular. Book ahead if you can.

Keeping the Peace

National Law Enforcement Officers Memorial

Like the military memorials on the National Mall that we visited in Chapter 11, this one is a sober reminder of the price some men and women have had to pay for our safety. The memorial itself is a quiet space in a busy part of town, across from the National Building Museum. In the square, bronze lions, male and female, keep watch over their cubs, an allegory on the job of police officer. Names of the more than 20,000 officers who have been killed on duty since the 18th century line the low walls; a book at each end will help you locate officers from your own home town, something I did on my visit.

The visitor center is on E Street between 6th and 7th, about two blocks from the actual park. There are souvenirs, books, and memorials to officers who lost their lives in the line of duty. Best, though, are activity books for kids in grades K through 8 with questions, puzzles, facts, and art projects that will allow youngsters to explore what it means to be a police officer, to get more out of the memorial, and to learn about their hometown heroes. The books are free and there are several versions, keyed to various ages. You'll also find an interactive video system that will let you learn about the many officers who died on duty. If there's a police officer in your family, something from the gift shop here would be an appreciated memento. *[4th and E streets NW. Metro: Judiciary Square. Free. The visitor center is at 605 E Street NW. Free.]*

Undercover Action

No, despite the subhead, this isn't a section about political peccadilloes: This is a family book. We're going to talk about spies here. It's a subject I've never been able to resist, and I'll bet there's a file on me somewhere because of that. Or am I just being paranoid?

I'm not going to try to get you into the CIA offices in this section, but we will visit a little public corner of the usually super-secret National Security Agency. Several years ago I had a student whose parents worked for the NSA, and I asked her what they did. "I asked them that once," she told me, "and my Dad said he could tell me... but then he'd have to kill me. I'm *pretty* sure he was joking."

Anyway, we'll save that for a bit and start with one of Washington's newest attractions.

The International Spy Museum

The first time I tried to visit this renovated building on F Street, the museum was not yet open. I talked to the security guard and was, I admit, prowling around a bit on the other side of the building to see what I could see. I'm glad to say I was tailed and told to clear off. These people really know their stuff. He even called for backup—in case I turned out to be dangerous, I guess.

Now anybody with the price of admission can get in, and you don't even have to sneak. There's no other museum like it. Even James Bond

Don't sneak into the Spy Museum—just buy a ticket

would be impressed. See bugs, cameras, and recording devices of all sorts, or things even a Hollywood screenwriter couldn't dream up (although Hollywood experts have played their part in providing disguise techniques for real spies).

You'll learn about spying through history, from Biblical to Medieval times, about George Washington's spies during the Revolution to Lincoln's during the Civil War—right up to the present day.

You'll see some of the weapons spies use to protect themselves when their backs are against the wall, and you will probably never look at a tube of lipstick, the heel of a shoe, or a fountain pen the same way again. There's lots of information about the Cold War era, and plenty of chances for you to observe, follow clues, and make deductions to see whether a career change is in order. Former CIA and KGB agents are on the staff here, and if you have any questions, just walk right up. There's no need to introduce yourself. They already know who you are. *[800 F St. NW. Metro: Gallery Place–Chinatown. Adm.]*

National Cryptologic Museum

Now let's get to the museum run by the NSA, the agency that's so secret the government denied its very existence until just a few years ago and agents joke that its initials stand for No Such Agency. (This is probably meriting another entry in the Lain dossier.)

In one not-all-that-easy-to-find corner of Fort Mead just north of Washington, you'll find this museum dedicated to America's cloak-and-dagger specialists. Actually there are signs on the highway for the museum, but you'll have to drive down an unpromising-looking road to find it tucked behind a Shell gas station. It's on the map on page 175.

Expect to see code books, machines that produce coded messages that even the senders can't read, and a display dedicated to the Navaho "Code Talkers" whose use of their own native language proved to be World War II's most unbreakable code.

In that war, the German High Command believed it had developed the world's most impenetrable coding machine, called Enigma. The museum gives you the story (or at least as much of it as they're willing to tell you) of how the code was broken, a discovery Germany didn't learn about until 30 years after the war. The museum is a tantalizing look at things that are usually deeply hidden. *[Fort George G. Meade. Follow the brown signs from the Route 32 exit of the Baltimore-Washington Parkway. The exit is about halfway between the cities. Closed Sun. Free.]*

Off Limits for Now

Before September 2001 there were a couple of other popular defense-related sites that you could tour. Right now visits to these have been eliminated or severely restricted, but they're interesting places, and if you keep an eye on their websites before your trip, you might find that you can get in. The situation is still very fluid.

The Pentagon *[Arlington, VA. Metro: Pentagon.]* has always had a popular tour. It's presently unavailable, but that could change. This is the headquarters of the Department of Defense and the world's largest office building, covering 29 acres, and enough interior space that you could store 100 million basketballs inside, though I don't know why you'd want to. For now, you'll have to tour the building by going to the website, but at least you'll come away loaded with trivia. (There are 691 drinking fountains, 4,900 toilets, 7,000 outlets for electric clocks, etc., etc.)

More interesting, I think, is the **Washington Navy Yard** *[8th and M streets, SE. Metro: Navy Yard.]* with its two first-rate military museums. **The Marine Corps Museum** *[Washington Navy Yard, Building 58.]* is open Mondays, Wednesdays, and Thursdays, but arrangements to enter the base must be made in advance by telephoning the museum. The museum traces the history of the Corps from 1775 to the present with outstanding displays of weapons, uniforms, and other artifacts. **The Navy Museum** *[Washington Navy Yard, Building 76.]* was considered one of Washington's nicest. It, too, is available only by appointment at the moment, unless you already have Department of Defense clearance to enter the base.

Access to these places will probably improve again as time goes by. If you're a family with a Navy or Marine Corps history, though, it might be worth it even now to make arrangements to visit. Phone numbers are on the museum websites.

Recommendations

✔ If you visit Arlington, plan to spend two or three hours. There's much to see and a lot of walking to do. It's worth the time.

✔ Remember to plan ahead and get advance tickets or security clearances for some places to avoid disappointment. Six months before your trip is not too early.

✔ Ask museum personnel plenty of questions. They have endless stories to tell that you won't find in the museum's printed guides.

14. Something for Everybody

W e did lots of research before we took our family to Washington for the first time, and everybody gave us the same advice: "Go to the Mall and stay there. Hit every attraction between the Capitol Building and the Lincoln Memorial and don't worry about anything else."

It's true that you'll have a memorable time if you do that, but I've never been very good at following advice, and the rest of the family is as independent-minded as I am. So while we did visit a lot of the Mall-area attractions, we went further afield, and were constantly surprised and delighted by what we found.

Because few cities anywhere attract the wonderful variety of people that Washington does, few cities have as many different sorts of museums, lots of them in places you might not think to look. In this chapter we'll look at a selection of places that are hard to categorize, but any one of which might be the highlight of somebody's trip. There's nothing here that at least one member of the Lain family wouldn't be fascinated by, and some have met with unanimous acclaim.

Textile
Museum

S St

Connecticut Ave

Dupont
Circle

15th St

Rhode Island Ave

Dolls' House &
Toy Museum

Massachusetts Ave

M St

Explorers
Hall

Washington Post

16th St

L St

K St

Capital
Children's
Museum

7th St

H St

3rd St

F St

Postal
Museum

Constitution Ave

The National Mall

C St

Voice of
America

Explorers Hall

The National Geographic Society is the world's largest nonprofit scientific and educational organization. People around the world are familiar with its stable of wonderful magazines, including *National Geographic, Traveler, NG for Kids*, and more. The Society sponsors expeditions to all parts of the world and among all its peoples. Its maps are definitive. The Society's headquarters is in Washington, where its first-rate museum, Explorers Hall, is an attraction that anybody with the slightest interest in natural science or culture is sure to enjoy.

It's hard to tell you exactly what you'll find, though. The exhibits change constantly. We've seen artifacts from explorers trying to reach the North Pole, great basalt heads from the Mexican jungle, the skeleton of a crocodile so large that it hunted and ate dinosaurs, the story of a year-long walk across the center of Africa, relics raised from the Titanic, and much more. One thing we'll bet everybody *will* want to see, though, is the globe—the largest in the world. You'll have an astronaut's view of things as it rotates beneath your gaze. *[1145 17th St. NW. Metro: Farragut North or Farragut West. Free.]*

The prehistoric crocodile at Explorers Hall won't eat you. He's extinct.

Capital Children's Museum

Before I went to a children's museum for the first time (in London, I think), I wasn't sure what I'd find. Kids in glass cases? Fortunately, they're always more interesting than that, and now I visit children's museums wherever I find them—although I sometimes get looked at as an oddity myself: a middle-aged man alone, without a kid in tow.

The Capital Children's Museum is a good place to stop if you've got little ones, although its admission price of around

> ***Tip:*** *If you visit between 10 a.m. and noon on Sunday, admission is half-price.*

$7 for everyone age 2 or more is steeper than most of its ilk. There are modest discounts for military personnel and those age 55 and over.

The museum has a nice variety of permanent exhibitions. One of the coolest is Brain Teasers, with challenges that will require everybody to throw another shovelful of coal on their mental furnaces as they work out a series of tests that show you how much fun it can be to learn. In fact, kids usually don't realize they're learning things here... they think they're playing!

Kids who like to watch cartoons can make their own animations right here, and the hands-on chemistry and physics lab will let your budding mad scientists perform their own experiments under the watchful eyes of real scientists. Youngsters can try out professions like firefighter or bus driver, or learn what it's like to be a kid in places like Japan or Mexico. It's a place for touching, trying, and tasting, not just looking.

The museum is housed in an old building (built as a convent and later used as a poorhouse) just a ten-minute walk from Union Station. Follow F Street around the east side of Union Station to 2nd Street and turn left. It's a two-block walk. Or from the Metro, enter Union station and walk through it. Leave by the back exit and turn right on H Street crossing above the railroad track. The museum is just a block away. *[800 N. 3rd St. NE. Metro: Union Station. Closed Mon. Adm. but half-price Sunday morning.]*

Washington Dolls' House & Toy Museum

This is very definitely not a hands-on museum, the founder and director, Mrs. Flora Gill Jacobs, emphasizes. It's rather old fashioned, with low lights and everything in glass cases, and the place has the look and feel of Victorian times. But what a marvelous place it is! Certainly no one in the world knows more about doll houses than Mrs. Jacobs (her book on the history of doll houses has been the standard work on the subject since it was first published in 1953) and her museum holds scores of them from all over the world: a 15-room house crammed with furniture; doll houses 4 feet tall; Victorian and Queen Anne style doll houses: more than you can possibly imagine. A large cabinet of miniature chairs. Noah's Arks. A miniature zoo. Humpty Dumpty's Circus. A Mexican doll house, complete with chapel and priest. Kitchens, forts, the U.S. Capitol, Mount Vernon.

You'll also find dolls and games of all sorts. Of the games, my favorite was "The Game of Cathedrals and Abbeys of England"— billed as a card game you could even play on Sunday.

There's a Victorian Tea Room where kids can book birthday parties, but generally this is a museum that may be more for adults than for kids. Mrs. Jacobs called it a museum of nostalgia and pointed out that it is definitely not a "touching museum." So very little ones will probably be bored, although there are plenty of small step-stools to allow the shorter members of your family to get a good look at things. But it will fascinate anyone from 5 to 95 who has ever taken her doll house seriously. Presidential daughters and granddaughters have visited here. The museum has been around since 1975 and looks like it ought to be good for another century at least. There are two shops upstairs that sell doll houses and accouterments.

It's out of central Washington a bit. Take the Metro Red train to

Friendship Heights, a 15-minute ride from the center of the city. Turn left off the train to the Jenifer St. exit. When you come out of the elevator turn left down the sidewalk and walk a few yards to Jenifer Street. Turn left and go 1 block to 44th Street. Cross 44th and turn left. Go half a block to a yellow Victorian building and you're there. *[5236 44th St. NW. Metro: Friendship Hts. Adm.]*

Two Surprises

If you had asked the young Larry Lain (an obnoxious kid, I seem to recall) to name the two most boring subjects on the planet, there's a fair chance he would have said stamps and cloth. Just goes to show how sometimes a guy *can* get smarter as he gets older. If any of your traveling companions show even the tiniest interest in either of the two places in this section, go there! You'll all be amazed at what interesting topics both are.

I'd start with the **National Postal Museum** (a Smithsonian museum). *[2 Massachusetts Ave. NE. Metro: Union Station. Free.]* This sounds pretty uninspiring, unless you're a collector. Stamps? So what! But like everything else the Smithsonian touches, this is done to perfection. You can see it in a half hour, but you'll probably have trouble getting the kids out in so little time. They can sort mail in a railroad mail car, test their flying skills on a simulation of an old mail plane (three old ones hang from the ceiling), and create their own postcards. They'll learn about Owney, the dog who became the mascot of the Postal Service, and walk through a forest as they learn how the first Post

Part of the campaign to stamp out boring museums

Roads were developed. There's a great exhibit on the pony express, and I would never have believed that an entire gallery on the evolution of the envelope could be so fascinating! Of course you can see thousands of stamps from all over the world, depicting every area of human interest. There's a stamp store and a museum shop, of course, and a Discovery Center that sponsors periodic educational activities for kids on Saturday mornings.

Another surprising stop is the **Textile Museum** *[2320 S St. NW. Metro: Dupont Circle. Daily but 1–4 only on Sun. Adm.]* This isn't as glitzy and interactive as the Postal Museum, but if you've ever wanted to drool over the intricacies of ancient Persian carpets, to look at South American tapestries that were old long before Columbus came to the New World, study the patterns and symbolism of Islamic, Chinese, and Indian fabrics, this is a place to pass an interesting 30 to 60 minutes. Kids will probably get the most out of the museum's learning center, where they can touch and compare different types of fabric, see how they're made (*I watched one 6-year-old look at his Mom and say with amazement, "You mean silk comes from worm spit?"*) and how they're colored (including dyes from ground-up bugs!) The museum also has family days periodically, where kids can try their hands at weaving, quilting, and more.

This and That

Washington, D.C., got rid of its streetcars in 1962. But you can still ride them just a few miles away at the **National Capital Trolley Museum** *[1313 Bonifant Rd, Wheaton, MD. Closed Mon-Tues. Adm.]* The museum has seventeen trolleys, some more than a hundred years old from Washington and four other countries, model trains running through the Washington of a half-century ago, and more. Ironically, driving is the easiest way to get there, but on weekends you can take the Metro Red line to Twinbrook or Glenmont and take a No. 26 bus to the museum. See the map on page 175.

Something for Everybody

It's a fun place for anybody who likes trains to spend an hour. You can learn about trolleys beginning with the horse-drawn version from Civil War days, and take a 1½-mile (2.8km) ride on one of the trolleys. If you visit on the third Sunday in October or April, all the museum's trolleys are out for your inspection, even though not all of them are in operating condition: It's not easy to get replacement parts to repair old trains. Volunteers are know-

Go for a ride on an old streetcar at the Capital Trolley Museum

ledgeable and enthusiastic; one was excited to hear that we were from Dayton, Ohio, where trolley buses still roll past our house, and wasn't satisfied until he'd dug out all the museum's photographs of Dayton trolleys.

Sports and entertainment fans will want to keep an eye on coming attractions at the **MCI Center** [601 F St. NW. Metro: Gallery Pl–Chinatown.] This is Washington's major indoor sports arena. They no longer give tours of the facility and the Discovery Channel store that used to be there is gone now, leaving a sporting goods shop as the only retail space. But it's the place to go if you can get a ticket to see the Washington Capitals of the National Hockey League or the Washington Wizards of the National Basketball Association. Watch for other special shows, too—concerts, professional wrestling, and figure skating championships.

Keeping in Touch

Some observers claim Washington, D.C., has three major industries. *Tourism* is obvious. That's why you're holding this book, right? The second is *Hot Air production*. After all, that's what governments do best. And finally is *News*. Probably more news stories carry a Washington dateline each year than that of any other city on earth. You can have a better insider's look at the news and how it's produced than anywhere else in the country through two fascinating tours.

The Washington Post *[15th and L streets NW. Metro: McPherson Square or Farragut North. Free tours Mon. by appointment.]* is one of the world's most respected and influential newspapers. You can take a guided 50-minute tour of the Post and see where news is written, edited, designed, and printed by telephoning (202) 334-7969 and arranging a time. Tours are on Mondays between 10 a.m. and 3 p.m. by appointment only and are free. Children must be at least 11 years old.

While it lacks some of the prestige of the BBC World Service, the **Voice of America** *[3rd and C streets. SE. Metro: Federal Center. Free tours M–F 10, 1, 2:40.]* can be heard all around the globe, carrying radio, television, and Internet news, information, opinion, and entertainment in 53 languages from its studios in Washington, D.C.

Recommendations

✔ Don't stick just to the area around the Mall. You'll miss some of Washington's neatest delights.

✔ Don't be too quick to judge. Even museums about things you don't think you'll like, like dollhouses or postage stamps, will surprise you if you let them. Be tolerant of other people's choices and they'll be tolerant of yours.

15. Unforgettable Art and Culture

I have to learn to write better chapter titles. This one, for instance, is not going to excite a lot of kids. Maybe I should have called it *"Places To See Pictures of Violence and Gore and Places Where They Keep All the Books—Even the Dirty Ones."* But that would be juvenile, exploitive, and probably unnecessary anyway: Kids can have a wonderful appreciation for art. They're more spontaneous than older folks, more whimsical, less worried about finding deep meanings and intellectual insights. They can just enjoy art, while the rest of us are trying to analyze brushstrokes, varnishes, and color palettes. We can learn a lot from our kids.

Art museums are hard to avoid anyway if you hang out near the National Mall, because the area is littered with them. I don't expect you to visit them all on this trip, although maybe you'll get to go through all of them over a period of several visits, as we have. Each person will have his or her own favorite. (Mine's the Sackler.) But let the kids decide which one or two you'll tackle on this trip.

We'll save the galleries for a little while, though, and start out in the library—or rather two of them: Two very remarkable libraries. Then we'll begin our tour of a dozen buildings packed with more great art than you'll ever have time to look at.

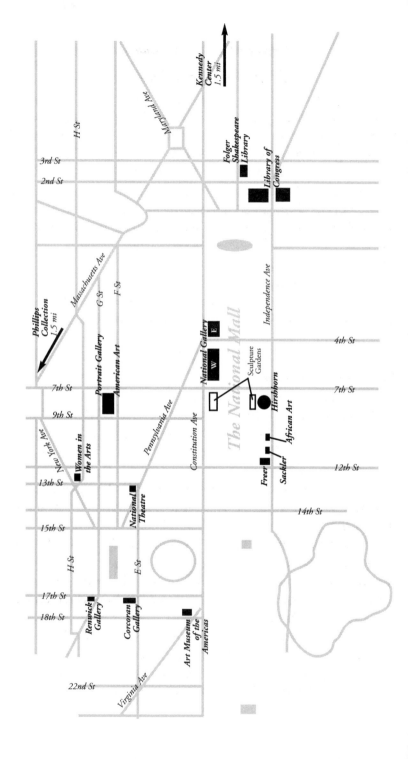

A Trip to the Library

Even today, when we really know better, we think of libraries as nothing more than repositories for books. That's probably because for 3,000 years, that's the only sort of permanent medium we had for storing information. Today, though, if I walk two blocks to our local public library branch, I'll find magazines, video tapes, DVDs, cassette tapes, CDs, computers connected to the Internet, maybe a few elderly phonograph records—and, oddly enough, some books. I've even lived in places where you could borrow paintings for your walls. Libraries aren't book repositories... they're *information* repositories.

Nowhere is that more obvious than at our first two stops, two of the great libraries of the world. There are books aplenty, but much, much more, and they are two of the most dazzling places in Washington.

The Library of Congress

Yes, the Library of Congress has books. In fact, a copy of every book published in the United States is on deposit here (including this one), because the Library of Congress directs the copyright office in the United States. So besides every book, the Library collects copies of every other copyrighted item in America—every musical composition, poem, photograph, map, play, motion picture, comic book, software program... an almost endless list!

You can't just browse among all these goodies, though, and check out the items you want for two weeks like you can from your library at home. First of all, this is the Library of *Congress*— it was set up primarily to allow legislators to do research on any subject they might need as they were enacting laws. So it's not really for the general public at all. Second, there's no browsing. The stacks are closed. Researchers must request the specific material they need, and a staff member will get it for them. It is possible for ordinary people like us to use the library, but we have to apply, explain the project we're working on, and describe the sorts of materials we need. It's probably not worth the bother for next year's history class term paper.

But there is so much to see. The exhibition galleries in the Thomas Jefferson Building (the oldest of the three buildings here, finished in 1897) make up one of the great museums of Washington. Even if it were completely empty, the building itself would be worth visiting for its grand marble and gold-leaf decoration. The Great Hall is breathtaking. The building is not empty, however, and there's something worth seeing on every floor.

You'll enter on the Ground Floor from the west side of the building. Stop at the visitor center and pick up a guide to the building, map, and information about the exhibitions. To the left of the visitor center there are a couple of small theaters, but kids will probably find the galleries more interesting, especially the Swann Gallery for Caricature and Cartoon and the Bob Hope Gallery of American Entertainment.

The Library of Congress houses unbelievable treasures

Go up the stairs to the First Floor and you can't help but be dazzled by the Great Hall. In the East Corridor at the back of the Great Hall are display cases containing two of the most valuable books in world. One is the Giant Bible of Mainz, written by hand in Mainz, Germany, in the 1450s, an incredible masterpiece of the scribe's art, and one of the last great works ever produced by hand. It was one of the last because also in Mainz in the 1450s Gutenberg developed the printing press, and his new technology put those scribes out of work. In the other display case is one of only three perfect copies in existence of the Gutenberg Bible.

Go up to the Second Floor, where you'll find, just off the South Corridor, the Treasures Gallery, the heart of the Library of Congress collection. It won't take you long to learn why they call it the Treasures Gallery. Maybe you'll see Thomas Jefferson's rough draft of the Declaration of Independence, written in his own hand, with additions and corrections jotted in by Benjamin Franklin and John Adams. Look for a copy book that the schoolboy George Washington used for his lessons as a teenager, or a map that he drew as a surveyor; the wallet Lincoln was carrying the night he was killed (he had $5 in Confederate money); Alexander Graham Bell's lab notebook from his invention of the telephone; Orville Wright's diary from December 1903 describing the first airplane flight. There's more: old baseball cards, Edison's first phonograph recordings, presidential diaries, the poem that became the National Anthem, books from Jefferson's own library (which formed the basis of the Library of Congress collection), and historic books, maps, and documents from around the world. It's about as close a personal encounter as you can have with history.

And while you're on the Second Floor, be sure to step into the Visitors' Gallery and watch the researchers below in the fabulous Main Reading Room. This is where you'll be working if you do get permission to work on that history term paper here. *[10 First St. SE. Metro: Capitol South. Closed Sun. Free.]*

Folger Shakespeare Library

Shouldn't one of the greatest Shakespeare libraries in the world be in England? Well, they have their own, after all. This one-of-a-kind place was created in 1932 by American businessman Henry Clay Folger, and is not part of the Smithsonian, the National Park Service, or anything else connected with the government.

Both the Folger's building and its collection are amazing. The 30-foot-high Exhibition Hall is paneled, Elizabethan-fashion, in dark wood and serves as a wonderful place to display pieces from the Folger's vast collection, which includes 79 of the 240 surviving first folios of Shakespeare's work, far more than any other library in the world. (A library in Tokyo is next, with 11.) The hall is home to numerous special exhibitions drawing from its collection of more than 300,000 books, including thousands of remarkable rare and one-of-a-kind items like books owned by England's King Henry VIII. The museum also owns thousands of playbills, costumes, paintings, films, musical instruments, and more.

The building itself is an art-deco masterpiece, with bas-reliefs of scenes from Shakespeare's plays. You can let your family scholar try his or her hand at identifying each. The Elizabethan Garden,

No telling who you'll run into on your way to the Folger

with plants and flowers mentioned in Shakespeare's plays, is a quiet place to take a breather after a hard morning of sightseeing.

But my favorite outdoor touch at the Folger is the statue of Puck in the fountain on the west side of the building. Puck, a character from *A Midsummer Night's Dream*, looks toward the halls of Congress just a few blocks away. And near him is inscribed a line from the play: "What fools these mortals be."

The Folger has frequent plays and recitals in its Elizabethan Theatre, which is made to look like the courtyard of a Medieval inn, the sort of place where Shakespeare's plays were often performed. If you're in Washington on the Sunday closest to Shakespeare's birthday on April 23, be sure to stop by the Folger for a day of games, stories, crafts, music, and other activities of the Bard's day. [*201 E. Capitol St. SE. Metro: Capitol South. Closed Sun. Free.*]

Art on the Mall

Now let's get to the art. The tour I'm going to lead you on in the next few pages can't begin to do justice to the magnificent and peculiar things you'll see, but I'll try to give you a little of the flavor of each building to help your family choose which ones it wants to visit. At least you know you can't make any wrong choices. Wherever you go, you'll see pictures even your younger kids will recognize, or things that will make their eyes bug out in amazement... or amusement.

National Gallery of Art
This is one of the few places on the National Mall that isn't part of the Smithsonian. These two buildings near the east end of the Mall probably hold enough canvas to wallpaper a medium-sized state, and the value of the collection is literally priceless. As you face the National from the Mall, you'll see two buildings. On your left is a very conventional building, the West Wing, with a low domed roof. On the right is a modern, angular structure, the East Wing.

Kids love the giant mobiles in the National Gallery East Wing

Do you want to guess which one hold the traditional art and which one holds the modern art?

Surprise! Unlike most things the government seems to do, the National Gallery gives you exactly what if implies. The traditional art is in the traditional building and the modern art is in the modern building.

Before you go in, though, the kids (and the parents) will enjoy a walk through the Sculpture Garden just to the left of the West Wing. There's nothing traditional about this sculpture! You might see a gigantic typewriter eraser—parents might have to explain what a typewriter was and why you couldn't just use a "delete" key— or something that looks like a huge pile of ice cubes. Whatever is on display is sure to provoke the incredulous question, "That's *art*?" Answer it however you think best. If you're here in the winter, there's ice skating, too.

Once you're inside the **West Wing**, though, it's like you've fallen down a rabbit hole into some sort of artistic Wonderland. You'll see paintings you recognize in every gallery, like coming face to face in a restaurant with a celebrity you admire. All the big names are here. Let me drop a few.

Do you like Impressionists? Then once you're inside, go to the beautiful rotunda and turn right. The third gallery on your left is filled with Monet masterworks, and the adjoining galleries are packed with paintings by Degas, Renoir, Pissarro, Toulouse-Lautrec, Van Gogh, and more.

I often go straight for the Leonardo. Leonardo da Vinci was probably one of the ten most brilliant and accomplished people our species has produced. Painting was one of his many talents, but fewer than twenty of his works (including the *Mona Lisa*) have survived. The National Gallery has the only Leonardo in the Western Hemisphere, the portrait of Ginevra de' Benci, painted almost twenty years before Columbus arrived in the New World. To see it, turn left at the rotunda and go to the third gallery on your right. Walk through that gallery, and in the one behind it, you'll find the Leonardo.

You will find numerous computers with touch screens that will help you locate things, and give you more information than you can hold in the Micro Gallery on your left as you

Tip: *Borrow a good art book from your public library and find pictures from Washington's great galleries. That will familiarize your kids with them. Then find them when you visit.*

enter from the Mall. If you're content with just an old-fashioned gallery map, there's an information counter there, too. And if your feet are tired, there's a pleasant sitting room with comfortable furniture on your right as you enter, near the coat check.

The **East Wing** is all sharp edges and odd angles, and the art here is much less traditional, with work by famous people like Picasso, Matisse, Pollack, and others. Kids will like the interesting (a generous word) sculptures and mobiles, often in unconventional materials and bright colors. *[Constitution Ave. and 3rd St. NW. Metro: Archives or Judiciary Square. Free.]*

The Hirshhorn fountain is a great place to cool off on a hot day

Hirshhorn Museum

If anybody liked the East Wing of the National, the Hirshhorn, a Smithsonian museum, is right across the Mall from the fountain in the National Gallery Sculpture Garden. You can't miss it—it's the big round building... looks like a huge drum.

It's got a sculpture garden of its own in front, and a big fountain in its central court. It's a very popular place to stand on a hot day, because the wind swirls around in the circular courtyard, scattering its cool mist in unexpected directions.

Things are pretty cool inside, too, and it's the unusual kid who won't like this collection of modern sculpture and painting, although pieces do go back to the post-impressionists. Paintings range from the classic to the frankly bizarre, but the sculpture is what everyone finds irresis-tible. You'll find old favorites like Andy Warhol on the first floor, Degas and Gauguin on the second, and Picasso on the third. *[Independence Ave. & 7th St. SW. Metro: L'Enfant. Free.]*

Freer Gallery of Art and Arthur M. Sackler Gallery

Are these two museums or one? It doesn't matter. This is the

Smithsonian's collection of Asian Art. The buildings are close together and are connected by an underground walkway, and when you pick up a gallery map, both are included. The **Freer** is older, opened in 1923, and has one of the finest collections of Asian art in the world. The building itself is a showplace, built like an Italian renaissance palace. One highlight is certainly the Peacock Room, an ornate dining room from a mansion in London that was decorated by American artist James McNeill Whistler. When the mansion's owner died, Charles Freer bought the room and had it taken apart and brought to the museum he had endowed in Washington. The Freer also has a nice collection of American art. *[Jefferson Dr. and 12th St. SW. Metro: Smithsonian. Free.]*

The **Sackler** was added in 1987 and also contains a wondrous collection of Asian art that stretches from the Mediterranean to Japan, from large Buddhas to tiny and delicate jade carvings. I especially like the comprehensive explanations the gallery gives, explaining the Islamic and Asian religions and cultures that gave rise to the art. *[1050 Independence Ave. SW. Metro: Smithsonian. Free.]*

National Museum of African Art

This was originally a private museum founded in 1964, but was adopted by the Smithsonian in 1979 and moved to this striking building on the Mall, near the Sackler Gallery, in 1987, unique among Smithsonian museums because it's mostly underground.

The three levels are filled with centuries of artifacts from all parts of Africa, and pays great attention to educating visitors to widely differing customs of the many peoples and tribes of the continent. You'll find masks, jewelry, fabrics, and carvings, but there's a real emphasis, too, on the ordinary things of everyday life—personal belongs, household objects, and ceramics. *[950 Independence Ave. SW. Metro: Smithsonian. Free.]*

Art off the Mall

Renwick Gallery

A branch of the Smithsonian's National Museum of American Art, the Renwick focuses on American crafts in wood, clay, metal, glass, and other media. I love the delicate glassware and blown glass. Displaying paintings is not the aim here, but some of the works from the National Museum of American Art are being displayed here during its renovation.

This building, just across the street from the White House, is a favorite of mine. Not as vast as those that house most other major galleries, the building was originally built for the Corcoran, which is now a couple of blocks away, in 1871. It's an elegant old building. Go in and you're faced with a grand staircase with a marvelous chandelier above and even handrails covered in velvet.

At the top of the stairs is a wonderful room, the Grand Salon, covered with art, and filled with elegant furniture. It's used for small concerts and receptions, and a glorious Christmas tree stands in the center in December. Even the security guards here are knowledgeable about the art and will gladly talk about it if you stand still too long.

By the way, do visit the room directly opposite the Grand Salon. It's called the Octagon Room. Count the sides. Is there a problem here? D.C. does seem to have a problem with polygons of more than five sides. [*17th St. and Pennsylvania Ave. NW. Metro: Farragut West. Free.*]

Corcoran Gallery of Art

The Corcoran Gallery of Art (which is not one of the Smithsonian's museums) focuses on 19th and 20th century American art—and does it marvelously well, although it also has an excellent European collection and many ancient Greek and Roman pieces.

Go up the grand staircase (apparently *de rigueur* for art museums) and find paintings and artists you'll recognize, like

Rembrandt Peale's *Washington Before Yorktown*, Gilbert Stuart's portrait of George Washington, or Samuel F. B. Morse's 1822 painting of the House of Representatives.

To have your breath all but taken away, go into a single magnificent room, the Salon Doré. This wonderful room, filled with inlay, gilding, mirrors, and an eye-popping ceiling mural, was part of a private residence in Paris built about 1770. American industrialist William Clark bought it and installed it in his New York City mansion in 1904 and bequeathed it

Washington's galleries are filled with memorable art

to the Corcoran in 1925. Clark, who was also a U.S. senator, donated many of the other artworks you'll see as well.

For a very un-art-museum experience, go to the Corcoran on Sunday morning for its weekly Gospel Brunch, with more music and singing and hand-clapping than most art galleries hear in a decade. The adjacent School of Art is one of the nation's most prestigious. *[17th & E St. NW. Metro: Farragut North or Farragut West. Adm.]*

National Museum of Women in the Arts

This isn't just an art museum, it's an arts gallery. I say *arts* because the exhibits here go beyond painting and sculpture and the other standard forms of art. You'll also find work by women filmmakers, silversmiths, poets, videographers, performance artists, composers, playwrights, and more. And it's more than a museum, which too often implies just displaying things that are finished, static. The NMWA is a place where the arts live and grow through its presentations and its educational outreach.

The museum presents a continuing progression of special exhibitions, often of interest to young people. One I saw on a recent visit was a series of books and illustrations from 150 years of versions, in four languages, of the Rapunzel fairy tale, ending with a rap music version.

The research library and archives contain more than 11,000 books and 16,000 files on women artists, as well as hundreds of video and audio tapes. Even the building, with its elegant white and salmon marble lobby and grand chandeliers, is a work of art. There's a lovely white tablecloth café on the mezzanine that's open for lunch. [1250 New York Ave. NW. Metro: Metro Center. Adm.]

Phillips Collection

If you like Impressionist paintings, the Phillips has one of the country's finest collections with major works by everyone you'd expect, and more modern masterpieces by artists like Picasso and Mondrian. It's a memorable outing for devotees of the genre, but at $12 to $15 per person, pricey for a family. Maybe best to save it for the dedicated art student in your group. [1600 21st at Q St. NW. Metro: Dupont Circle. Closed Mon. Open Sunday until 7 p.m. Adm.]

Art Museum of the Americas

Across the street from the Organization of American States—a sort of United Nations for the Western Hemisphere—is its small art museum. From descriptions I'd read, I had expected traditional arts and artifacts, but the museum is a showplace for modern artists, mostly from Latin America and the Caribbean. The building was once the residence of the OAS Secretary-General. [201 18th St. NW. Metro: Farragut West or Farragut North. Closed Mon. Free.]

Artless

Two Smithsonian art museums are closed for major refurbishment until 2005. Until then, some works from the

National Portrait Gallery and the National Museum of American Art will be seen on loan at other museums in Washington and around the country.

On Stage

People don't generally go to Washington for evenings at the theater, but there are plays and concerts all over town. We mentioned Ford's Theatre in Chapter 10, but there's also the National Theatre *[1321 Pennsylvania Ave. NW. Metro: Federal Triangle or Metro Center.]* which has frequent Saturday morning programs for kids. Of course the Kennedy Center for the Performing Arts *[New Hampshire Ave. and Rock Creek Pkwy. NW. Metro: Foggy Bottom.]* is one of the country's great performance spaces. And during the holiday season or during the summer, look for temporary stages set up on the National Mall or the Ellipse. I've been treated to patriotic concerts in the summertime on the Mall and carols near the national Christmas tree on the Ellipse in December, and it's always a nice surprise to come across something like that. Another theater on the Mall, the Sylvan Theater near the Washington Monument, presents free family-oriented programming all summer long.

Recommendations

✔ Many of the buildings in this chapter are works of art themselves. Talk about the architectural details with your kids as you pass by or walk through—construction materials, decorative stone or woodwork, inlays, floors, windows.

✔ Kids of junior high age and older will get a lot out of a visit to one of the libraries we talked about. Seeing genuine books and documents owned by history's most influential people is always a treat.

16. Living Heritage

Washington, D.C., is one of the most ethnically, culturally, and religiously diverse places in the country. That should come as no surprise. Washington is the national capital, and embassies and legations from 200 or more countries are located here, each with dozens of staff members from the country.

Add to that the fact that 535 U.S. Senators and Representatives are here from every state in the country, each bringing along who-knows-how-many staff members, relatives, lawyers, and associated hangers-on. Every industry, labor group, fraternal organization, and charity known to humankind has a lobbyist here (with a full staff, of course). More print and electronic journalists (and staff members) from every corner of the country and around the globe are based here than there are people in some entire countries.

And tourists! They come from everywhere! Yes—in Washington, D.C., you can find every language, religion, race, cuisine, attire, and interest that you like, a marvelous hodge-podge of humanity. In this chapter, we're going to visit a few of the most significant of Washington's many ethnic and religious sites, and I'll take you to one or two of my own out-of-the-way favorites as well.

National Cathedral

Kahlil Gibran Garden

U St

Islamic Center

Massachusetts Ave

Immaculate Conception Basilica

14th St

Franciscan Monastery

4th St

Rhode Island Ave

K St

H St

Chinatown

F St

Constitution Ave

OAS Bldg

The National Mall

Independence Ave

Holocaust Memorial

14th St

11th St

11th St. Bridge

M.L. King Ave

W St

Frederick Douglass Home

Morris Rd

Erie St

Anacostia Museum

African-American Heritage

The city of Washington has one of the nation's largest and most vibrant African-American communities, so it's appropriate that there are two important museums here showcasing the contributions of black Americans. Unfortunately, they're not near the National Mall, but in the Anacostia section of southeast Washington, one of Washington's poorest areas. They're not well served by public transportation, but if you have a car available, you can drive—I'll give you directions in a moment. If you don't have a car and want to visit, a taxi ride should be no more than about $8.

Anacostia Museum

The Anacostia Museum for African American Heritage and Culture has just gone through a complete renovation and reopened in 2002. This is one of the smallest Smithsonian museums, but it's packed with things you won't find anywhere else. We all know enough history to know that it happened, but it's still unsettling to see the actual bill of sale for one slave, and manumission papers that granted freedom to another. There are scores of photographs depicting the lives of black Americans over the past hundred years, and artifacts that range from some of Frederick Douglass's possessions to original manuscripts of the great poets Paul Laurence Dunbar and Langston Hughes.

The museum pays a lot of attention to folk art and the daily life of America's African American communities, and has an obvious focus on teaching people how to preserve their heritage. Because it is something I've done in my own family and classrooms, I especially liked the emphasis on oral history, complete with detailed suggestions about how visitors can create oral histories of their own family and community members. *[901 Fort Place SE. Metro: Anacostia then transfer to W2 or W3 bus. Free. A safer choice is to drive, if possible. Take Pennsylvania Ave. to 11th St. SE. Turn right (south) on 11th Street and cross the bridge. Follow the signs to*

The Anacostia Museum traces the history of black America

Martin Luther King Jr. Ave. Take MLK to Morris St.—about ½ mile—and turn left. Follow Morris for about 1 mile. It will curve to the left and the name will change to Erie St. Four blocks later the name changes again to Fort Place. The museum will be on the right. There is also sometimes a free shuttle bus from the Mall. Ask at the Information Desk in the Castle.]

Frederick Douglass National Historic Site
At the top of a tall hill near the appropriately-named High Street in Anacostia is the home, Cedar Hill, where former slave and Abolitionist leader Frederick Douglass lived the last eighteen years of his life. Run by the National Park Service, Cedar Hill is still filled with Douglass's belongings. Almost everything in the house is original, from his eyeglasses to the furnishings to the exercise weights to the checkers set he carved himself.

Be sure to see the cane that once belonged to President Lincoln, presented by Mrs. Lincoln to Douglass after the president was assassinated. The small building in the garden is not original, however. The original "Growlery," where Douglass often did his writing, was destroyed in a 1956 hurricane. This is a reconstruction.

If you have Tourmobile tickets, Cedar Hill is easy to get to, because it's on the route. If not, driving is again the best approach. *[1141 W St. SE. Free. To drive, take Pennsylvania Ave. to 11th St. SE. Turn right (south) on 11th Street and cross the bridge. Follow the signs to Martin Luther King Jr. Ave. Take MLK about 5 blocks to W St. Turn left. Cedar Hill is between 14th and 15th streets.]*

The City Within a City

That's what the community around 14th and U street calls itself, and the term is well deserved. If you're familiar with New York City, you'll understand when I say that U Street is to Washington what 125th Street is to Harlem. U Street is the Main Street of this community, once known as Black Broadway because of the number of theaters, jazz clubs, restaurants, and dance halls that lined the street. Of course it couldn't miss being an entertainment center: Duke Ellington was born in this neighborhood, at 1212 T St. NW. **The Lincoln Theatre** at 1215 U St. NW was the area's leading vaudeville theater and cinema, and has been carefully restored.

We try to come through this area at lunchtime, because there's nothing like a stop at **Ben's Chili Bowl** at 1213 U. St. NW next to the theater. Get the half smoke sausage or order up a chili dog with mustard, onions, and Ben's spicy chili. Just grab a seat at the counter or join the line for take-out, which can be long at lunchtime. Ben's has been an institution in the neighborhood for decades. Oh, you can get vegetarian chili and turkey subs here, too—but why would you want to?

Just up the street, near one of the Metro exits, is the **African American Civil War Memorial**, inscribed with the names of tens of thousands of black soldiers who fought for the Union Army during the Civil War. *[Take the Metro to the U St–Cardozo station.]*

Religious Heritage

Washington has some of the most remarkable places of worship in the country. If you're a churchgoing family, make it a point to attend services, or at least visit, your faith's principal house of worship. But even it you're not, a tour of one or two of these places will give you a spectacular hour. In a city crammed tight with architectural and historical wonders, the places we'll visit next rank near the top.

National Cathedral

If you've toured Europe and wandered through the cavernous Gothic cathedrals there, a stop here can make you feel like you're back in France. If you're from Europe, you'll feel right at home. And if you haven't seen the memorable European versions, then you'll be just as dazzled here as you would be in Chartres or Notre-Dame. This is the sixth largest cathedral on the planet!

National Cathedral took 83 years to build, from 1907 to 1990, and its central tower is the highest point in Washington at 676 feet (207m). I especially love the stained glass windows, a mix of modern and traditional styles. Look for the Space Window about halfway along the right side of the nave as you face the altar. It commemorates the Apollo XI moon landing and incorporates a fragment of moon rock!

In St. John's Chapel to the right of the high altar, you'll find red needlepoint kneelers that commemorate great Americans in sciences, the arts, and in politics. Of course we had to find Dayton's Wright Brothers. One guide told us that there is a kneeler here dedicated to every U.S. president, but there was considerable debate whether there should be one for President Nixon, who resigned in disgrace in 1974. The cathedral ultimately came down in favor of traditional forgiveness—and not breaking up a complete set.

The High Altar is made of stone from Jerusalem quarries, and

National Cathedral is the sixth largest church in the world

even though this is an Episcopal church, a wall carving on the left side of the nave honors the Roman Catholic Pope John XXIII. There's more than just the church itself, as well. The Close—the area around the church—has pleasant walks, memorable views, and the serene Bishop's Garden.

This 20th-century church has one notable advantage over many of its 12th-and 14th-century European sisters, and you'll appreciate it on the sort of hot day we had on one visit. It's fully air-conditioned! *[Wisconsin & Massachusetts aves. NW. Free. Metro: The Cleveland Park station is more than a mile away. A taxi from the Mall area will cost $7–8.]*

Basilica of the National Shrine of the Immaculate Conception

This is the principal Roman Catholic church in Washington, and it's another visually stunning one. I can't decide which I like better, but it might be this one, because while I've seen many wonderful Gothic Churches, this one is quite different, although not as large (but it still holds 6,000 people—more than lived in the town where I grew up).

This church's mosaics are some of the most dazzling I've ever seen, and they're everywhere, from the great tiled dome to the 3,600-square-foot "Christ in Majesty" behind the High Altar. You'll find ceiling mosaics, mosaics in many of the beautiful side chapels, even in the crypt.

The side chapels and statuary here are some of the most beautiful of any of the hundreds of churches I've visited. But whatever you do, don't miss the crypt. The lack of windows aside, this doesn't feel like a crypt. Walk along the memorial wall and see the remembrances to thousands of lay people and clerics alike. You'll undoubtedly find names you recognize. See if you can spot the one to Babe Ruth!

You'll find auxiliary chapels down here, too. My favorite is the African Chapel with its Black Madonna. The area also serves as a small museum, with mementoes of all sorts, plus objects like the coronation crown of Pope Paul VI. There's a sizable café down here and the largest church gift shop I've ever seen. [*Michigan Ave. & 4th St. NE. Metro: Brookland–CUA. Free.*]

Islamic Center

One of the clearest memories I have of our first family trip to Washington is laying in bed in our apartment near Rock Creek Park, listening to the *Mu'azzin* chanting the Muslim call to prayer from the minaret at the mosque a few blocks away, a new experience for this Midwestern boy. Even then, it was no longer necessary for the caller to climb to the top of the 160-foot (49m) minaret. His microphone and loudspeaker saved him the effort. But the call to prayer, either by loudspeaker or by voice, is a centuries-old ritual of prayer five times each day as instructed in the *Qur'an*.

You'll hear that call today if you're in the neighborhood of one of Washington's most beautiful places of worship and one of the finest mosques in America. You know my feelings about mosaics, and those on the buildings are as beautiful as any in Washington.

The Islamic Center welcomes visitors of every faith

Non-Muslims are welcome to enter the Mosque except during prayer. Leave your shoes at the entrance outside.

Inside you'll discover a space so ornate and highly decorated that you won't know where to look. Muslim nations from around the world donated money, labor, and furnishings to make the mosque in America's capital city something special. Arabic calligraphy adorns the walls with passages from the *Qur'an*. The enormous copper chandelier was a gift from Egypt. The unbelievably plush carpets could have come from nowhere but Iran. The ornate tiles and the men to install them came from Turkey. When the mosque opened in 1957, the money and materials to build it had come from every corner of the Islamic world.

It's a sophisticated building as well. Mosques are oriented toward the Islamic holy city of Mecca, and in this part of the world, mosques have always faced east. This one does not.

While Mecca appears almost due east of Washington on a map, the shortest distance follows the curvature of the earth in what's called a Great Circle route. (If one of the kids took geometry last

> *Tip:* When visiting the mosque, women should not wear shorts, short skirts, or sleeveless or midriff tops. These are expectations quite similar to those of many other places of worship, like St. Peter's Basilica in Rome.

year, he or she will be glad to explain it.) So the mosque actually faces along that path, to the northeast.

The Islamic Center also contains a library, classrooms, offices, and—of course—a gift shop. *[2551 Massachusetts Ave. NW. Metro: Dupont Circle. Closed Fri afternoons to non-Muslims. Free.]*

St. John's Church

This old Episcopal church is just across Lafayette Square from the White House, and it's possible that you can catch a glimpse of the President near here on Sunday, no matter what his religion might be. Every President of the United States since James Madison has gone to church here occasionally. If you slip inside at other times, pew 54 is the presidential pew. The church is open daily and there are free tours on Sunday after the 11 a.m. service. *[1525 H St. NW. Metro: McPherson Sq. Free.]*

Places for Contemplation

I like places that make me think, or leave me in peace so I can spend time thinking my own thoughts. The next three places will do that. The first is one of the most difficult sites in the book to experience, and I thought about not including it. A family vacation is supposed to be nonstop fun, right?

Well, maybe you want a little education thrown in, too. If you're going to Washington, probably it's at least partly because you want everybody, including yourself, to learn something.

The first place in this section is by no means fun. But it deeply affects everybody who visits it, and it certainly gives them plenty to think about.

U.S. Holocaust Memorial Museum

Despite the fact that this is a place that will leave visitors shaken and depressed, the Holocaust Museum has become one of Washington's most popular attractions, but I have to tell you, it's very intense. The museum itself recommends its permanent exhibition only for visitors 11 and older, and even that might be a stretch. I'd want to make sure that any child I took to the Holocaust Museum, but especially any who were younger than 12 or 13, were very well prepared for the experience, that we'd talked beforehand, in explicit terms, about what they could expect to see, and that they wanted to visit.

The museum will take at least 90 minutes to tour and, because there's so much to see, read, and watch, it can take twice that, if you want. When you enter, an elevator will take you up to the fourth floor, where the exhibition begins. You follow a prescribed route that's arranged chronologically through the most horrific fifteen years of the 20th century.

As you begin, you're given an identity booklet recounting the life of a real person who lived during the Holocaust, and are instructed to turn pages at certain intervals to learn how that person was affected by the events depicted in each section of the museum.

The fourth floor, covering the years 1933 to 1939, tells the story of the Nazi rise to power and the beginnings and escalation of the Jewish persecution in Germany and nearby countries. On the third floor, visitors are taken through the ghettos of Europe, through Jews' transportation to concentration camps, and shown how 6 million men, women, and children were methodically murdered—shot, worked to death, gassed, used for medical experiments, and worse.

The second floor recounts the war's end, the liberation of the survivors from the death camps, and their efforts to begin their lives again. It also contains the solemn Hall of Remembrance and a learning center. The first floor is devoted to temporary exhibitions.

Exhibits are graphic. There are photographs, audio descriptions, and films of families being torn apart, of medical experiments, of the inside of death camps, of mass executions. The most shocking photos and films are not within easy eye gaze, but are sunken in wells or situated behind partitions where audiences must choose to

Tip: *The museum is always packed, and admission is by timed ticket. Arrive early in the day or you risk all that day's tickets being gone. If the admission time on your ticket is an hour or more away, you can look at the temporary exhibits, or go see another attraction and return at the appointed time.*

see them. But you inevitably come face to face with much that is disturbing anyway—films from Dachau, the voices of Auschwitz survivors, the photographs of children, a pit filled with thousands of shoes stripped from the victims of the gas chambers.

Hundreds of people crowd the exhibits, but they are so quiet! Even in open spaces without exhibits, people talk only in hushed tones that are both reverential and unbelieving. Should you go? I can only say that if your children are old enough and are prepared for what they'll see, and if this is part of your heritage—either because of your religious or cultural background or because of your membership in the human race that both performed and suffered these atrocities—then it's a place worth seeing. You'll never forget it, no matter how much you wish you could. *[100 Raoul Wallenberg at 14th St. SW. Metro: Smithsonian. Free.]*

Franciscan Monastery

One of Washington's truly unknown gems is tucked away in the northeast corner of the city. Built in 1897, this monastery of the Catholic religious order of St. Francis contains quiet cloistered walks and serene courtyards, all open to the public. What most people come for, though, is a trip to the Holy Land.

Monks of this monastery are trained to help care for religious sites in the Holy Land. So here are replicas of many of the shrines that visitors flock to see in and around Jerusalem, including those identified as Calvary, Mount Thabor, and Nazareth. There's also a replica of part of the Catacombs in Rome, including crypts and chapels where early Christians hid beneath the Eternal City.

Visitors are free to stroll around the quiet grounds, or can take one of the hourly tours (9–4 except noon Mon.–Sat., 1–4 Sun.) to learn more about the shrines and the work of the order. *[1400 Quincy St. NE. Metro: Brookland–CUA. Free.]*

Kahlil Gibran Memorial Garden

Washington has dozens of parks and squares, mostly crowded and surrounded by traffic. This is one of my own favorite places, though, just a quiet place to sit and think... or talk... or relax and recharge. Odds are against your ending up here; it's used mostly by locals because it's away from most tourist traffic.

But if you've walked up Massachusetts Avenue looking at embassies, crossed the bridge over Rock Creek, and maybe peeked at the house President Bill and Senator Hillary Clinton bought on Whitehaven Street after he left office, you'll need someplace to sit down—it's been a long walk and there are no Metro stations nearby.

Dedicated to the great Lebanese poet Kahlil Gibran, this is one of D.C.'s most serene spots. The garden includes a bust of the poet and inscriptions from his work, including his best-known prose-poem *The Prophet*. While many Americans know

Kahlil Gibran Gardens are great for relaxing

his literary work, not all know that he was also an accomplished artist. While he lived most of his life in the United States after coming here at age 12, he returned to Lebanon for his education and is buried there, revered as one of the most important Arabic-language writers of the 20th century. I've sat in this park and read an idle hour away, enjoying the peace and my book. I think Gibran would approve. *[30th St. and Massachusetts Ave. NW.]*

And Don't Forget...

While it's not nearly as extensive as those in San Francisco or New York, Washington's **Chinatown** *[6th to 8th and G to H streets NW. Metro: Gallery Pl.–Chinatown.]* is fun to walk through and a great place to eat. When you get off the Metro, take the Chinatown exit and gawk at the ornate Friendship Gate, a staple of the entrance to every Chinatown I've visited. Kids always enjoy wandering around a Chinatown, looking at the decorations, shops, and signs.

In Chapter 15 I directed you to the art museum of the Organization of American States. Its headquarters is in the **OAS Building** *[17th St. & Constitution Ave. NW. Metro: Farragut West or Farragut North.]*. Tours have been suspended, except for school groups. But if you'd like to visit, keep an eye on the OAS website for the latest information on when they might resume.

You can find all sorts of unexpected cultural experiences if you keep your eyes and ears open. One friend, a noted jazz pianist, recounted a visit a few years ago:

We'd parked near Chinatown and were walking near a church where over 200 black people were gathered outside for a funeral. But it was perfectly, I mean absolutely, quiet. I'm a musician and I make my living with my ears, but I've never heard that kind of silence. Then we saw they were all signing—all those people talking with their hands! It was the funeral of a deaf brother or sister, and the whole black deaf community and their friends had turned out.

Although smaller than some, Washington's Chinatown is filled with color and good food

That's a great example of a culture within a culture. In fact the deaf community is unusually active in the D.C. area, which is home to Gallaudet University, the country's chief deaf institution of higher education. Pay attention: The world is more diverse than we realize, and Washington proves it to you every day.

Recommendations

✔ Washington presents unlimited opportunities to learn more about your own heritage, or about other religions and cultures. It's one good reason to go.

✔ Places of worship of almost any denomination welcome visitors and have brochures about the building or denomination that are free or cost only a nominal amount. Whenever we travel, we use places like this to rest tired legs and learn about the beliefs of others.

✔ Many other museums have exhibits about the contributions of various cultures and creeds. Have the kids seek out those exhibits.

17. The Great Outdoors

One of our favorite parts of any big city vacation is the chance to get out into the wide open spaces—fresh air... long grassy lawns... groves of trees... flowing streams or thundering rivers or expansive lakes. There's nothing like a trip to the big city for a chance to enjoy nature.

Don't be confused. The heat hasn't gotten to me. We enjoy nature *away* from the urban bustle, too, but there's something wonderful about being in the middle of a city of a million people, planted in the center of a great park, far from traffic noise and fumes, shoes off, shaded by a tree, relaxing on the plush grass.

We *do* enjoy the hubbub of major cities, but we always find a place we can go for an evening picnic, for a cool respite on a hot day, for a romp in the sunshine (or in the snow, depending on the time of year), to reconnect with green growing things after all the miles of gray concrete sidewalks, or just to have a place to escape to when the urban commotion gets to us. We love Chicago's Grant Park, London's Regent's Park, Manhattan's Central Park all the more because of the furor of activity that surrounds them—and that can't touch us as long as we're sheltered inside them.

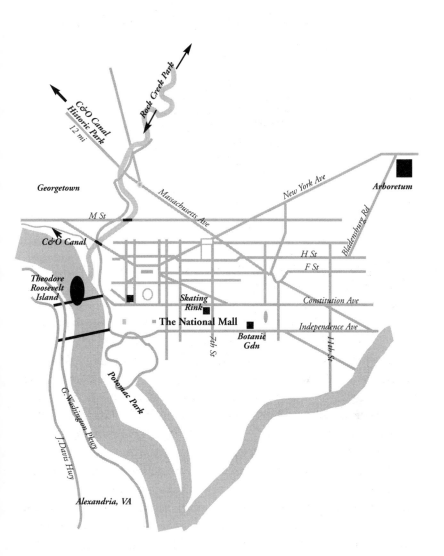

Rock Creek Park

C&O Canal
Historic Park
12 mi

Georgetown

Massachusetts Ave

New York Ave

Arboretum

M St

C&O Canal

Bladensburg Rd

H St

F St

Theodore
Roosevelt
Island

Skating
Rink

Constitution Ave

The National Mall

Independence Ave

7th St

Botanic
Gdn

11th St

Potomac Park

G. Washington Pkwy

J. Davis Hwy

Alexandria, VA

Washington, D.C., has places like that, too, where you can spend a half hour or a full day, and where you might find us sprawled under a tree. If you stop and say Hi, we might even share our ham sandwiches with you.

C&O Canal National Historic Park

Here in the 21st century, we know next to nothing about the enterprise President John Quincy Adams called "The Great National Project." The United States was growing into a nation of unprecedented physical size, and of unimaginable natural resources. The problem was to get all those resources and an increasing amount of farm produce from the vast open lands of the West to the great population centers of the East, as well as to make it easier for some of those Easterners to help populate the West.

Take a ride on a genuine canal boat at the C&O Canal Historic Park

Canals seemed like the answer. They were in use throughout Europe; they ought to work here as well.

Adams hadn't reckoned on the vast size his young nation was becoming. The United States, although much smaller than it is now, was already much larger than European nations, and a canal long enough to span an entire European country would hardly make a dent in the enormous North American landmass.

Still, the project was begun. In the North, canals like the Erie could be short enough to be successful in relatively little time. But the Chesapeake and Ohio Canal was to run 460 miles, connecting Chesapeake Bay near Washington, D.C., with Pittsburgh, on the Ohio River. Adams broke ground for the canal on July 4, 1828: It was supposed to take ten years and cost $3 million to build.

By 1850 the canal stretched only about 180 miles, from Washington to Cumberland, Maryland, and had cost more than $13 million, but that was enough. It was declared finished. By 1850 the railroad had taken over the job of long-distance moving anyway, and could be built at far lower cost. The canal was obsolete before it even opened.

Still, canal boats moved coal and agricultural products from Cumberland to the Chesapeake for 74 years, not shutting down forever until 1924.

But it wasn't forever, after all. Now a 22-mile stretch of the canal is open again, not to move coal, but to show your family about life in the canal days. The C&O Park is a wonderful place for an outing.

The park stretches for miles along the Potomac River north of Washington. The visitor center is the Great Falls Tavern, a canal-side inn built in 1831 and a popular local dining spot even a century later. Rangers here can give you maps of the trails along the canal and adjacent Potomac River. They'll even show you how to get to the remains of an old gold mine.

You ask: Why not just use the river for shipping goods? One look will tell you why. The Potomac here is shallow, fast, and filled with rocks. A boat couldn't survive a hundred yards in this water. In fact George Washington, a surveyor himself, was one of the first to advocate building a canal alongside the river.

The best part of the park is the chance to take an hour-long ride on a canal boat, going through the old locks, and listening to the stories about the men who worked the cargo barges. Your boat will be pulled by

Tip: *You'll be cautioned to stay on the trails. Do it! This stretch of river averages seven drownings per year. Stick to the paths and overlooks.*

mules, just as it would have been 150 years ago. (Make a note: If you go for a stroll along the towpath, watch your step. Mules walk here, too, leaving behind the sorts of deposits you might expect.)

Don't feel sorry for the mules. Two will pull your boat down the canal for half an hour. Then the mules will be changed and the two that were riding in the front of the boat will bring the boat back while the first pair rests. Do they mind? The driver says they sense they've got it easy. Nowadays, a mule works for half an hour towing a 25-ton boat. But a century ago, the mule's ancestors might have worked all day towing a 125-ton coal barge.

There's no Metro near the park, but I'll give you driving directions. The park is only about 15 miles (25km) northwest of central Washington. See the map on page 175. No car? No problem. You can still take a canal boat ride. I'll tell you how in a minute when you get to the section on Georgetown. *[11710 MacArthur Blvd., Potomac, MD. Free, but there's a charge for canal boat rides available Wed–Sun., Apr–Oct. Take the Beltway to Exit 41, then north on about MacArthur Blvd. less than 5 miles (8km) to the park entrance on the left.]*

Around the Mall

The National Mall itself is a nice place for everyone to run off excess energy. (Maybe just the kids, come to think of it. Barb and I stopped having excess energy about the time the kids started to walk. It took every bit of energy we had just to keep up with them.) The Mall has wide open spaces and plenty of room to toss a ball (or kick one) or a Frisbee disc. It doesn't have a lot of trees—mostly around the edges—and much of the grass gets trodden down to dust by midsummer. You'll find a few places nearby, though, that will give you a taste of Mother Nature's best.

U.S. Botanic Garden

The kids had better not run around in here; they'll trample somebody and you'll all get tossed out. This is not one of your large, spread-out botanic gardens. But if you'd like to see the marvelous variety of flora the world has to offer, you've come to the best place in Washington.

Have the kids come in and try it out, even if they whine that it's going to be boring. It's not. There's lots of cool stuff, and I always see alert parents who can find things to point out to the kids about some of the 20,000 plants here:

Mom: "Smell this plant, Wendy."
Wendy (amazed): "It smells like root beer!"
Mom: Right! This is the plant they make root beer from.

The Botanic Garden has really huge lily pads

Watch the water misting from the ceiling. Find plants with huge, incredible leaves. Look for carnivorous plants and read about how they capture and eat bugs. See the huge lily pads. Find the plants with the nastiest-looking thorns or the biggest flowers. Walk through the jungle. Find the plants that provide familiar products like bananas, coffee, tea, and rice. I was wearing a straw hat in the garden one day, against the furious summer sun we'd been having, and I'm almost sure I saw the plant labeled "Panama Hat Plant" shrink back in horror as I passed it while wearing the dried carcass of its cousin.

You have to follow the crowded path through the greenhouses, but it doesn't take long to go through them. By 2007, though, they will be much more extensive. The conservatory has been getting some much-needed refurbishment since the late 1990s, but the grounds outside are now being developed with a rose garden, water garden, learning center, and more. *[Maryland Ave. & First St. SW. Metro: Federal Center SW. Free.]*

The Ice Rink

If you're in Washington in the winter, ice skating on the Mall is a great way to warm up. The ice rink, which doubles as a fountain in the summer, is in the Sculpture Garden of the National Gallery of Art, straight across the Mall from the Hirshhorn.

You can rent skates for less than $3 if you've unaccountably forgotten to pack yours, and ice time is about $5 for two hours. There's a café nearby where everybody can warm up with hot chocolate, and the rink is open until late at night. *[9th St. and Constitution Ave. Metro: Smithsonian or Archives–Navy Memorial. Open until 9 p.m. Sun, 11 p.m. Mon–Thurs, Midnight Fri–Sat. Fees for skate rental and ice time.]*

For wintertime fun, rent ice skates at the rink next to the National Gallery

Potomac Park

Trying to decide where one park ends and another begins isn't always an easy task. Locals in Boston make a clear distinction between Boston Common and the Public Garden. Londoners insist on the difference between Hyde Park and Kensington Gardens. To the rest of us, it doesn't matter very much.

The National Mall runs from the Capitol Building to the Lincoln Memorial, but hanging down from its west end, following the river, is an appendix-like green space called Potomac Park. (It's actually West Potomac Park. East Potomac Park is a little further along, beyond the Tidal Basin. It's not especially important to care about this.)

Unlike your appendix, Potomac Park is very useful indeed. This is where the Jefferson and FDR memorials are, and in the spring, the Japanese cherry trees planted around the Tidal Basin bloom with a beauty that's impossible to describe. You have to fight your way through traffic to see them, if you insist on using a car, but the walk from the Lincoln Memorial isn't a long one and is more than worth the fifteen or twenty minutes it takes.

During the rest of the year, Potomac Park is green, shady, and quiet, at least until you get to the golf course at the far east end of the park. *[1100 Ohio Dr. SW. Metro: a mile away south of the Mall. Free.]*

Theodore Roosevelt Island

If you really want to get back to nature without going too far into the wilderness, this is your place. With almost 3 miles (5km) of hiking trails through swamp and forest, and places to sit quietly, to fish, to watch for small animals and water birds, and to picnic, this is the sort of scenic getaway you don't expect in the city. Since Roosevelt was a noted outdoorsman and conservationist, this park suits his memory perfectly. Of course there's the obligatory statue of TR, arm upraised, evidently in full throat. Note that the public toilets are not open in the winter.

To get here you have to take a footbridge from the parking area adjacent to the northbound lane of the George Washington Memorial Parkway, just north of Arlington National Cemetery. It's also possible to walk from the Rosslyn Metro station. From the station on Moore Street (That's the street you're facing if you come up the elevator. If you use the escalator, Moore Street is behind you when you reach the top) go a block east to Lynn Street, turn left and go about a quarter mile (400m) north. After you cross both lanes of the Lee Highway that runs on each side of Gateway Park, you'll come to the Bike & Hike Trail. Follow that to the right and it will lead you to the footbridge. *[Roosevelt Bridge from the George Washington Memorial Pkwy. Metro: Rosslyn. Free.]*

Out and About

If you'd like wide open spaces that are a little more wide open than those around the Mall, here are a couple of nice choices. Unfortunately, they're most easily accessible by automobile, but you can get the flavor of the first, at least, via Metro.

Rock Creek Park

Twice as large as New York's Central Park, Rock Creek Park is larger than at least two of the world's countries (have the kids figure out which ones) and, if it had a population of something other than furry little animals, it could probably petition for representation in Congress. It stretches along Rock Creek for more than 5 miles (8km) and provides some of the capital's best walking, bike riding, skateboarding, and loafing possibilities.

If you go to the National Zoo, you'll find yourself in Rock Creek Park. But if you're just looking for a day out under the trees, take the Metro to Cleveland Park. Walk north up Connecticut Avenue and watch for a sign on the right leading you into the park. About a half mile along that trail will take you to Rock Creek itself, and turning left along the trail running beside the creek will take you to one of the park's attractions, **Pierce Mill** *[Closed Mon–Tue. Free.]*, the last gristmill in the city, which was operational from the 1820 until 1897. There's a small art gallery near the mill. From here, walkers can take the West Ridge trail down to the Zoo, about a half-hour's walk south.

If you have a car, there's a **Nature Center** *[Closed Mon–Tue. Free.]* with a planetarium show and short nature walk designed especially for kids in the center of the park, as well as the **Rock Creek Horse Center** *[Closed Mon. Fee for rides.]*, where riders 12 and older can get horses to take out on the park trails, and younger kids can ride ponies on weekends.

U.S. National Arboretum

No matter what time of year you visit, there's a lot of Mother Nature to be seen at the National Arboretum. Wintertime is optimum for hollies and holly berries. Early spring brings out the magnolias, and by April the cherry blossoms, dogwoods, azaleas, and wildflowers are blooming and the grass has turned that particular shade of green you see only just after it wakes from its winter nap. In the summer, everything is gloriously

The old columns of the Capitol Building are a strange, compelling sight at the Arboretum

leafed out, and the roses, water lilies, and crape myrtles are in bloom. In the fall, the leaves are vibrant and the fields are full of gold. Who can resist?

You can walk or drive for miles through the Arboretum, and there's always something to see. No one will be able to resist the bonsai museum. The picnic area is in a grove of state trees, representing all 50 states and D.C. Fern Valley has varieties of this ancient plant from all over the country, and a cool and quiet half-mile path that takes you through them.

One of the most interesting corners of the Arboretum is a hilltop with 22 sandstone columns standing regally alone. These columns were once part of the east portico of the U.S. Capitol Building. They were replaced during a renovation in 1958 and placed here in 1990, creating an interesting landmark and photo opportunity. *[3501 New York Ave. NE. Metro: None. Free.]*

Neighborhood Strolls

Now that we've gotten all the way to Chapter 17 together, I've walked you pretty much all over Washington, both the big-city parts and the wide-open-spaces parts. I've got a couple of other places to take you before we're finished, though. The first of these is actually part of D.C. and the other, while across the river in Virginia, is still very much a part of Washington's urban landscape. But both have a small-town feel to them that can almost be village-like.

What's more, if there are dedicated shoppers in your family, you'll score major points with them by taking them here. Countless credit cards have died honorable deaths in the shops and boutiques of Georgetown and Alexandria.

Georgetown

The village of Georgetown existed almost half a century before Washington City was carved out of the Potomac swamps, which means it wasn't named for George Washington, as most people think, but for England's King George II. It wasn't annexed to Washington City until after the Civil War. Now it's an expensive and trendy place to live, filled with some of the country's most powerful and influential people. Throw a rock in Georgetown and you'll probably hit a senator, a lobbiest, or political correspondent. Hmmm. Pass the rocks....

The Metro doesn't serve Georgetown. Maybe too many people here have chauffeurs to make it worthwhile. But it's just a short walk from the Foggy Bottom station, and if you don't want to walk, there are shuttle buses every 10 minutes from the Foggy Bottom, Dupont Circle, and Rosslyn stations. Cost is just 25 cents with a Metro transfer, 50 cents otherwise.

Georgetown has two "Main Streets," M Street and Wisconsin Avenue NW. I can't even begin to run down the restaurants, antique shops, clothing stores, galleries, music stores, chocolate and ice cream shops... pretty much everything even the fussiest of shoppers could want. There's even a big shopping mall on M Street.

If shopping isn't your thing, there's plenty of historical and architectural interest here, like **Dumbarton Oaks and Gardens** *[1703 32nd St. NW, Georgetown. Metro: None. House and art museum open 2–5 p.m. except Mon. Free. Gardens open 2–5 daily. Adm.]*, a beautiful mansion and grounds where the conference that set up the United Nations was held in 1944. A few blocks away is **Tudor Place** *[1644 31st St., Georgetown. Metro: None. Closed Sun–Mon. Adm.]*, a mansion that belonged to Martha Washington's granddaughter. Dignitaries like Lafayette and Robert E. Lee have stayed here.

A walk along N Street will give you a real feel for what Georgetown looked like in the 19th century, with its blocks of Federal style houses and apartments. But my favorite place is along the same canal that opened this chapter. South of M Street and north of the river is the end of the **C & O Canal** *[1057 Thomas Jefferson St. NW, Georgetown. Free, but there's a charge for canal boat rides available Wed–Sun., Apr–Oct.]*. You can walk along the towpath here, beside the old 19th century houses–some are still residences and some are shops and restaurants now. Walk past old factories and pass under old bridges. Or ride! If you don't get to the historic park, you can take a canal boat ride here instead. Whatever you do, Georgetown is a great place to spend an afternoon.

Alexandria, Virginia

If it's more convenient, you might spend that afternoon in Alexandria instead. It's almost as old, just as historic, equally charming, and no less filled with good food and good shopping. It's a little closer to the Metro than Georgetown: The King Street station is a 10- to 15-minute walk west of the historic district.

The best part of Alexandria for me is just looking at the old homes and businesses in the Old Town, although it got me into trouble once. I like to stroll along quiet streets, looking at houses and into the rooms behind their windows. (No, I'm not some sort of pervert, honestly! I don't stop and stare, just look as I pass at the chandeliers, décor, pictures—the sort of things easily visible from the street that anybody could see. I don't even slow down!) As I was doing this along Royal Street one evening, a homeowner spotted me, leaped to his wide-open window, shouted an unkind remark about my ancestry, and slammed the window. So enjoy the lovely architecture but be careful—some Alexandrians are touchy.

Attractions in Alexandria include **Gadsby's Tavern** *[121 N. Fairfax St. Closed Mon. Adm.]*, a 1770 hotel; the **Old Presbyterian Meeting House** *[321 S. Fairfax St.*

18th-century buildings line the streets of Alexandria's Old Town

Closed Sat–Sun. Free.], which dates to 1772; and **Christ Church** *[N. Washington and Cameron streets. Free.]*, a 1773 church where you can see the pews of George Washington and Robert E. Lee.

Washington used to send produce from his plantation to the **Farmer's Market** that has been running for more than 250 years at its spot near King and Fairfax streets. Mount Vernon was less than 10 miles away, after all. And Lee grew up here. You can visit **Lee's Boyhood Home** *[607 Oronoco St. Closed Dec 15–Jan 31. Adm.]*. The neatest place to shop, in my opinion is the Torpedo Factory Art Center *[105 N. Union St.]*, where you can watch artists and craftspeople of all sorts at work, and buy directly from them.

There's a lot to see and do on the Alexandria waterfront

This was a real torpedo factory, making munitions for World Wars I and II. We also saw some of the best street entertainers I've ever encountered right outside the building, an a cappella doo-wop group. In fact, the entire riverfront area here is a delight.

If you still think the Washington, D.C., area is just about museums, ornate government buildings, and crowded streets, go back to the beginning of the chapter and read it again.

Recommendations

✔ Spend at least a half day away from the noise and bustle of urban life. It will refresh you.

✔ Pick an area to walk—Georgetown, Alexandria, or a nice neighborhood you've chosen yourself, and look at its history, its architecture, its parks, its shops, and its people.

✔ Ride a canal boat!

III

The Planning Pages

By this time you should know about everything there is to know about Washington except what color socks the President is wearing today. In this section we'll put it all together. Chapter 18 lists all the attractions we've talked about so your family can discuss them and make some decisions. Chapter 19 shows you how to take that discussion and turn it into a well-paced, efficient, and fun itinerary. And Chapter 20 will help you find reasonably-priced airfare and accommodations, then walk you through the budgeting process so you come home with money still in your bank account. Finally the appendix lists about 140 websites where you can get reservations, help, and the latest information about almost everything we've talked about in these pages.

All of this is to ensure that your family has as great a time in Washington as mine has had. Have a great trip, and if you see the President, tell him Larry says Hi!

18. Top Attractions

Now you're faced with the most difficult part of your trip—aside from paying for it, of course! You've read about all the things to see and do in the previous chapters and some members of your family might be feeling a little intimidated by the size of the list. That's okay—it *is* an intimidating list: It contains more than 130 things to see and do!

No matter how dedicated a tourist you are, you're not likely to get everywhere on that list unless you get elected to Congress and get to live there at my expense. But take comfort in this: The list could have been much longer. I left out many places that were on my preliminary list because they were too hard to get to, of interest to too few people, or were too much like some of the attractions I had already included.

Of course I added some things that weren't on that first list, either. I'm always on the lookout for new things I think will appeal to families like yours, and I love the nice surprises I get when I find something cool that other visitors or guidebooks have overlooked.

But back to your dilemma. How can you sift through all the things we've talked about and narrow the list down to something you can manage in a week or two? Well, every family has its own way of dealing with these things. If the kids are 1, 2, and 3 years old, voting is pointless; Mom and Dad will have to make the decisions. But 11, 12, and 13? That's another matter.

For a major expedition like this, where at some degree of cost and inconvenience you take your family hundreds or thousands of miles from home to a place where there's way more than they can possibly see and do, it's critical for the success of the trip that everybody be involved in the planning. There's nothing you can do that will ensure the success of the trip more than that. People who have helped plan a trip have a real stake in its success and will inevitably be much more agreeable and flexible traveling partners.

Maybe the Lains were too organized, but Barb and I are teachers, and if you're not well organized in a job like that, you are well and truly doomed. So we're careful planners by nature. Before a major trip, beginning with our first vacation in Washington, our approach was always the same. We'd do lots of reading about our destination and make lists of all the possible things we could see and do. Then, as a family, we'd talk about each of the things on the list, often at dinner. We'd summarize what we learned from the guidebooks and from talking to people who had been to wherever we were planning to visit, and we'd find things for the kids to read, too, if possible.

Next we'd make copies of our list of attractions and everybody from oldest to youngest was asked to mark each attraction in one of three ways:
- I really want to see/do this
- I don't care about this one way or the other
- I don't find this interesting at all

We also asked each person to mark the one attraction or activity he or she thought was most important, the thing that it would be really disappointing to miss.

When we counted the votes it became clear at once that there were a lot of things we could leave out. *Everybody* hated them!

It was also obvious that certain attractions were must-do places because everyone liked them. They formed the core of our trip. We also added the items from everybody's list that he or she had said was their Number One choice—even if nobody else voted for it—and these went to the very top of the chart. That left us with a list of musts, a bunch of things we could toss out, and a large group of maybes. Then the task became roughing out an itinerary. That's what the next chapter is for. But we kept three principles in mind as we did it:

• Get to everybody's No. 1 attraction early in the trip so no one will be disappointed.

• Use the overall voting as a guide but make sure everybody's ideas are included.

• Don't over-plan, because you're sure to find attractions and opportunities you hadn't thought of.

The last of those points is important. I can't tell you how many spontaneous things we saw and did that we just discovered on the spot. We've done spur-of-the-moment boat rides, cave tours, picnics, and more so often that an itinerary sometimes seems superfluous. But to make the trip a success, you've got to have a starting point.

On the next few pages is a list of all the attractions we've talked about in earlier chapters. You can copy these pages for each member of the family to use for voting, or just use them as an outline for the family discussions. The chapters in which each was featured is in brackets, if you'd like to refresh your memories, and I've highlighted in **bold** type the attractions that probably have the widest appeal to most families, or those I think you might especially like.

I've also marked which attractions are located in Maryland [MD] and Virginia [VA] because some of the highlights of a trip to Washington, D.C., aren't in Washington at all.

❏ African American Civil War Memorial [16]
❏ Alexandria [17] [VA]
❏ Anacostia Museum for African American Heritage and Culture [16]
❏ Anderson House [10]
❏ Arlington House [13] [VA]
❏ **Arlington National Cemetery [13] [VA]**
❏ Art Museum of the Americas [15]
❏ Arthur M. Sackler Gallery [15]
❏ Arts and Industries Building [12]
❏ **Attend a Session of Congress [9]**
❏ Baltimore Civil War Museum [12] [Baltimore, MD]
❏ Basilica of the National Shrine of the Immaculate Conception [16]
❏ Ben's Chili Bowl [16]
❏ Bureau of Engraving and Printing [9]
❏ Busch Gardens [10] [Williamsburg, VA, area]
❏ C&O Canal, Georgetown [17]
❏ C&O Canal National Historic Park [17] [VA]
❏ Capital Children's Museum [14]
❏ **Capitol Building [9]**
❏ Castle, The [11]
❏ Christ Church [17] [Alexandria, VA]
❏ Claude Moore Colonial Farm [10] [VA]
❏ **Colonial Williamsburg [10] [VA]**
❏ Corcoran Gallery of Art [15]
❏ DAR Museum [10]
❏ Decatur House [11]
❏ Department of the Interior Museum [9]
❏ Dragon Paddleboat [12] [Baltimore, MD]
❏ Dumbarton Oaks and Gardens [17]
❏ Eisenhower Executive Office Building [9]
❏ Embassy District [9]

- ❏ Explorers Hall [14]
- ❏ Farmer's Market [17] [Alexandria, VA]
- ❏ FBI Headquarters [13]
- ❏ Folger Shakespeare Library [15]
- ❏ **Ford's Theatre [10]**
- ❏ Fort McHenry [12] [Baltimore, MD]
- ❏ Franciscan Monastery [16]
- ❏ Franklin D. Roosevelt Memorial [11]
- ❏ Frederick Douglass National Historic Site [16]
- ❏ Freer Gallery of Art [15]
- ❏ Gadsby's Tavern [17] [Alexandria, VA]
- ❏ Georgetown [17]
- ❏ Harborplace [12] [Baltimore, MD]
- ❏ HiFlyer Balloon ride [12] [Baltimore, MD]
- ❏ Hirshhorn Museum [15]
- ❏ Historical Society of Washington, D.C. [10]
- ❏ Ice Rink [17]
- ❏ International Spy Museum [13]
- ❏ Islamic Center [16]
- ❏ Jamestown Colony [10] [Williamsburg, VA, area]
- ❏ **Jefferson Memorial [11]**
- ❏ Kahlil Gibran Memorial Garden [16]
- ❏ Kennedy Center for the Performing Arts [15]
- ❏ Korean War Veterans Memorial [11]
- ❏ **Lain Walk [5]**
- ❏ Lee's Boyhood Home [17] [Alexandria, VA]
- ❏ Leesburg Animal Park [12] [VA]
- ❏ **Library of Congress [15]**
- ❏ **Lincoln Memorial [11]**
- ❏ Lincoln Theatre [16]
- ❏ M Street, Georgetown [17]
- ❏ Manassas National Battlefield Park [10] [VA]
- ❏ Marine Corps Museum [13]

Top Attractions

❏ Maryland Science Center [12] [Baltimore, MD]
❏ MCI Center [14]
❏ **Mount Vernon [10] [VA]**
❏ **National Air and Space Museum [12]**
❏ National Aquarium (Washington) [12]
❏ **National Aquarium [12] [Baltimore, MD]**
❏ **National Archives [10]**
❏ National Building Museum [11]
❏ National Capital Trolley Museum [14] [MD]
❏ National Cathedral [16]
❏ National Cryptologic Museum [13] [MD]
❏ National Gallery of Art [15]
❏ National Law Enforcement Officers Memorial [13]
❏ National Museum of African Art [15]
❏ National Museum of American Art [15]
❏ **National Museum of American History [10]**
❏ **National Museum of Natural History [12]**
❏ National Museum of Women in the Arts [15]
❏ National Portrait Gallery [15]
❏ National Postal Museum [14]
❏ National Theatre [15]
❏ National Wildlife Visitor Center [12] [MD]
❏ National Zoo [12]
❏ Navy Museum [13]
❏ New York Avenue Presbyterian Church [10]
❏ OAS Building [16]
❏ Octagon [11]
❏ Old Post Office Tower [11]
❏ Old Presbyterian Meeting House [17] [Alexandria, VA]
❏ Old Stone House [11]
❏ Pentagon [13] [VA]
❏ Petersen House [10]
❏ Phillips Collection [15]

❑ Pierce Mill [17]
❑ Port Discovery [12] [Baltimore, MD]
❑ Potomac Park [17]
❑ Powerhouse [12] [Baltimore, MD]
❑ Renwick Gallery [15]
❑ Rock Creek Horse Center [17]
❑ Rock Creek Nature Center [17]
❑ Rock Creek Park [17]
❑ St. John's Church [16]
❑ St. Matthew's Cathedral [10]
❑ Star Spangled Banner House [12] [Baltimore, MD]
❑ State Department Reception Rooms [9]
❑ Supreme Court Building [9]
❑ Textile Museum [14]
❑ Theodore Roosevelt Island [17]
❑ Top of the World [12] [Baltimore, MD]
❑ Torpedo Factory Art Center [17] [Alexandria, VA]
❑ Treasury Building [9]
❑ Tudor Place [17]
❑ U Street [16]
❑ Union Station [4]
❑ U.S. Botanic Garden [17]
❑ U.S. Holocaust Memorial Museum [16]
❑ U.S. National Arboretum [17]
❑ U.S.S. Constellation [12] [Baltimore, MD]
❑ Vietnam Veterans Memorial [11]
❑ Virginia Beach [10] [VA]
❑ Voice of America [14]
❑ Washington Dolls' House & Toy Museum [14]
❑ **Washington Monument [11]**
❑ Washington Navy Yard [13]
❑ Washington Post [14]
❑ **White House [9]**

Top Attractions

❑ Woodrow Wilson House [10]
❑ Yorktown Battlefield [10] [Williamsburg, VA, area]

That's the list. Now, in the tradition of Washington, D.C., America's most ballot-driven city, let the voting begin!

19. Sample Itineraries

Since I started writing a couple of hundred pages ago, I've been operating under the assumption than you're not insane. That's right, isn't it? (Yes, I agree that taking a lengthy holiday with your family and expecting it to be fun isn't necessarily evidence of sanity—only optimism. But fun and optimism are what the Family Travel series is all about!)

OK—it's stipulated that you're probably not insane. That means you won't even attempt to see all 130+ attractions in this book on your vacation. That would truly be crazy. In the previous chapter we talked about how to discover the important things on your list. Now let's discuss how to actually structure a week or two in Washington.

I'm going to suggest some itineraries you can start with, just to show you how you might put together a trip to the city. While you're welcome to just follow one of the itineraries in this chapter step by step, I hope you won't. You should do what works best for your family, not mine!

What are important here are the principles you use in putting an itinerary together. Here are the principles I use in planning:

- Everybody gets his or her first choice, no matter what.
- Don't try to see more than two or three really major attractions in one day.
- Look for things in the same part of town, where possible, to minimize travel time between attractions.
- Vary your activities; don't do two grand churches, two art museums, or two tall observation towers in one day: They'll dilute each other.
- Try to have both indoor and outdoor activities each day.
- Build the major places into your itinerary first, and look for interesting walks, buildings, historic sites, or minor attractions nearby or along your route from place to place.
- Look for ways to go into some depth about a specific person or event by finding a variety of activities that share the same theme.
- Have a backup plan in case the weather is really foul on a day you'd planned to be outdoors, or you wake to an especially gorgeous day when you were going to be inside most of the time.
- Be flexible enough to abandon your plans when something is closed or you run across something neat you hadn't known about. It will happen on every trip—guaranteed!

You'll be able to see those ideas at work as you peruse the itineraries I've set down in this chapter. What's important is that, once you're home again, nobody feels that something really essential has been left out of the trip. Of course there will be activities left undone and sites left unvisited. That's inevitable… unless you *are* insane. That just gives you a good excuse to go back again one day! Traveling is very similar to dining: It's much better to get up from the table wanting just a little more than it is to stuff yourself to the point of discomfort. Washington is a real feast for travelers. Savor it.

I've given you itineraries for both one and two weeks in this chapter to make it easy for you to see how to design a trip for your family. Notice a couple of things: First, I've tried to include as many of the seventeen key attractions (the ones in bold type in the list in Chapter 18) as possible. But it's just not possible to get everything in. You'd be crazy to try. Second, I've built in a lot of choices. Which of them you pick will depend on what you and your traveling companions like to do. You'll certainly add things that aren't on my lists.

It will make a difference whether you have access to a car while you're in the city. While you'd have to be insane after all to decide to drive to the places around the National Mall and downtown, some outlying places in the District, or in neighboring Virginia or Maryland, are much easier to get to by car... and sometimes it's the only way. The itineraries here always provide options for people without their own wheels. I've also provided a couple of optional days you can add at either the beginning or end of your trip, if you have the time and energy. I haven't specified any particular days of the week for activities, but remember that some attractions are closed one or two days a week, open afternoons only, or stay open late some evenings, so check the listings before you go.

Ready, then? Let's go!

One-Week Itinerary

Arrival Day—How much you do today depends pretty much on when you arrive. The first time the Lains visited, we spent a full day driving from Ohio and got in about 7 p.m. I've flown in as early as 9 a.m. and as late at 10 p.m. and arrived by car at every time in between. If you're driving (and are not insane) you'll try to arrive between 10 a.m. and 4 p.m., between the morning and evening rush hours, or after 7 p.m. when even the Beltway gets relatively calm. Arriving too early in the morning can mean that your accommodations aren't available yet. If you're flying, international flights are most likely to arrive in the early afternoon, but flights get in around the clock, of course.

The first thing you have to do once you're in, though, is to get organized. You're tired from traveling and you need a little time to unpack. Remember what we talked about in Chapter 4 about unpacking, napping, and so on. But what next? Everybody will be eager to see the famous sights, and you can't disappoint them. So unless it's very late and bedtime is at hand, let's do something spectacular.

If you've arrived in the evening after most attractions are closed, this is a perfect time to take the Lain Walk from Chapter 5. You'll see the Capitol, the White House, the National Mall and more, and if it grows dark while you're walking, you'll see one of the country's most spectacular nighttime scenes as all the famous buildings bask in brilliant illumination.

If you know you'll arrive early in the day, why not start out with a real rush? Make arrangements to get tickets for a tour of the Capitol Building your very first day. If that doesn't get your trip off on a high note, I can't imagine what would. Plan months ahead of time for this; the sidebar *Go to the Head of the Line* in Chapter 9 gives you the details.

After spending a couple of hours in the Capitol, I'd suggest getting a great overall view of the Mall and the city by walking West down the Mall toward the Washington Monument and turning right on 12th Street (just past the Museum of Natural History) and strolling up to the Old Post Office Tower for a breathtaking eyeful. The food court here would be a great place to have lunch, too.

From there, turning left on Pennsylvania Avenue will take you past the White House. You can't go in, but be sure you walk around the block to see it from both sides. If you got an early start today, you might stop off, on your walk from the Capitol, to visit the National Archives, once they reopen (check my website) to see the original copies of America's three most important documents: the Declaration of Independence, the Constitution, and the Bill of Rights.

Day 2—What an exciting day yesterday was! You saw the three most famous buildings in Washington all at once—the Capitol, the White House, and the Washington Monument. Can it get any better than that? Just wait!

This morning let's devote some time to Abraham Lincoln. No president governed in more difficult and turbulent times, and none left a bigger impact on the country. He was willing to subject the nation to civil war in order to preserve it, and treated the defeated secessionist states with great compassion when the war was over. He emancipated a people enslaved on the continent for 300 years, and was the first American president to die by an assassin's hand. Yes, Lincoln is worth a morning of our time.

You might begin at the New York Avenue Presbyterian Church at New York and 13th NW, someplace tourists less savvy than you almost always miss. You'll probably have to ring the bell to be admitted, but don't be shy: You'll be welcomed. Let them know you've come to see the church and Lincoln Parlor. You'll be shown to the sanctuary and be able to sit in the pew where Lincoln sat on so many Sunday mornings, and then will be directed to the parlor the president often visited to see the Emancipation Proclamation written out and signed by Lincoln himself. From there it's just a short walk to Ford's Theatre, where Lincoln was shot, and the house across the street where he died just a few hours later.

After lunch you've got several possibilities. If you have a car available and would like to pursue the theme of the morning, drive down to the Anacostia section of Washington. Visit the home of Frederick Douglass, himself a former slave and great driving force for Abolition, and who was a good friend of Lincoln. After that, visit the Anacostia Museum to delve deeper into centuries of black life and culture.

If you don't have a car, or feel like doing something else, you could return to the Mall area and stroll to its west end, pausing at the Lincoln Memorial, the memorials dedicated to veterans of

Vietnam and Korea, and continuing around the Tidal Basin to the FDR and Jefferson memorials. That's a lot of walking, but it's a beautiful stroll and there's no need to hurry. If the weather is really nasty, though, an afternoon at either the American History or Natural History museum, which are on your route, is always time well spent. When you're finished, there might still be time to slip into the Octagon or Decatur House, if grand old houses interest you.

Day 3—If you spent yesterday with Lincoln, it seems only fair to give equal time to George Washington today. Make the first stop the Washington Monument for an unforgettable view of your vacation city. We like to get there first thing in the morning to give ourselves plenty of time for other things. And today will be a busy day. Don't forget to get your tickets ahead of time or you might find it hard to get in.

Next take your first venture out of Washington and get in the car or on the Tourmobile bus and go to Mount Vernon. You can spend several hours here, because there's a lot to see, and when you start to wear down, it's refreshing to sit behind the house and watch the Potomac roll by. When you return, you'll probably have time for an afternoon visit to Arlington National Cemetery, making sure to pause for the Changing of the Guard at the Tomb of the Unknowns.

If you haven't had a chance yet to walk through the Mall area at night after all the buildings are lit, tonight's the perfect night for it.

Day 4—You were up early yesterday, so maybe you should sleep in a little this morning and take today a little easier. After everybody's had a good breakfast, take the Metro up to Dupont Circle and use the cool of the morning to stroll up Massachusetts Avenue, gawking at the big houses, mostly embassies representing nations from all over the world. If you haven't had your fill of presidents yet, the Woodrow Wilson house is about a fifteen-minute stroll up the street, at 24th and S streets. (The Textile Museum is just a couple of doors down, if some people would rather stop there.) Ten minutes beyond that is the Islamic Center and, whatever your faith, you won't regret stopping in the mosque.

Most of the time I turn back when I reach Rock Creek, although sometimes I stroll on and rest for awhile at Kahlil Gibran Gardens. Either way, by the time I've walked back to Dupont Circle, I'm ready for lunch and there's a lot to choose from in this neighborhood. You'll be faced with the same choices, and there are no wrong answers. If all yesterday's attention to George Washington got you thinking about the Revolutionary War, you could go back up to Anderson House, which doesn't open until after lunch, to learn more.

When you're finished in this area, get back on the Metro and spend an afternoon looking at some art on the Mall. (Actually, the wonderful Impressionist paintings of the Phillips Collection are near Dupont Circle, but it's horribly expensive.) Depending on where you're going, you'll change trains at Metro Center or at Gallery Place–Chinatown. Use the latter if you're going to the National Gallery of Art, probably your best bet if you haven't been there before. It's got a little bit of everything. No… it has a *lot* of everything!

Spend the afternoon at the National (or wherever else you choose) and if some people get bored looking at marvelous paintings and sculpture (hard to believe, but it sometimes happens) they can go on the Mall and run themselves silly. Lots of places to get an ice cream treat there, too.

When you've finished your art excursion, you can get back on the Metro (or even easier, take a 15-minute stroll) and go to Chinatown for dinner, a relaxing end to a relaxed day.

Day 5—If you're visiting from overseas, remember that you should reconfirm your flight home today. Just a quick phone call will do it.

Today you might start with one of the most popular museums in the world. That means you should be up and out the door early this morning because while you don't need a ticket, you can wind up in a long line at the security desks if you're not there until mid-morning or later. Of course I'm talking about the Air and Space Museum.

If you're here when the museum opens at 9:30, you'll be ready to leave by 11:30 or so (remember the 2-hour rule), and that's a perfect time to walk up to Union Station for lunch, where the lower level food court offers what seems like almost unlimited choices. Everyone will want to be well-fortified, because after lunch you've got a special opportunity, if you've planned carefully: attending a session of Congress.

Visitors from other countries might not be as interested in this (although we've enjoyed sitting in a session of Parliament in England), and it isn't something you want to do with little ones, but if the kids are older, today would be perfect for taking them to a session of Congress. Again, you'll want to plan well ahead of time and write for passes, but sitting in the gallery in the Senate or House chamber where so many distinguished and influential men and women have worked (and a few scalawags, too) watching the people's representatives charting the course of their nation is an experience that makes an American history class or civics lesson come alive. (Of course you take the risk that when you visit they'll be debating something as earth-shattering as whether to allow the Department of Agriculture to regulate the size of heads of cabbage being shipped to Asia—but it's the being there that matters. We've seen the House discussing national parks and the Senate debating something about bridges. Neither were inspiring topics, but it was neat to actually be there.)

If Congress isn't in session during your visit, or you decide that visiting the chamber isn't right for your family, there are lots of other terrific ways to spend your afternoon. If you had lunch at Union Station, look at some of the things that are within a 5- to 15-minute stroll from there:

- The Supreme Court
- The Library of Congress
- The Folger Shakespeare Library
- The Capital Children's Museum
- The National Postal Museum

Here's a plan: This would be a good time to split up so everybody gets to go somewhere they think is especially neat. Spend a couple of hours seeing something special, then meet again at Union Station. Have a cold drink or some ice cream as a mid-afternoon pick-me-up, and walk over to the National Building Museum. (Just walk straight west on E St. for about 10 minutes. When you get to the National Law Enforcement Officers Memorial, cut through the plaza. The Building Museum is across the street on the other side of the Memorial.) You will be the only family you know to have visited this museum, unless you know somebody else who bought this book. And you'll have some photos of an amazing place none of your friends knew existed.

Day 6—Don't be surprised if you wake up feeling a little depressed today. The vacation is almost over! And how can you possibly see all the rest of the things you want to see? Sorry— you can't. In Washington, there's *never* enough time to see and do everything on your list. So what can you do today?

Yesterday was pretty busy. Maybe you should slow the pace a bit and visit the National Zoo this morning, always a popular outing, especially if you think about the idea that turned up in Chapter 12 about wild elephants rampaging through Indiana cornfields. Since there's plenty to see and eat and drink at the zoo, stay until after lunch.

Sample Itineraries

You've got several choices this afternoon, all of them appealing. We can spend the afternoon frolicking (OK, probably Mom and Dad will be resting) in Rock Creek Park. But seeing one of Washington's (and America's) great cathedrals is an appealing idea, especially if you're not from Europe (or haven't visited there) where they're almost as common as McDonald's. If you have a car you can go to National Cathedral, or you can take the Metro to the Basilica of the Immaculate Conception.

But you might decide that a good way to spend the last afternoon and evening of your trip is to do some shopping, taking a leisurely stroll through some picturesque neighborhoods, and going someplace nice for dinner. Either Georgetown or Alexandria is perfect for that. Georgetown has the added advantage of a canal boat ride, so that might be my own choice, if there's time (last ride starts at 3 o'clock). But I like both places so much that I know you won't be disappointed either way. You'll come home with your arms full of purchases, your stomachs full of good food, and your memories full of a great time in Washington, D.C.

Day 7—I don't know what you'll have time for today. You might get in another full day of sightseeing, or you might have to get up before dawn and head home. If you're flying home, you might have an early morning flight, although most transatlantic flights leave in the evening. You'll probably have to check out of your accommodations between 11 a.m. and 1 p.m. If you're driving, that doesn't matter because you can stash your gear in the car and visit a few more places, if you have the time. If you have to check out of your rooms long before it's time to go to the airport, though, you can almost always make arrangements to have your luggage stored at the hotel for a few hours.

So if you *do* have time, what can you work into your last day? If you've planned ahead for tickets, good choices for the morning might be the Bureau of Engraving and Printing, the FBI

Building, the International Spy Museum, or the Holocaust Museum. If there's time this afternoon, visit the American History or Natural History museum, if you haven't done that yet.

But leave yourself plenty of time to get to the airport (at least 2 hours) or to catch the train (at least 30 minutes), and if you're driving, avoid rush hour. Leave at midday, or wait until evening when the Beltway calms down a bit.

Two Excursions

If you have a day or two to spare and would like to add something special to your trip (like going to Washington isn't already special enough....), here are two ideas for outings that can be such fun that they're really worth separate vacations all to themselves.

These trips will work either before or after the Washington, D.C., portion of your trip, and if you want to, you could consider shortening your Washington visit to get one of them in. To tell you the truth, though, it's hard to imagine what to leave out in Washington! The first excursion below could even be done as a daytrip from D.C., something I'll suggest in the two-week itinerary for families that have that much time to spend.

We've even taken one excursion on our way into Washington and the other after we'd finished with the city and were on our way out. That can be pretty rigorous for kids, though, so unless they're really hardy travelers, you might want to choose just one.

Washington to Baltimore
Remember the Baltimore sidebar in Chapter 12? You probably got the idea there that you could easily spend all day. So why not? If you have a car, you can drive straight to the Inner Harbor area in little more than an hour. If you don't have a car, it's even easier: You take the MARC train from Union Station to Camden Station, just a 5-minute walk from the waterfront. Once you're there, you'll find all the things we talked about in Chapter

12–and more–within an easy stroll. There's a tourist information building about halfway between the U.S.S. Constellation and the Maryland Science Center.

The advantage to having a car, though, is that you can easily stop off at the attractions that lay between the cities. We've spent an active day in Baltimore, stayed the night there, and set out for Washington first thing in the morning. But we've made a morning stop at the National Wildlife Visitor Center, and visited the Cryptologic Museum and the National Capital Trolley Museum in the afternoon, getting into D.C. after the furor of rush hour is over. It's just as easy to do in reverse order, too.

Washington to Williamsburg

The Virginia excursion is just as much fun, although it's longer and really does require a car. You can leave Washington in the morning and work your way south, toward Colonial Williamsburg. Along the way you can choose from among several places we've talked about in this book:

• Mount Vernon, in case you don't get another opportunity to get there;

• the Claude Moore Colonial Farm, to get everyone into the mood for looking at life in the 1770s;

• the Leesburg Animal Park;

• Manassas National Battlefield Park to learn about the Civil War on the ground where two important battles took place.

In fact, if there are real Civil War buffs in your family, you'll find battlefield sites at other places on your drive down to Williamsburg, including Fredericksburg and Richmond.

Williamsburg is about 150 miles from Washington, about three hours' drive. We had planned to make the trip at the end of our first Washington family trip, but ran out of energy before we got there. We've done it since, though, and it was a great way to wrap up a trip.

Two Week Itinerary

If you have two weeks to spend in Washington, you can see some of the attractions you just can't squeeze into a one-week visit, and you can take things at just a little slower pace. On a trip this long, we always try to work in a daytrip, or a relaxed day in a park, or something else very different from the usual urban attractions, at least every five or six days. Also remember special evening activities like a river cruise, dinner in Chinatown, and certainly a walk after dark to see the brilliantly lit buildings. Here is one possible way to put together a two-week trip to the Capitol.

Arrival Day—I think I'll just stick with what I said for Arrival Day in the one-week itinerary. It's hard to beat that as a way to start the week.

Day 2—Go to the Mall this morning, pick up all sorts of local information at the Smithsonian "Castle," and get ready for your day. If you had to name the Smithsonian museums most visitors would call their "Big 3," you'd probably come up with Air and Space, American History, and Natural History. Let's start with Air and Space this morning, the most popular of them all. After lunch at Union Station, I'm still in favor or attending a session of Congress. If that's not possible or your family voted that one down, you can visit the Supreme Court, which is nearby (and perhaps watch a case being argued for a little while). Or hop a Red Line train to Farragut North and explore part of Downtown Washington. Near here are St. John's Church, St. Matthew's Cathedral, and the cool exhibits at National Geographic's Explorers Hall.

Day 3—I've got two suggestions for today, one indoors and one outdoors. If you're here in the heat of the summer, do the outdoor ramble in the morning and spent the hot afternoon in air-conditioned comfort. If it's wintertime, start indoors and take advantage of the afternoon sun outside.

The outdoor activity is a walk through the west end of the National Mall and around the Tidal Basin to see the Lincoln, Jefferson, FDR, Vietnam War, and Korean War memorials. The indoor choice is inspecting some of the world's greatest art at the National Gallery or, if you're in the mood for something less conventional, the Hirshhorn.

Day 4—Start this morning with a tour of the FBI Building, the International Spy Museum, or the Bureau of Engraving and Printing, then, after lunch at Dupont Circle, walk through the Embassy District, stopping along the way at whatever catches your interest from among Anderson House, Woodrow Wilson House, and the Islamic Center.

Day 5—For a refreshing change of pace, plan to spend the day outdoors. If you have a car, the C&O Canal National Historic Park is a perfect choice–dramatic scenery, interesting trails, even a gold mine... and canal boat rides, of course. Closer in is Rock Creek Park with Pierce Mill, the Nature Trail–and horseback riding! The Arboretum is quite a bit tamer, but some people like tamer... especially parents on vacation. If you have no car but still yearn for the gentle touch of Mother Nature, the western end of Rock Creek Park is still accessible, and it's possible to get to Theodore Roosevelt Island on the Metro and just a little leg power. Even if you choose to stick close to the Mall, the Botanic Garden can be a respite from the concrete-and-steel environment of the urban landscape.

Day 6—Going to the library isn't usually a thrilling experience... unless the library in question is the Library of Congress, where the Treasures Gallery is not to be missed. The only thing better will be when the National Archives reopens–keep an eye on my website for that information.

The snack bars on the Mall serve great big fat hot dogs, and that would be a cheap and easy choice for lunch. Then, after a walk through one of the sculpture gardens, it's time to head for another of the "Big 3" Smithsonian museums. This time it's my personal favorite, the National Museum of American History, a perfect follow-up to what you saw this morning. There's something for everybody here, but don't forget to visit the ice cream parlor… and be careful about sitting outside along Constitution Avenue at 5 o'clock!

Day 7—To get off the beaten track a little, you might visit the Frederick Douglass home and Anacostia Museum this morning, if you have a car. If you're wheel-less, today might be a good time for less togetherness. Why not split up for awhile? Older kids will enjoy the freedom to wander, and Mom and Dad might want to take younger kids to places that are of special interest just to them. There are lots of possible destinations. A few that come to mind:

- the Capital Children's Museum
- the Folger Shakespeare Library
- the Navy and Marine Corps museums at the Navy Yard, if they're open
- the National Postal Museum
- the Washington Dolls' House and Toy Museum
- the Textile Museum
- media tours of the Washington Post or Voice of America
- the National Aquarium (Commerce Department Building branch)

When you get back together, this might be a nice afternoon and evening to spend in Georgetown–shopping, gawking, dining, even taking a canal boat ride if you can't get out to the C&O Park. For dinner, choose an ethnic restaurant of some sort (We know a great Vietnamese place on M Street) and stop for ice cream before you head back for bed.

Sample Itineraries

Day 8—Time for another day out of the city. You might visit attractions in northern Virginia today. If you have a car, you can start the day at the Claude Moore Colonial Farm, just outside the city. If you have no car, don't worry. Just sleep late this morning and linger over your breakfast. The other stops on today's itinerary are accessible either by car or by Tourmobile. Mount Vernon, home and burial place of George and Martha Washington is first, and will take at least two hours, perhaps more. On the way back you'll have to pass near Arlington National Cemetery, and it's worth whatever you have left of this leisurely day.

Day 9—Time has flown by–your vacation in Washington is more than half over and you've probably crossed off only about 10 percent of the things on your list! What can you do today to get caught up? Well–Nothing. The list of things to do in Washington is endless, and your holiday isn't.

On your first day you had an aerial view from the Old Post Office Tower. Early in your second week, why not do the same thing, but from the top of the Washington Monument this time, provided you were savvy enough to get your tickets ahead of time. You were, weren't you?

By 10 o'clock you're ready for something else, and you couldn't do better than the last of the Big 3–the Natural History Museum. After lunch you might visit the Supreme Court, if you haven't done that, the DAR Museum, the FBI, the Spy Museum, or Bureau of Engraving and Printing, or perhaps visit one of the historic houses we talked about–Decatur House or the Octagon. All those are easily walkable from here.

If clean clothes are getting scarce, this might be a good evening to do a couple of loads of laundry.

Day 10—A good follow-up to a busy day like yesterday would be a trip to the Zoo. With your own transportation you could go to the National Wildlife Visitor Center and the Cryptologic Museum or Trolley Museum instead.

Day 11—You might make today a day for contemplation by getting an early start and visiting the Holocaust Memorial, followed by a visit to the National Cathedral, or Immaculate Conception Basilica and the Franciscan Monastery. If that seems a little heavy or isn't suitable for your family, try one of the art museums–the Freer, Sackler, or African are good choices today, and follow up with another one of the more specialized places we talked about for Day 7, maybe splitting up again.

Day 12—All Aboard! Today you can really get out of Washington. Get to Union Station first thing, grab a quick breakfast, and take a run up to Baltimore to experience the attractions of that great city. The sidebar in Chapter 12 will give you more ideas than you can squeeze in.

Want to stay in Washington instead? If I were choosing, I'd wander along U Street (making sure to stop for a chili dog at Ben's for lunch) perhaps visiting the church we didn't make it to yesterday, or driving out to the Arboretum, if I had a car handy. International visitors should be sure to reconfirm their flights home today.

Day 13—Today you might visit the Lincoln sights we talked about on Day 2 of the One Week Itinerary: the church on New York Avenue, Ford's Theatre, Petersen House. After lunch (the Hard Rock Café is just down the street from Ford's Theatre) you could go up to U Street, if you haven't been there, visit the Museum of Women in the Arts or another art museum, or go to the DAR Museum.

Day 14—Two weeks gone already–where did the time go! Your family will remember this forever. How shall you finish the trip?

Maybe you'll have to leave early. If you've got the time today, though, you can use it as a catch-up day, visiting some of the things we'd listed as alternatives for the days above that you just haven't gotten to yet. This afternoon and this evening you can spend shopping and walking the old streets of Alexandria, a quiet end to a vacation that will be something your family will talk about whenever you get together for years to come.

20. Budget Worksheets

I've heard from a number of readers of other books in this series who have found the forms in this chapter especially helpful, especially if they haven't set up a complicated family trip like this before. This is exactly the way we planned holidays with our own family and, being a little conservative and more than a little compulsive, I even do it this way when I travel alone.

First is a form you can fill out as you search for airfare. It includes all the things we talked about in Chapter 4, and you can use it in talking with your travel agent or while cruising travel and airline sites on the Internet.

Next are two forms that incorporate the accommodations advice we covered in Chapter 3. Fill out one of these for every place you're investigating and you'll be able to compare them easily. They're best for using while you talk on the phone with the manager, but if you need to, you can use them by mail or fax, especially if you're coming from outside North America.

Finally, the chapter contains a simple budget-planning form you can use to project your expenses. It's exactly what I do every time I take a major trip, and probably had more to do with keeping us out of debtor's prison than any other single thing. Because I am conservative and compulsive, the budget is designed to estimate on the high end of your expenses. I'd much rather have money left over at the end of the trip than to run out just as I'm about to pay for dinner on our next-to-last day of the trip.

Finding the Fairest Fare

Answer these questions for your travel agent or before you sit down to check websites and airlines. They'll help you get the best deal.

Form 1–Air travel requirements. Give to travel agent or use with websites.

1. How many people travelling? _____
   _____Adults_____Children under 18 (ages:_____)
   _____How many students?
   Depending on the route and the time of year, discounts may be available to students or children under a certain age

2. Departure date: _____
   Is this date ❑Fixed or is it ❑Flexible?
   If you can travel during Low Season, airfares may be half or less of High Season (summer months) fares. Avoid Friday, Saturday, Sunday flights for better prices.

3. Length of stay? _____days/weeks
   Stays of 7 to 30 days usually qualify for the cheapest rates because business travellers usually stay for less than a week. Avoid return flights on Friday, Saturday, Sunday for better rates.

4. Preferred airline, if any?_____
   If you or another family member works for an airline, you may be eligible for deep discounts. Do you have a frequent flier account with an airline? Do you have enough miles in an account to get one or more tickets free?

5. Preferred airports, if any?_____

You might save money by driving to a more distant airport where cheaper fares are offered. Price flights from all nearby airports. And remember that prices to all three Washington-area airports will probably be different.

6. Non-stop flight required or connection okay?

❏ Non-stop only; ❏ connection okay

Unless you live near a city with non-stop service, this isn't an issue: you'll have to connect. But if there's a choice, the connection might be cheaper.

7. Check consolidators.

Some companies buy blocks of tickets from airlines and resell them at a discount. These can be great value, but check companies carefully: some very low advertised prices are scams. Travel agents may know who are the most reputable consolidators.

You should be able to use this information to find the best fares available. Keep checking prices even after you've made your arrangements, though. Airlines have sales just like grocery stores do and usually will reissue more expensive tickets at sale prices for a service charge.

Accommodations at Manageable Prices

Apartments are ideal if you're staying in Washington for a week or more; they're far more home-like than any hotel room. Apartments are nicer, too, because they're roomier and more comfortable. You can also save money by cooking some of your own meals instead of eating in restaurants three times a day. But if you decide on a hotel, motel, or suite, get one with a kitchenette and you can still save money. Always talk or write directly to the manager to get the best information and the best price.

Budget Worksheets

Once you've compiled a list of several possible apartments or hotels, start talking to managers. Telephoning is the best way to gather basic information, with a follow-up letter or fax to the manager of the place you select. There are two forms on the next two pages, one for apartments and one for hotels, suites, and motels.

Form 2a–Finding an apartment

1. Hello. I am looking for an apartment in Washington for ___ people. We will arrive on this date, _____ and will leave on _____, a total of ___ nights. There will be ___adults and children whose ages are _____.

2. We would like a...
   ❏ studio apartment ❏1-bedroom apartment ❏ 2-bedroom apartment
Please describe the apartment, the building, and the neighborhood:
3. What is the address of the apartment? How far is the nearest Metro station? Which station?
4. How large is the apartment? What floor is it on? How many beds?
5. What kind of bath/toilet facilities are in the apartment?
6. Does the apartment face the street? How quiet is it? Describe the building and apartment security features.
7. Describe the furnishings and appliances in the apartment. Is there a telephone? A television?
8. Describe the cooking facilities in the apartment. How much storage space is there?
9. Does the apartment have laundry facilities? Air conditioning?
10. Describe the building. How old is it? When was it last remodeled? Is there an elevator?
11. How often is the apartment cleaned and linens changed?
12. Describe the neighborhood. Is it residential, commercial, industrial?
13. How far away is the nearest self-service laundry? Grocery store? Bakery?
14. How do we pick up the keys?
15. What is the best price you can give me, including all taxes?
16. Is there any way to reduce it further? (like length of stay, weekend specials, bringing our own linens for extra cots, sleeping bags so we won't require an extra bed, cleaning the apartment ourselves and laundering the sheets and towels, etc.)
17. Are there other dates in about the same time period when the rate would be lower?
18. What credit cards do you accept? How much deposit do you require and when is the balance due?

Thank you. If we decide to rent this apartment, I will confirm this with you within one week.

Form 2b–Finding a hotel, motel, or suite

1. Hello. I am looking for a hotel in Washington for ___ people. We will arrive on this date, _____ and will leave on _____, a total of ___ nights. There will be ___adults and children whose ages are _____.

2. Where is the hotel? How far is the nearest Metro station? Which station?

3. Do you have a room or suite with cooking facilities? A refrigerator?

4. How large is the room?

5. How is the room furnished? Can we control the heating and cooling in our own room?

6. What kind of bath/toilet facilities are in the room?

7. What is the additional charge for two adjoining rooms connected by an interior door?

8. Are rollaway beds available for extra people?

9. If we don't use a rollaway or bring our own linens for it, is there a deduction? How much?

10. Is there an elevator?

11. Does the room have an alarm clock? Coffee maker? Hair dryer? Refrigerator? Safe?

12. Is breakfast provided? What does it consist of?

13. How far away is the nearest self-service laundry? Grocery store? Bakery?

14. What is the best price you can give me, including all taxes?

15. Is there any way to reduce it further? (like length of stay, weekend specials, bringing our own linens for extra cots, sleeping bags so we won't require an extra bed, cleaning the room ourselves and laundering the sheets and towels, etc.)

16. Are there other dates in about the same time period when the rate would be lower?

17. What credit cards do you accept? Do you require a deposit?

Thank you. If we decide to rent this room, I will confirm this with you within one week.

After you've gathered information about three or four apartments or hotels, you're ready to choose your Washington home. Contact the manager again and make the booking, and follow up in writing with a letter or fax.

Your Holiday Budget

Now we get to the bottom line: What will it cost to take your family on a vacation it will never forget? The form is set up to estimate on the high side, because it's a wonderful feeling to come home from a great trip with money left over.

Form 3–Your travel budget

_____1. Travel expenses
  Airfare, train tickets, or driving expenses, including meals during layovers or on the train or road, and overnight accommodation if you're driving a long distance.

_____2. Accommodations
  from Form 2a or 2b. If you're driving, include the cost of parking your car in this category.

_____3. Food: meals and snacks
  ■ *If you're staying in a hotel, you'll probably eat two or three meals per day in restaurants. If that's the case, allow $15 to $35 per person, per day for meals, depending on the ages of your children.*

  ■ *If you're renting an apartment and plan to fix breakfast and supper at home most of the time, eating only lunch out, figure $10 to $20 per person, per day, a figure which also takes the purchase of groceries into account. It's possible to spend much more, of course,*

but these figures will provide for you comfortably.
Per person/per day ___x number of days ____x
number in family = $_____

_____4. Attractions and sightseeing
*There are a vast number of free attractions, and kids
get in free to some places that cost their parents. You'll
probably spend less than this but let's figure an average
of $5 per person per day.*
$5 x ____people x ____days = $_____

_____5. Shopping and souvenirs
*This is a very personal category. We suggest you give
each child a fixed amount, perhaps $20 to $50, or a
sum of perhaps $5 to $10 per day to pay for souvenirs,
snacks, etc. They can, of course, supplement that with
their own money if they wish. Mom and Dad can set
their own budget in this category. However, it is best to
set a fixed amount in advance. Give the money to your
children when you arrive, perhaps a little at a time for
younger ones.*

_____6. Local Transportation
■ *The Metro: If you buy a 1-week Metro pass, the cost
is $17.50 per week. If that's more than you need, you
can buy cards for a any lesser amount you choose and
add more money to them as needed.*
$17.50 x ___ people x ___ weeks = $_____

■ *Airport Transportation: If you fly into IAD or BWI
and take a taxi to your accommodations, it will cost
you at least $50, much less from DCA. Public
transportation is great from DCA and reasonable from
BWI, less convenient but possible from IAD. The first*

rate will get you anywhere on the Metro from DCA or via bus/Metro from IAD. The second involves a taxi from DCA, train/Metro from BWI, or taxi from IAD. $3.50 x ___people = $_____ or $15 to $60

■ *Taxi: You might take a taxi occasionally during your visit. Let's budget $30.*

Total Expenses in Categories 1 through 6 above $_____

Appendix
1. Photography

About the only thing that's easier to find in Washington, D.C., than politicians is cameras. Everybody's got them. I fully expect to watch a presidential press conference some day and see the President appear with a camera slung around his neck. Let's talk for a few minutes about taking memorable pictures. You have a lot of choices: video cameras, photographs, slides, digital photos. Things were easier when everybody just had old brownie box cameras, but even I'm not that old! Washington is worth going to a bit of trouble for, however; it's probably the most photogenic city in the United States.

Let me give you one very good piece of advice, something I learned from my college photo instructor: Take lots of pictures. Film is cheap, or at least much cheaper than missing the one shot you really wish you had. You may never get another chance to shoot what you see in front of you right now. Don't miss it! No matter how many pictures you take, film and processing still account for only a tiny percentage of the cost of the trip.

I should say that my own bias is toward prints—easy to organize and to look at whenever I want them, ideal for making the enlargements that cover the walls of my office and our home, simple to share with others. But I use all the available technologies: prints for personal use, slides for my books and lectures, digital images for books, websites, and e-mail, and video for family events. So I have thoughts on the plusses and minuses of each. And excuse me if I'm a tiny bit technical here. Skip over the parts that don't pertain to you.

Photographs and Slides: Unless I know I'm going to be making large prints of my negatives, I use a fast general purpose film for most things, ISO 400. I can shoot almost anything outdoors, even on very gray days, and often don't need a flash indoors. If it's a bright day and I plan to be shooting buildings and landscapes I might want to enlarge, I'll use a slower, finer-grained film like ISO 100, which will produce better big enlargements.

On the other hand, if the day is very dark, if I'm doing night photography, or if I plan to do a lot of shooting indoors, I may use a faster film. Fuji makes wonderful ISO 800 and 1600 speed print films that have good color and surprisingly fine grain. While I do a lot of night photography (Washington is stunningly beautiful at night) I never travel with a tripod. I can hand-hold slow shutter speeds, but at night or in dark interiors I'll find something to set the camera on, or something to brace myself against.

Of course a flash is pointless for a photo of the Capitol Building or Lincoln Memorial at night, and many museums that permit photography do not allow you to use flash. Turn it off.

For slides, I use slower film because I find the colors more true-to-life, so I avoid the ISO 400 Ektachrome unless I know light is going to be a problem. On the other hand, ISO 25 Kodachrome produces brilliant color that can be enlarged as much as you want, but you need lots of light. Speeds of 64 to 200 are a good middle ground.

I'm not a big fan of disposable cameras because they're bulky and image quality is just mediocre most of the time. I've used them once or twice in a pinch when my own camera was unavailable, but they can cause real problems for fliers, because they're not easy to protect from airport x-rays, especially if you have several. The family trip of a lifetime deserves more, in my opinion, than flimsy cameras with plastic lenses that will pile up in a landfill.

Digital Cameras: This emerging technology is getting better every day. Digicams that produce 3-megapixel images or better can yield stunningly beautiful images that can enlarge to billboard size, almost. Printers have not quite caught up with the technology, but that's changing, so prints made from digital images are not quite photographic quality yet—but that day is coming, and soon. I still find it more of a nuisance than an advantage to have people gather 'round the computer to look at photos. Passing around a photo album is more my speed. But I suspect I'm fighting a losing battle on this one… and I do love looking at my best pictures on a big, bright monitor instead of in a 4- x 6-inch print.

For the very best pictures, use your camera's top-quality setting, and, if it's available on your camera, save the images in a TIFF (or TIF) format in 150 to 300 dots per inch. Those settings will produce the largest files, however, so you'll get far fewer images on your memory card or stick that way. The difference in the quality of enlarged prints will be obvious, though. Furthermore, if you use computer software to edit or enhance your pictures, you really do want TIFs. The other format used by most digital cameras, JPEG (or JPG) is a compressed format. Each time you open the image to edit it or change its size, and re-save it, you're compressing the compression, and the quality deteriorates a little further.

On the other hand, if you only intend to look at them on your computer, to post them on the Web, or to e-mail them to others, the JPEG format at 72 dpi is just fine. It produces the smallest files, and computer monitors and Web pages won't be able to use the higher resolution anyway. I usually shoot at the highest setting, then convert to lower-quality JPGs anything I plan to mail or post on the Web.

Video: Camcorders have become smaller, lighter, and more portable over recent years, and less likely to cause the backache or sore shoulder you would have suffered from them even a few years ago. Video is great for capturing the antics of your kids romping on the Mall or shooting luscious panoramic shots from the steps of the Lincoln Memorial.

The biggest downside is that you can't quickly zip to just one part of the tape you want to see as you can flip to a page in an album–you have to go through the tape in a linear fashion. Video isn't easy to edit, either–certainly not as simple as deciding what photos to put in an album, what slides to put in a tray, or what digital images not to delete. But it does provide a good overall look at your trip. It's also easy to narrate the tape as you shoot, to tell viewers what they're seeing. That's less easy with still images. (I carry a small notebook to remind myself what I've taken so I can write it in the album later. Otherwise captions are apt to run along the lines of "Here's Barb in front of some building … Here's Barb in front of a different building…")

Just don't pan your camera too fast unless you own stock in the motion-sickness medicine Dramamine, and don't let your cuts go on too long. Two minutes of the Capitol Building doesn't seem very long when you're shooting it, but two minutes of just watching people walk up and down its steps on your TV at home will seem like an eternity.

Security Checkpoints: X-ray machines have become a reality of the 21st century for travelers, and that can cause terrible problems for photographers. Film can be fogged by x-ray machines and photographs ruined, despite what security screeners may say. The problem is less acute with slower films, but the faster the film, the greater the danger. Because the effect is cumulative, a 100-speed film can survive a few passes through x-ray machines, while a roll of ISO 1600 will be ruined the first time.

What's more, it's not just airports you have to worry about. Many museums, galleries, and public buildings now x-ray everything carried in. I even saw a security guard x-ray a soft-drink in a plastic cup from a nearby fast-food restaurant.

I always request a hand inspection at airports. In the United States, screeners are supposed to comply with that request, according to Federal Aviation Authority guidelines, but many are understandably reluctant to do so because it slows the line at the checkpoint. Rules vary outside the U.S., however, and screeners may flatly refuse any request for hand inspection.

But I have to protect my work as a professional or there would be no photos in my books. So I invested $30 in a lead-lined film bag. When the opaque bag turns up on the x-ray screen, they hand-inspect it anyway. I also travel with high speed film and tell them so. They are much more willing to do the inspection if they know you have film that's more than ISO 1000. Keep your film in your carry-on bag, never in checked luggage. The much more powerful x-ray machines used to scan those bags will toast all your film, lead bag or no lead bag.

But government buildings are less likely to grant hand inspections, even for high-speed film, so I carry my lead bag in my daypack for those times I can't avoid the x-ray. Or I'll just take my digital camera, which is not affected.

2. *Washington Websites*

L isted below are helpful links and official websites of attractions, as well as selected unofficial websites I think are especially useful. If you find a broken link, or a web address that's changed, please let me know so it can be updated. A page of clickable hotlinks will be posted at the author's *Washington D.C. for Families* update page, accessible through www.interlinkbooks.com/dcforfamilies.html

General Information

DC Pages
www.dcpages.com

The District
www.thedistrict.com

Official D.C. Government Website
www.dc.gov

Washington, D.C. Chamber of Commerce
www.dcchamber.org

Washington, D.C. Convention and Visitors Association
www.washington.org

Getting There

Amtrak
fares, schedules, and other information about the national passenger rail service
www.amtrak.com

Cheaptickets
discount airfare
www.cheaptickets.com

Internet Travel Network
travel information from American Express
www.itn.com

Lowestfare
discount airfare
www.lowestfare.com

Microsoft Expedia
popular general travel site
www.expedia.com

Priceline
name your own price for airfare and hotels, but watch restrictions
www.priceline.com

Travelocity
good general travel site
www.travelocity.com

Accommodations—Apartment Services & Suites

Access Accommodations
www.washingtondc.accessaccommodations.com

Apartment Site featuring privately-owned places
www.dmoz.org/Regional/North_America/United_States/
Washington,_DC/Travel_and_Tourism/Lodging/Vacation_Rentals

DcLux Apartments
www.dcluxe.com

Endless Summer Vacations
www.esvflorida.com/dc.htm

Executive Club Suites
in nearby Virginia suburbs
www.dcexeclub.com

Appendix: Washington Websites

1st Washington Hotels
www.1stwashingtondchotels.com

No More Hotels
www.nomorehotels.com

Northernwood Travel
www.washington.dc.northernwoodtravel.com/washington_suites

Accommodations—Hotel and Motel Listings

I always check several sites. The prices are usually different. Then I call the property directly.

Best Lodging
www.bestlodging.com/usa/dc

Capitol Reservations
www.capitolreservations.com

D.C. Accommodations
www.dcaccommodations.com

Northernwood Travel
www.washington.dc.northernwoodtravel.com

Smoothhound
www.smoothhound.co.uk/usa/district-of-columbia/washington

Washington-DC-Hotel Net
www.washington-dc-hotel.net

Washington.org hotel list
www.washington.org/index

Media

Washington Post
daily newspaper
www.washingtonpost.com

Washington Times
small daily newspaper
www.washtimes.com

The Washingtonian
comprehensive monthly magazine
www.washingtonian.com

Radio Stations
formats, frequencies, and links to station websites
www.washingtondc.com/media/radio

Television
local TV stations and links to station websites
www.washingtondc.com/media/television

Arrival
Immigration and Naturalization Service
U.S. government site with free downloadable forms, but hard to navigate
www.ins.gov

Immigration Services
visa requirements. Also offers immigration forms for a fee
www.visa-forms.com

Baltimore-Washington International Airport Information
www.bwiairport.com

Dulles Airport Information
www.mwaa.com/dulles

Reagan National Airport Information
www.mwaa.com/national

Getting Around
Metro (Washington Metropolitan Area Transport Authority)
www.wmata.com

Appendix: Washington Websites

MARC Trains (commuter rail from BWI and Baltimore)
www.mtamaryland.com/schedules/index.cfm

Tourmobile
www.Tourmobile.com

Washington Flyer Coach Service
www.washfly.com

Attractions

Alexandria
www.ci.alexandria.va.us

Anacostia Museum
www.si.edu/anacostia

Arlington House
www.nps.gov/arho

Arlington National Cemetery
www.arlingtoncemetery.org

Art Museum of the Americas
www.oas.org/museum

Arts & Industries Building
www.si.edu/ai

Basilica of the National Shrine of the Immaculate Conception
www.nationalshrineinteractive.com

Bureau of Engraving and Printing
www.bep.treas.gov

C&O Canal National Historic Park
www.nps.gov/choh

Capital Children's Museum
www.ccm.org

Claude Moore Colonial Farm
www.1771.org

Colonial Williamsburg
www.colonialwilliamsburg.org

Corcoran Gallery of Art
www.corcoran.org

DAR Museum
www.dar.org/museum

Decatur House
www.decaturhouse.org

Department of the Interior Museum
www.doi.gov/museum

Dumbarton Oaks and Gardens
www.doaks.org

Embassy Row
www.embassy.org/embassies

Explorers Hall, National Geographic Society
www.nationalgeographic.com
www.nationalgeographic.com/explorer

FBI Building Tour
www.fbi.gov/aboutus/tour

Folger Shakespeare Library
www.folger.edu

Appendix: Washington Websites

Ford's Theatre
www.nps.gov/foth [as a historic site]
www.fordstheatre.org [as a working theater]

Franciscan Monastery
www.pressroom.com/~franciscan

Frederick Douglass National Historic Site
www.nps.gov/frdo

Freer Gallery of Art
www.asia.si.edu

Georgetown
www.georgetowndc.com

Hirshhorn Museum
www.hirshhorn.si.edu

Historical Society of Washington, D.C
www.hswdc.org

International Spy Museum
www.spymuseum.org

Jefferson Memorial
www.nps.gov/thje

Kennedy Center for the Performing Arts
www.kennedy-center.org

Korean War Veterans Memorial
www.nps.gov/kowa

Leesburg Animal Park
www.leesburganimalpark.com

Library of Congress
www.loc.gov

Lincoln Memorial
www.nps.gov/linc/

Marine Corps Museum
www.hqinet001.hqmc.usmc.mil/HD/General/Visitors_Researchers_Navy_Yard

Maryland Science Center
www.mdsci.org

MCI Center
www.mcicenter.com

Mount Vernon
www.mountvernon.org

National Air and Space Museum
www.nasm.si.edu

National Aquarium (Washington)
www.nationalaquarium.com

National Aquarium (Baltimore)
www.aqua.org

National Archives
www.archives.gov

National Building Museum
www.nbm.org

National Capital Trolley Museum
www.dctrolley.org

Appendix: Washington Websites

National Cryptologic Museum
www.nsa.gov/museum

National Gallery of Art
www.nga.gov

National Law Enforcement Officers Memorial
www.nleomf.com

National Mall
www.nps.gov/nama

National Museum of African Art
www.nmafa.si.edu

National Museum of American Art
www.americanart.si.edu

National Museum of American History
www.americanhistory.si.edu

National Museum of Natural History
www.mnh.si.edu

National Museum of Women in the Arts
www.nmwa.org

National Portrait Gallery
www.npg.si.edu/

National Postal Museum
www.si.edu/postal

National Theatre
www.nationaltheatre.org

National Wildlife Visitor Center
www.patuxent.fws.gov

National Zoo
www.natzoo.si.edu

Navy Museum
www.ndw.navy.mil/Visitors/NavyMuseum

New York Avenue Presbyterian Church
www.nyapc.org

OAS Building
www.oas.org

Octagon
www.cr.nps.gov/nr/travel/wash/dc22.htm

Old Post Office
www.oldpostofficedc.com

Old Stone House
www.nps.gov/rocr/oldstonehouse

Pentagon
www.defenselink.mil/pubs/pentagon

Petersen House
www.nps.gov/foth/hwld.htm

Phillips Collection
www.phillipscollection.org

Port Discovery
www.portdiscovery.org

Franklin D. Roosevelt Memorial
www.nps.gov/frde

Renwick Gallery
www.americanart.si.edu/collections/renwick

Appendix: Washington Websites

Sackler Gallery
www.asia.si.edu

St. Matthew's Cathedral
www.stmatthewscathedral.org

Smithsonian Institution
www.si.edu

Smithsonian Institution "Castle"
www.si.edu/activity/planvis/museums/i-sib.htm

State Department Tours
www.state.gov

Supreme Court Building
www.supremecourtus.gov

Textile Museum
www.textilemuseum.org

Theodore Roosevelt Island
www.nps.gov/this

Treasury Department Tours
www.ustreas.gov/curator/tours.htm

U.S. Botanic Garden
www.usbg.gov

U.S. Capitol Building
www.aoc.gov [Architect of the Capitol]
www.senate.gov [U.S. Senate]
www.house.gov [U.S. House of Representatives]

U.S. Holocaust Memorial Museum
www.ushmm.org

U.S. National Arboretum
www.usna.usda.gov

Vietnam Veterans Memorial
www.nps.gov/vive/index.htm

Voice of America
www.voa.gov

Washington Monument
www.nps.gov/wamo

Washington National Cathedral
www.cathedral:org

Washington Navy Yard
www.ndw.navy.mil/Visitors/visitors

Washington Post
www.washingtonpost.com

White House
www.nps.gov/whho
www.whitehouse.gov

Woodrow Wilson House
www.woodrowwilsonhouse.org

		DATE DUE	
			11/07
		WITHDRAWN	